THE BLUE YEARS

ERIN ROSE BLACQUE BELAIR

THE BLUE YEARS

Line editing, proofreading, cover design, and interior book design provided by Indigo: Editing, Design, and More:

- Line editor: Kristen Hall-Geisler
- Book design: Vinnie Kinsella

www.indigoediting.com

"To live near the ocean is to live twice."
—My Grandfather

These pages were written during the few years where I lived so near the ocean, so close to it, I didn't know how to separate myself from it. These pages are presented here in the same linear timeline in which they were written, but I do not much believe in time, and there is little linear about them. These things I struggle with here—love, grief, guilt, and the responsibility to ourselves to be who we are—they are not linear. You can read this in any way that feels true to you, and I hope in these pages you find moments in which you are reminded that we never truly ache alone, that there is mystery in the mundane, and that life is both stunning and tragic, often in the same moments. We are never just one thing. We are, as is the color blue, one of life's great paradoxes.

I must give thanks to the women who came before me, particularly: Maggie Nelson, her words in *Bluets*, and the permission it gave me to fall madly in love with this color; Rebecca Solnit and her work "The Blue of Distance" in *A Field Guide to Getting Lost*; and Carol Mavor and her meticulous research and devotion in *Blue Mythologies: Reflections on a Colour*. Without these works I never would have been able to find the way to access my own blue years.

It must be said that this book would not exist without the men I have loved and who have taught me so much in return. Thank you. I am sorry. I love you.

—Erin Rose Blacque Belair

WE STILL PRAY SOUTH—
written a year before I would live at the ocean

I keep on dreaming of places where the sea stretches so far ahead of me I lose my footing. Places where time seems to have stopped, the world grown up around it, ivy-vined and sun-leached. It's here where I love you, and here where I leave you. We count the days we have together knowing, as we did back then, they are always numbered. We are always finding a way to distract ourselves from the big universal truths. Time ebbs and faces grow old.

I feel myself constantly pirouetting in my own memories; now is an isolated event, a snow globe filled with sand. There is sand in everything, a grit between my teeth while I sleep, a film across the pillow case. Everything is so promising when you dust off the sheets and we sleep straight through until morning.

Everyone is curious about what is going to be made next, but all I want is to slow the passage and stay this age forever. There is a lot left for us to squeeze from each other.

Lately people from my past keep on telling me how nothing is turning out the way they wanted it to. You're living in your parents' basement again, and I doubt it will be the last time. I wish I could spoon-feed everyone the knowingness that it all turns around, picks up, and becomes something else. But I am not too shy to know that sooner or later it will be me again out to pasture and wondering where things went wrong. I'm worried about being happy, but then I'm happy about being worried. It means there is still a compass, still a way north, and still a good reason to pray south.

WE ARE HERE

A new place in my life has been marked. I strip the wallpaper down to the scaffolding. I rebuild, but still the old life remains in the bones. We are forever pressed into one another, hairline fractures and horseshoes. We never really start over.

I can remember something you said in every single dress I own.

I have just arrived, and this is what I already know about this place: there is always a bird, always sand stuck to the bottom of my feet, always windows open. There is the sound of water so constant soon I will not even hear it. There is salt on my lips and the color blue.

I have been of want. Things I now have, and yet I want what I had before. I must learn how to be where I am and not to be where I have been. Perhaps you were right in saying it's a writer's curse. Perhaps I am only settled when I am unsettled.

The last six months are a fever dream, and I have woken up at the sea. There is a mild and urgent sense of forever in his presence that makes me tired. I am more aware than ever before that I have both been here and have never been here.
Nothing is the same.
Everything is the same.
There are always divers in the cove out front, and I sit and watch them swim. They are being pulled closer toward the shore one moment and pushed farther out to sea the next.

I imagine this might be what it feels like to love me.

I am one year older, and I do not have anything special it say about it. I suppose this is because every day I am one year older. What this does make me think about, though, is my mother. She was in the same stretch of time that I am now in when she had me. Sometimes I imagine two separate linear stretches of time. In one I had the baby, and in this one I did not. This also makes me tired.

We rarely understand the choices we make until it is too late to unmake them.

WORDS FOR THE COLOR BLUE

I imagine her sitting in the front seat of your car. Then I go for a walk. I decide there aren't enough words for the color blue and I should start a list.

Miss-me-blue
So-long-blue
Kiss-my-neck-blue
I-used-to-love-you-blue

Everything you say to me rattles like pennies in a glass jar. I never settle back to where I was before.

I think about going out to the desert to learn something, but I don't know what. Out there the ideas have always come more clearly; there is less to get in their way. Perhaps this place will be like that too. Maybe the ideas will come in like the waves from some unknown place.

I can see now how many times you were right about me. The only thing I was really afraid of was hard work. I blamed the rest of the circus for letting the tigers out after dark. Does it make you feel better if I say it was all my fault?

I am going to stop worrying about what I have done and think rather on what I am going to do. The work, like prayer, will add up. Everyone, eventually, is going to be okay.

People teach us who they are;
It is our job to listen.
Life teaches us the lessons we ask for;
It is our job to learn them.

Love teaches us how to navigate both.

no. 0

First, we have to note that the ocean is not blue—not of blue, but appears to be blue. Like so many things in our world, I begin to learn. Blue is the most elusive of all colors. The sky and the sea are blue because they reflect blue light back at us. They absorb every other color besides the blue. Because blue light vibrates at a higher frequency than any other color on the spectrum. It escapes when all else remains trapped and hidden. This feels important.

no. 1

I lose myself in learning of the color blue. I think it is important to say I am not even nearly the only one. That my obsession runs like a blue vein through all of time. We are drawn mysteriously to the color over and over again, and the more you learn, the more you are drawn to it. Blue is a paradox, as Carol Mavor says in her collection *Blue Mythologies*. "Paradoxically Blue" is her introduction. She says, "I am trying to be a connoisseur of blue." Me too, Carol, me too.

no. 2

If you search for facts about the color blue, the first thing the internet tells you is that blue is the least common of the colors we eat. That blueberries are the favorite of all blue foods. Favorite to whom it doesn't say. Also that mosquitos are twice as attracted to the color blue. And also that blue birds cannot see the color blue. This stops me.

This fact is followed by: Owls are the only bird who can see the color blue.

None of this is true. After reading more I learn birds can see blues we cannot see. They can see ultraviolet light. They can see even more blues than we know of.

If I could tell you anything, I would tell you I left the screen door open, so I wouldn't make noise when I left late at night. I would tell you about planting tomatoes in June and about the smell of their leaves on my burnt fingertips, and about cutting celery with the windows open. I would tell you about sleeping near the river, or about how I always reached out to touch his arm while he drove.

BURN IT. BURY IT.

In New Mexico, in September, there is always the promise of a storm somewhere near, a thunder that rarely reaches you. There is always mud between your toes, always something to eat. I am stilled by the landscape and the intention in everything they do, from how they till the soil to how they pray. And still I think of only you.

There is a story told to children here, folklore to keep them from swimming in the ditch bank. A story of a woman who drowned her children in the water and cries there at night. La Lorona. They say you can hear her if you listen quietly. They say don't swim. There are dangers and beauty in equal measure, it seems, everywhere I turn of late.

An old friend takes me up into the mountains to sleep in a cave carved from sandstone so mother earth can literally wrap herself around us. In the morning, when we wake, we walk down to the river, cloudy with clay and silt and low for the season. I stand in the mud and toss a rock as far as I can, intending to let go of the things I don't know how to let go of. But walking back to the cave, you're still with me, and so is she.

So we dig a hole with a shovel in the soft earth, and I write it all down, I burn the paper, and then I bury it. We say a prayer and leave it there. A storm wants to come, but it never does. When I go back to the ocean, I do not feel any better. I sense I am only starting to think about the things I don't think about. I am only now seventeen months later talking about it out loud.

We do not grow up into the kind of women we think we will be. We grow up into the only kind of women we know how to be.

IN A DIFFERENT LIFE

Sometimes there aren't words for how I feel. There are colors, but not enough words for the colors either. I always imagine that in a little while I will be all right. I will learn to look out to the sea and wonder what comes next rather than turn over the stones of what I left. I imagine in a little bit I'll be someone else.

In a different life, I live on an island and I am less worried about everything, and I string seashells on fishing line and hang them around the edge of my home. I eat greens from the garden with table salt and only cry when I cut myself. In a different life, I didn't leave you.

I buy hydrangeas and put them in the north-facing window to bring in new ideas. I put the dream catcher in the west-facing windows to stop the things that scare me. And I sleep in the east corner of the house. And in the mornings, I pray south. Because this isn't a different life.

A friend writes a poem in which she says, *I could have been so many people.* I find myself reciting this line for days on end as the tide comes in and goes out, as it muddies and clears. I can make sense of everything in life with an analogy about the ocean. It does what we do, it comes and it goes.

ON DREAMING

Sometimes I speak of something, and then I dream it. Other times I dream of something, and then I see it. Since I was young, my dreamscape has been a tangible place in which I am taught. I carry back with me moments, lessons. I learn in ways that are backward and strange, but the message is clear. The message is always clear, even when everything else is muddy.

Keep your eyes open.
No one can live like this for very long.
Remember you did the right thing.

In the mornings, I tell you about my dreams, but you do not know how long I have been doing this. You do not yet own the context of how important this part of the day is, and I am reminded that we are sometimes still strangers.

You tell me — and you are right in telling me — that's no way to live a life as lovely as mine. "I wonder if anyone else enjoys being themselves as much as I do." I wrote that once, but I a hardly remember who that girl was. It sounds nice though.

I wish I knew what she was like. But that's never going to change.

In my dreams it is easier to learn because my window of focus is so narrow. So I try to do that here. I read something you told me four months ago, something along the lines of how you must be very deliberate in where you place your focus. It's the duty you have to being alive this one time.

I should be able to learn the waking lessons, too, even though they are always muddy and the message is not always so clear.

There is something still
in coffee rings or paper cups
the rise of your back
while you slept.

The gate would clatter
the offshore winds shift
bougainvillea and sand drifts
moods
like tides
and your blue eyes.

There are back roads and right turns
I still make in my sleep.

no. 3

Birds can navigate over incredibly long distances using the earth's magnetic field. Their ability to see ultraviolet light, particularly blue light, is what allows them to do this. There is a lot of science behind all of this, but essentially an evolutionary protein in their eyes has been discovered and believed to be responsible. I read most of this in *The Eye: A Natural History* by Simon Ings. I pass days like this.

No big animals see far into the ultraviolet. The larger the eye, the more light it takes in, and there must be a point at which the potential damage ultraviolet light can do when focused outweighs its usefulness. Many birds and insects have evolved to see ultraviolet wave length, but they only live for a short time, dying before the damage becomes significant.

no. 4

I have wondered for years how birds, particularly the albatross, navigate overseas and never get lost. They are so precise they can stay on course with a five degree of variation. A bird's ability to see the magnetic field of the earth and use it for navigation is a relatively new discovery of the past decade. How they read the field, communicate it, or discover it remains unknown.

no. 5

An albatross can circumnavigate the globe in forty-six days. They are capable of traveling over ten thousand miles in a single journey. They spend the first six years of their lives flying over the ocean; after that they land only to mate. The breed for life, finding one another year after year as they return to the same nest every year, no matter how far they fly from it. It's also believed they can predict the weather and change their flight patterns an entire day ahead of a storm.

DEAD LETTER OFFICE

I try not to think about it all of the time. I am hard to be around, my edges snag, my touch pickles those close to me. Vinegar in my veins. I keep boxes inside of boxes, folded pieces of paper and cassette tapes in my glove box. I tag my thoughts—past, future, past conditional—so I can start to understand how often I am not really here.

At coffee, she tells me I have a lot going for me but I squander my days more often than not. I wonder at people who get things done. I read a book about a girl who wanted to sleep for a year, and I understand it so much I have to put it away. The sentiment rattles around inside me until I get sick, and then I blame it on the season.

Of the things I have been taught, or studied, or have picked up along the way, moving on is not one of them. She tells me, maybe it makes you a better writer, but not much better at anything else. This is the truest thing anyone has told me in six months. I look back at photographs taken in bathroom mirrors of myself living in Vermont, and all I can remember is the water on the windowsill and the rattle in my lungs.

The day before I left Vermont, it was raining, and I mailed myself home three packages. The boxes were so full I had to cover the tops in clear tape so they wouldn't split at the seams, leaving your sleeping bag and my winter jeans on the side of a road somewhere. It didn't matter. The one filled with the things most special to me—my notes from the work that month, the letter you wrote on the typewriter, the signed copy of the *California Field Atlas*, my books, my love notes—that one went missing anyway.

In the hazy month when I returned from Vermont and lived on my sister's couch, I could do nothing but talk in circles, cut things out of magazines, and get high. I one day filed a query with the post office online to find the package. It went unanswered. I was losing so much it felt right to let it go. I remained unfazed. Instead, I watched YouTube videos of tarot card readers because I was desperate for anyone to tell me what to do. I also cut more things out of magazines.

Today I got a notice that said the package is un-retrievable. It most likely sits in the Dead Letter Office—a place for lost, undelivered, and unreadable mail. I look it up, and the center is in Atlanta, Georgia, and over 20,000 pieces of mail pass through there daily. I read the word *un-retrievable* so many times it begins to look like another language. I lie on the couch while the sun goes down, and I imagine driving there only to lay down in a pile of letters and sleep there for a year.

ON THE RIGHT THING

What they do tell you—but you do not believe them for a very long time—is that doing the right thing is hard. Doing the right thing can be so hard it twists itself into feeling like the wrong thing. The right thing will keep you up at night months later and remind you of being so sick of the desert you couldn't see straight.

I try not to think about you there with her. I try not to think about the things that were once mine belonging to someone else. He tells me it's a part of the letting go, tells me it's a part of the process, tells me *replace* is an ugly word to use for something like this. He can smell it on me when I wake up angry, when I wake up adrift and out to sea.

I have to right my compass, fly back home again, try and do the right thing.

I read an essay about how possessions can hold certain power over us. How a duvet cover bought on a Tuesday in a different life is like a talisman linking us together. And maybe that's why I feel it so severely. Maybe it's her touching my things in your car that wakes me up in the night. But it shouldn't matter. We have to find new things to care about and new places to sleep at night. Nothing is mine save for this view.

In October the sea is less electric blue and more a steely, woolen blue. Still when the clouds clear, and they always do, still it glitters like piles of halite. But what does the sea care what color of blue it may be? Does it even know it? And if it did, would it want to be a bluer blue, or does it even care to glitter in the afternoon?

At the end of the conversation, his advice and my mother's advice are the same. "Come from a place of love. Do the right thing and send love."

AN INVITATION

I tell myself, *I am unaccustomed to this*. I tell myself, *That isn't true*.

We know it is fall now because there is no one on the beaches, because the backroads smell dry, and because the winds blow off-shore. I say it is winter, he says, not quite yet. Fall seems to be less of a season in California and more of a waiting space, a holding place for the things to come out of this.

We are told growing up every action has an opposite and equal reaction. I never truly understood that until now. How we make ripples and how they rock someone else's boat. How irreversibly everything can, will, and should change. I start to recite my own advice to myself: *earth time is hard time, show up for the change, you are only ever exactly where you are supposed to be.*

We have to believe the things we have sworn to be true. We have to turn pages and build houses and find new ways to spend mornings. We make beds, but we don't always sleep well in them, and still we have to go to sleep.

I can only imagine how the next year will look, and still, in ways, I will be wrong. I will be wrong about much of it, and I will be right about other things. About early mornings and new eyes and the smell of the sea in the middle of the night. This was to be, and we have to get in line with what life gives us.

I wonder if everyone is as affected by the seasons as I am, if everyone else prays to weather vanes, and if they dream in ways that twist them even when they are awake. All I want is a ranch in Montana where I can make huckleberry jam and tell the kids to come inside.

But eventually we put everything else to sleep, and we learn how to show up and do what needs to be done.

ON TIDES—

For two days the ocean has been calm. It is important for you to know about this place. That the ocean outside my window and the beach below make world unto itself. The rocky cliffs cut in and out of this coastline creating coves, a small sheltered bay. I feel that. Small and sheltered here.

If the moon can affect the tides, can the tides affect my mood? If the sea is calm, then so am I.

In the mornings, the water is a vice-grip grey-blue, dull, dim, and quiet. Other times, it's too bright to look at. It glitters and leaves you blind in spots for moments afterward. And still I look. But this morning there are clouds, and the water is still and looks like she's keeping secrets. I can see all the way to the horizon from here.

I had a teacher once who told me to never talk about my work, never tell anyone what your story is about. But early in the morning, I was having dreams that I had new ideas for stories, and now I cannot remember what they were, and that has only happened once before. Do you remember, in that basement in New York, how it was on the tip of mind?

When a story idea escapes you and goes on to find someone else, it leaves only its feeling, it's mood and the way it would have felt to write it. A mood you now cannot access no matter how hard you try. The impression is there, but the details are gone, and as any good reader knows, it's all in the details. I can tell you it has something to do with a younger older woman living in a facility for older people. But that isn't it at all; that is from a movie I watched three days ago.

The point is unless we sit down and invite it in, there are never going to be any more good ideas. So I sit here and sometimes a sailboat goes by, and the other day a dead harbor seal floated by, and sometimes there are divers in the cove. At high tide, you cannot see any rocks, and at low tide there are two clusters that come peeking out.

I think every day I should get myself some binoculars and learn the names of the birds. But again I am missing the point. Someone told me recently that being a writer sounded romantic in that lonely sort of way, cups of coffee and staring off into the distance.

When the sky changes, so does the color of the water.

No one tells you how to do it,
Only that it must be done.

The hard work is the heart work.

no. 6

I go back to the start. Blue is the rarest occurring color in nature. I follow this lead because it feels true. Blue does not just occur. It is a trick most of the time. Blueberries are actually purple, a variation of red, the color produced by a natural pigment called anthocyanins. The red pigment changes, appearing blue when the PH level changes. This is true of blue flowers too. Cornflower, bellflower, delphinium, hydrangea, iris.... I go to the market and try to buy some, but they're not in season.

no. 7

The same is true for animals, though the reason is different. What you see as blue is an evolutionary trick. Rather than adapting to produce a blue pigment, cellular structures changed to reflect blue light. A blue jay's feathers are made of tiny little beads that reflect blue light back to you, much like the scales on the wings of a butterfly or a peacock feather. If you were to get close enough, there really is no blue at all.

no. 8

There is always an exception. I watch a video online about the obrina olivewing butterfly. It naturally produces a blue pigment, and it is the only known animal to do so. I wonder how she figured it out when no one else could. I keep looking and find an article written in 2012 by Stephen D. Facccio on a website called Northern Woodlands. It's titled, "Why Most Animals Aren't Blue," and it reaffirms all the reading I've been doing. It also tells me, and I quote, "Only two vertebrates have been found that have blue coloring as a result of cellular pigment called *cyanophores*. Both the Mandarin fish and the closely related psychedelic Mandarin are the only animals worthy of being called true blue." I think, two fish and one butterfly.

IF YOU'RE READING

I am sick. It is a blessing. Something to point at and put my finger on. It's only natural to want to know why and what goes on. I was convinced for days that I was dying or losing my mind but didn't want to say either out loud. I've been stripped of what little sense I have and, even worse, what talent I possess. I sit blurry-eyed and watch the ocean move or the fire dance for five days straight. And I think about you.

I am someone who will talk a lot about how they hurt and what ails them, but it takes a lot to reach out and ask for help. I call a woman, Anne, on the telephone. She does energy clearings of the ties that bind us. She tells me my sadness, possibly even my sickness, isn't mine at all. I think about this a lot and try to pin down the places where it leaks in. I've thought it before: *this isn't mine, this isn't mine.*

I cannot imagine what the two of you say to one another. Nor do I want to think of how you think of me, and yet still I worry. Anne tells me a hex can come just from one person wishing ill for you enough that the energy binds itself and it gets hard to wriggle free from. If I could tell you anything, I'd say I am not trying to keep love from you. Perhaps under different circumstances, we even would have been friends.

The last seven months have tried to teach me the importance of being where you are. Because no matter how hard a time, we will eventually look back on it with some kind of nostalgia and want, even if that want is laced with ache. We inevitably move on to new spaces, and the thought will always be: I wish I had let myself be there more. If I could tell you anything, I would tell you this as well.

There will never be a life in which we do not ache, never again be so simple a time. As we grow older, we collect rooms, spaces, times of our life that when revisited induce a kind of wonder at who we once were, who we once loved, and how badly we once hurt. Even when you move on, the rooms remain the same.

There is something to be had here, and there is something you will miss here. Because even a sickness has something to teach us, bleary-eyed and staring out at the sea for days on end.

Nothing is small.

THIS PEACE—

Being calm has never suited me well. Or I have never suited myself to it. I am not sure which is true. I crave long stretches of time to myself and my ocean view. The world is a place I do not care to be a part of, and still I am pulled from this space stealing away only days at a time. Perhaps something in me knows this peace won't be mine forever.

I still think of the same things, of you, of her, of tide pools in Australia, and about June. But they seem now like familiar places I drive by, fixtures outside the window as I pass. Nothing holds the same weight. Even when the dreams come, they don't get in the car and ride alongside me like they used to. I know you, but I am not of you anymore.

During a different heartbreak in a different life in a different state where there was no ocean view, I remember telling someone that I didn't want to get over it. That my sadness meant we were still embroiled in something. Even if the link between us was the ache and the pain, it was still a link. I nurtured that pain for years, afraid it too would one day leave me.

Sometimes the ocean is so bright I cannot look at it.
Even blueberries can be sour if you have them at the wrong time.

If someone asks me when else have you felt this way, there is an afternoon that comes quickly to mind. I am in Bali and have been for weeks and have shed layers of self and skin and am in a small fishing village where I have to stay the night to catch a boat in the morning. I am alone, as I always was, and I walk to find a small restaurant, sit, and order gado-gado because it is the only thing I order in a new place. And I am writing in my journal and sitting on a floor cushion. It is so hot that everything I am wearing clings to my body, but I have moved past that bothering me. There are two men sitting not far away, and besides them the place is empty, but it is a strange hour in the afternoon. They are having a smoke and I cannot understand a single word they are saying, but the sound of their language has become so familiar to me that I wrap myself up it in. When the woman brings me my food, she is beautiful and small and slight. I thank her. And I am struck by the overwhelming realization that I am in this moment precisely the sort of person I always wanted to be. I have passed into a place of myself in which my projection and my actual being have aligned. And in that is the greatest sense of peace I had ever known, even so far from everything familiar.

In the morning I boarded a boat and crossed a dangerous straight of water and thought most certainly I was going to die. The boat rolled and rocked, and I tried to imagine I was somewhere else. The ocean outside the windows was too bright, the floors too slick with water. The blueberries had gone sour, and I could hardly even look at it.

We look so young in old photographs

It does not always occur to us there is another life waiting behind the one we have. Because we do not yet know what it looks like, what it tastes like, and who we are in other places.

BLUE FOR YOU

In the early morning hours, the sea is a loud silence. It is the only thing you hear, save a for a seagull, save for the sound of your own breath as you walk carefully along the path toward the water. The lilies have grown in, making you slip as you walk; they cling to the seagrass where they can. Buttercups bloom early.

Before the sun rises, the sea is a sleeping beauty, massive and rocking even in this small cove. Where it meets the horizon, there is a belt of baby bonnet, a lighter shade where the sun will crest through. From there it fades back to the heavens, a gradient darker until the midnight where a few stars still shine.

Nothing will teach you how many shades of blue there are like living at the sea in the winter.

In the cove, the water moves in every direction and all at once, a swirling basin that obscures everything beneath. When the tide drops, there are clusters of chocolate-colored sea rocks so sharp they'll cut your fingertips, covered in mussels and barnacles that cling to the rock when the water recedes. Carpets of vibrant green seaweed swell around the edges—a color you see only in the sea that reminds me of coastlines I've never seen. So wet it looks like you could drink it.

We too have tides, I tell myself, but they do not show so easily. There are times when we are nothing but swell and circumstance, and others where everything recedes and shows our sharp edges, the things that cling even when the waters are gone.

The birds fly so near to the water I cannot tell the difference between their lithe bodies and their shadows skirting the waves. At the full moon, the sea rises up as if it wants to press itself against the sky. A full moon is a full sea; you can feel the conversation between the two.

They say the whales are migrating right now, but I sit here every day and haven't seen one. They are heading south to Mexico, and when they come back, they will have babies with them. It seems to be the case with everything these days. Perhaps it is just the season. Perhaps it is just what I pay attention to. Perhaps it doesn't mean anything at all.

When the sun finally rises, the sea wears murky glass-bottle-green ribbons, a vase left in a window sill too long. The belt along the horizon glows a muted buttercream, perhaps a shade of ivory. Then it fades back into a sky blue we know so well that we see it even when our eyes are closed. Everything settles a little when the lights are on, or perhaps it just becomes more familiar.

The tide will drop in a few hours, and I'll walk the tide pools looking for starfish and sea urchins in deep swollen purples and spindly black needles. Every time the sea goes out, it takes something with it and shows us something new.

Same but different. I have a feeling that makes sense to you.

THE TROUBLE WITH WRITING IS

Years ago, in Idaho, Leslie Jamison came to read and speak with us. She taught a workshop where I wrote a very bad story. She was kind about it and chose one scene which I might extract and reuse: a dinner scene. I told her I'd recently been fixated with maraschino cherries, and later that night when she signed my book, she adorned her name with hand-drawn cherries. I felt the swell of being seen.

In the evening when she read, I was transfixed, in love, sworn by allegiance to read everything she would publish in the coming years. She read from *The Empathy Exams*, which were still underway at the time. She read of the Loneliest Whale. I could relate. But more than anything, I understood that nonfiction had nothing to do with me and everything to do with me at once, bound up into a single sentence.

When the questions came, someone asked, How do you reckon with writing about other people, about your family, about strangers, about anyone? Because the question that remains at the heart of all nonfiction writers is: What is true, and who am I to tell that truth?

Is my truth truer than your truth because it is mine? But say you remember things differently. Your perception your own. Your experience your own. And mine, mine. What if I wasn't even there? Is the barn yellow or red, and does it matter? What if you are nothing more than are a passing detail in the night: a hairclip on a nightstand, a story he tells me in the afternoon with the blinds drawn so the neighbors cannot see us?

Her answer to the question went something like this: You have to weigh it. Someone will be upset more often than not. You have to write it, but then you must weigh what you will lose by allowing the world to see it. One should often push forth now and then, but there will always be pieces that remain in desk drawers, written but never read.

I have my drawers too. Not everything gets read. And still I sit here, and I write and weigh, and I count the waves. My world is mine, and all that passes through is a lens in which to examine myself, my beliefs, and my hurt. Is it not the point to render the random into something meaningful in which we might use as a road map to something more? The passing details, the hairclip on a dresser, the stories he tells with the blinds drawn in the afternoon so the neighbors cannot see us.

There is a softness to the morning,
a quiet blue
a hush and a still,
not saved for the other hours.
A gift for those
who wake, cold toes and bleary eyes,
and come to the window
to see who they are
before everything else.

JUST A BIT OF BLOOD

You were in my dream last night, and I was bleeding in the living room of a house neither of us knew. I ruined the rug, but we didn't seem to care, neither that we'd broken in nor that they would know we were there. Spots like Rorschach tests along the edge near a piano. If I say you wanted to fuck me, does that give away what the dream was about?

This morning the ocean is so calm there are no waves, not even small ones that lap the shoreline, just flat and shades of blue to the impossibly near horizon where one boat has sat all morning. I met a fisherman who told me that an albatross is good luck, that the winds have different names, and that he only felt at home when he was out on the water. Sailors have superstitions, fisherman even more so. The ocean has its own language.

I am reading a book on reclaiming your creativity. I write morning pages. I wonder where I set it aside, so I feel so inclined to go looking for it. Someone originally handed me the book in the basement library in Vermont, the one with the window near the river where I had all of my hard conversations that month. Perhaps I left it there. Vermont feels like a lifetime ago and, in ways, just a moment. How can everything change so little and so entirely all at once?

The boat has gone beyond the horizon, and I can no longer see it.

In my dream you kissed me well and told me not to worry, it was just a bit of blood. I understood in the dream that what you said was not about what I ruined, but rather that I still had so much left give.

I do not know why
I love what I love
or why I have to ask for forgiveness
from the night.

In the morning it is still here,
the world
waiting for us.
As if to say, it is all right.

At daybreak the swimmers swim
and the birds fly
so close to the surface
each one is two.

no. 9

When I search *cyanaphores*, the internet asks me if I meant cyano-type. A cyanotype is a photographic printing process that creates cyan-blue print. There is a variety of recipes you can use; you can store the solution in glass bottles for months. "Making a cyanotype involves placing a negative image—which could be a photographic negative, or an object, as in a photogram—on treated paper or fabric. After an iron-based solution is brushed on, the paper is placed under ultraviolet light, or in direct sun, to develop."* You can print on almost anything. The shelf life is around two years. No matter how beautiful the blue image you create, it will fade in two years. This feels important. I order a kit online to make my own cyanotype imagery

New York Times, Ted Loos, 2016

no. 10

You once bought me a bracelet set with small rounds of perfectly blue lapis lazuli. Lapis lazuli is one of the only naturally occurring blue pigments on earth, and for much of time was only found in one place: a mine in the mountains of northern Afghanistan. The pigment, once extracted from the stone, produces what is known as ultramarine, or true blue. Also called the most precious pigment.

no. 11

Ultramarine first appeared as a pigment in the sixth century in Buddhist paintings in Bamiyan, Afghanistan, where the stone lapis is mined. From there the stone traveled four thousand miles in trade routes and appeared in ancient Egypt, where they adorned statues and tombs with the stone.

no. 12

The Egyptians failed to turn the lapis into a pigment and rather kept it whole. Because of this they were driven to create Egyptian blue, the first known synthetic blue, in 2,200 BCE. They made it from a mixture of limestone, sand, and a copper-containing mineral like azurite or malachite. They heated it until it became an opaque blue glass they could crush and combine with egg whites to use as a paint or glaze.

I WORRY AND I WAIT

I think it is easy to worry.

They say you can worry yourself sick over something. Perhaps that's what I've done.

I worry about polar bears in the doorways of small houses in a remote archipelago. The feeling of something so extraordinary made ordinary before your eyes.

And why was I crying in that restaurant in Paris? I cannot remember. I cannot remember no matter how hard I try. You bought me an expensive coat the next morning to make me feel better, though I do not think either of us knew why. I worry about this too.

I worry I will not take well to growing old. That I will be the sort of woman who loses everything when she loses her good looks. Unable to navigate and negotiate the world without them.

I am afraid but I do not know of what, and everything I write begins with the same few lines. About the baby. About Paris. And about my mother's hands.

These three ideas are strung together somehow, but I cannot decipher why or what their relation is to one another. It leaves me swimming in my dreams.

It seems like a silly time to worry. But I am predisposed to this, and I look up words in other languages to try and explain myself. I think the Russians call it *toska*. They say no single word in the English language renders all the shades of *toska*. And I feel that. I feel in shades.

FOR ME

I am sitting on the kitchen floor when he comes in. He tells me all of the time that it's just perspective. He wants so badly for me to find a new one. I want so badly to do the same. He sits with me even though he doesn't have to. Is this what it means to be in love? To sit with someone on the kitchen floor while they cry about someone else?

I whittle the days into a fine point. I do not write. Someone once told me, you have to get to a place where the shame of not writing outweighs the desire not to write. I'm waiting to cross that threshold. I worry so much it is making me heavy. Worried I made too many mistakes. Worried I wasted too much time. Worried I am in the wrong place. Worried I will never finish anything. Worried that I worry too much.

Is this thought true? In order to become the kind of person you want to be, you have to make peace with the person you've been? There is some kind of coming together that needs to happen, but I am not entirely sure how that is. I don't know how to meet myself in the middle. I have no doubt there is an answer in the act.

Perhaps I will go to the coast of Spain, but airplanes remind me of you. And I have already learned this lesson. You can put an entire world between you and what you'd like to forget, and still it finds you when you wake. We cannot outrun our own thoughts nor the fractures in our heart.

If I am being very honest, I know the answer, and I've known it for ten months. I have always thought you have to look at what is behind you in order to see where you are going. In this one thing, I worry I am very wrong. Because perhaps he is right, and it is all perspective. I should know this by now: you cannot drive forward by watching what is in the rearview mirror.

THE GOOD WORK

In the mornings the tide is so high you cannot see the rocks just beneath the surface, but they are there. You could not swim through nor sail over them even if you tried. They are most dangerous when hidden from view.

Someone tells me, what you exclude shapes your life just as much as what you include. That boundaries are not for keeping other people out but rather for reminding you what is actually yours to tend to. The queen of cups pays attention only to the ground beneath her feet, knowing that all she has control of is the seeds she plants and the water she gives them. Beyond this, nothing is hers.

I think it is easy for us to forget the singularity of our lives. To take in too much and worry about those who are not ours to worry about. We think of each other more than we should, distracted by where the other goes, left speaking to one another in smoke signals and parallel language for our parallel lives.

My mother and I listen to a woman read tarot cards on TV, and we eat salads of basil and grapefruit, and the baby is sleeping. Something about the afternoon is so common, and in that it will stay with me forever. I hope someday I am the sort of mother who listens to a woman read tarot cards with my daughter while we eat salads of basil and grapefruit.

All I can do is get the words down. Fill my days with the good work that makes my life work. In the morning I walk down to the shoreline, and in the afternoon I make pickles and the entire house smells like vinegar until the sun goes down. All I can do is plant the seeds, pray south, and sit back down to work.

Does everyone pray to weather vanes?

THIS HOUSE

This winter it does nothing but rain, and when we move out of this house I imagine I will say, all I did was lie next to the fire that winter, wait for the rain to stop so I could go down to the water. That's what I'll say. What else will I say about this house—there was a lot of love but there was a lot of grief? In the spring we will pack up our things and move two houses down, two houses closer to the sea. Change the view by a degree. Sometimes it's good to get out of places, to inhabit new spaces. I'm working a lot on letting go.

When I was a child, I used to cry when the bathwater drained. I tell him, I've always been like this.

She tells me, Mountains are waves. Soften your focus—you do not have to choose. It makes so much sense to me I think seriously of getting it tattooed on my body. Dream messages are like that; they get in no matter what you do while you're awake. I imagine she and I are so similar we might slip into one another's shadow if we were in the same room.

There was a time when I thought about her so often it bled the light out of the good parts of my days. I think that's the big lesson lately. Be where you are and not where you've been. I don't think other people have to deal with it like this. I think it's specific to my makeup. Does everyone else dwell in such detail that you might as well be able to time travel? That's no way to live a good life or the right life. I lie down in my car for forty-five minutes and pretend I'm somewhere else.

But pretty soon the spring is going to come, and the rain is going to stop, and I'll grow snap peas out on the deck. I suppose what is being asked is, what is the point of building a house if you don't even live in it?

ON THE HORIZON

There are sailboats on the horizon in the morning. From so far away, it looks as if they're sitting still, but I know once aboard you'd feel the movement beneath your body. We are moved even when no one else can see it. In the plain, stark morning, the sea and the sky seem to be a pair of lovers reflecting one another. Waves roll in across the coast like corduroy.

He once whispered in my ear, they come in sets of threes and fives. Then there is a break. There is always a break. You can count on that to catch your breath. I could never imagine myself out there waiting in the water for waves to come, no matter how many times I watched from the shoreline.

Lately I think, *Is this the break? Is this the part where I catch my breath? Is it why I feel so still and worry I will never move again?* I tell him from the shower, I just don't recognize myself sometimes. I don't have to see his face to know this is disappointing. If I've learned anything this year, it is how easy it is to disappoint other people simply by being yourself.

I try to imagine myself a year ago and the things I knew and didn't know and the thing I could sense but didn't want to look at. I try to reach back through time and tell her it's going to be ok, and it's not going to be ok. And then I think of myself a year from now, and I try to reach forward and ask her the same things. We so often forget who we are becoming. I tell myself I'll have to work harder this time to make sure she is all right.

The gravitational pull of the moon creates waves. There is something mysterious about that. Perhaps that's why when the good ones came, they always felt heaven-sent. Perhaps that's why we pulled over and watched them for hours. They were sent to us by the moon.

ON HERE

Here there are black-eyed Susans that grow clinging to the cliff. Here there is crumbling sandstone and quartz crystal that glitters in the afternoon. There is overgrown sea grass and someone calling for their dog in the distance. Everything smells of salt and stays damp, and my hair will have to be pinned back all of the time.

Here there is so much more ocean, and the sounds it makes are something I will begin to learn. Here it feels like an ocean and no longer like a sea. The horizon stretches for a lifetime. It is not all mine. Here there is a hawk in the palm across the cove. Here there are birds that sing and waves that roll. It feels as if I am the last person and as if something in me asked long ago to be the one that sits at the very edge and looks off into the big distance.

Here there is jasmine that grows along the walkway and outside of our bedroom. I am struck when moving in that the smell tethers me back to a different time, a time when perhaps I knew I would be here, but I didn't know how to look at it nor ask for it. One year ago I was writing from Vermont, and I was sitting on that river. A year can fold itself in half like a piece of paper, two moments happening exactly at once.

I wonder if back then the smell of jasmine was not reaching back to something I remembered but rather reaching forward and tethering me to a memory I did not yet have. To a time I did not yet know.

Here I walk barefoot on cold floors and drink tea in bed and count birds that go by. There is a clear sense here that this is where we were always going.

Here there is a single white sailboat on the horizon, and the sky is a deep grey and the ocean a mirror blue.

I am learning by the day
how to settle into what is mine.

And how to read the sea—

It can feel anywhere
from a muted charcoal grey
to a swirling sea-glass blue.

I imagine we are the same.

WE MUST BE WILLING

I think it has a lot to do with being willing. More than I ever thought before.

I go away for the weekend and stare out at a different sea. Channels like moods weave through the islands, and everything is mossy green and heartfelt, all honeysuckle and daffodils and cold, salty shores. I burrow away into my writer life in a way that feels familiar, the cloak of work, a purpose so clear it permeates everything. I sip coffee and say things like, it's not easy, and, I've never been good at anything else.

What I mean is I don't know how to finish anything and I am always afraid of running out of time. What I mean is I'm terrified the work is in vain or worse just not all that good. Sometimes I can't see the trees from the woods or make out the horizon, and if you asked me what it was worth, I'd probably look out the window and make comment on the color of the sky. What is the weight of being a writer?

When you introduce yourself, you tell me over a cup of coffee you are afraid, as an artist, you missed the boat. It is almost as if I am talking with myself. They say people come along and they are mirrors, show us what we need to see. I tell you it's not true, but secretly I think it is. I tell you can will another boat near.

We are in a bookstore in Seattle, and I am telling you what I want is a watercolor painting of whales, but what I mean is, please kiss me. Just because something feels good does not mean it's going to fit. Does not mean anything besides it feels good. This isn't a secret. But I am pretty sure it's a dream.

What I want is to go upstairs to your apartment even though I do not know where that is. What I want is to wake up with you and play with words and walk down the street and drink coffee and watch it rain, and drink bourbon early in the afternoon, and reads books out loud in my underwear with the windows open so all the noise gets in. If we had a life, I'd wear sandalwood and be the sort of person who throws away dishes instead of washing them. I'd be careless and adorable and shop at the corner store.

But this is not my life to want, nor is it enough to want something for five minutes. It is not enough to run my fingers over finished books; I cannot wish my work onto the shelf. What I am thinking is that we must be willing. We must will our lives in the direction of the very want that holds us. We must right our sails and get on the boat or, better yet, will the boat ashore by getting up in the morning and getting back to work.

We do not grow up into the kind of women we think we will be. We grow up into the only kind of women we know how to be.

ON MY WAY

I am made more by the day. I try to put into practice lessons I have been learning for the last five years. I read over my own words only to realize I have been talking to myself, right now, this entire time. It is nothing to hurt if we do not learn from it, and there is nothing to learn if we do not change from it.

If what I wanted was a full life—I have had it. If what I wanted was to test my heart—I have done it. If what I wanted was to see the world—I have seen it. What I want is to make peace with who and where I have been. What I want is to be here now.

There is a simple rhythm to these days that I will miss later. So I try to measure it. Water the plants, walk down to the shore, boil the water. I edit and read. I read and edit. The nature of this work is so circular. But the words, like the body, work better when you take care of them.

In a piece from three years ago, I said, I dream of a place where the sea stretches so far to the horizon I lose my footing. Ivy-lined and sun-bleached.

Maybe I was always on my way here.

Isn't this always the case? Isn't this what we whispered in the dark? This is not a destination. This too is just a time. But here there are ribbons of blue and shells to collect and string on fishing line in the window. Here I sleep and I dream and I work, and I make love in the afternoon and sit outside as the sun goes down.

TO LEARN

I ask myself, *why is nothing different?*

No one is going to write the book for you, mend your heart, or water the plants.

We have to relearn ourselves, and what we learn is we are not who we once were. This is a hard lesson. But so is origami, keeping maidenhair ferns alive, and Italian.

Everything I begin to understand in these months hinges on when the tide is going out, what kind of birds are going by, and whether or not I remember to eat lunch. The big lesson comes in making peace with how things fall apart. How we age, how we fall out of love, how we lose people.

I learn to trust myself more, to listen in the dark, and to lay out in the sun. It seems the things I am concerned about are actually and truly the signs of a good life. This is part of the learning, he tells me, just finding a different way to look at the very same things.

It's May now, and I keep on saying, any day. Any day now.

Sometimes I am so impressed by everything that has already been.

It moves slowly or not at all.
We work on laying to rest the small grievances
that make us too tired to roll over
in the night.
We smooth our evenings down
to a polished pearl.
We take tea sown by the water
in the mornings, and for one week
the waves are so big
we can hear them in our sleep.

TOO LONG COMING

I hear a voice say, you've been here too long.

I agree.

Even the things we care deeply about have a way of wearing themselves thin with the waves and the wind. I thought I would feel more. I thought I would care more, or ache more, or feel that ugly menagerie of feelings we get because we are, in fact, only human.

I am wondering less what you say to one another and worrying less about my mistakes. I think about things like how long the greens will last, deadlines for poems, and when the tide will go back out. I narrow my focus to a window of only what is right in front of me. The world becomes a place to play again.

My feelings wear one another, hide behind and inside themselves, and chase each another down in the dark of night. Relief and jealousy.

I do not know if it is a sign of being a woman or a sign of being me, but I sense now and then I am wholly unentitled to my own feelings. Does saying that out loud make me a different kind of woman than the one I want to be?

I feel myself entirely edged out of the room. There is no space left. You and her, and her. Life has a way of teaching you how to live it. How to make room, close doors, and swim in the water even when it's cold. There is relief in this, in my total absence. In my new life. In the plants I hang in the windows.

I make a list of the things I wanted to do instead. I let go of the name I had chosen. I stop saying what if we had. I learn the lesson that things are the way they are. There is no other path, no parallel.

I can no longer imagine it having gone another way. She is so little in your hands. Life has a way of teaching you how to live it. I have to lay my love down and get along. I've been here too long.

What if.

What if I told the sea of you?
And it didn't care?
If it came and went anyway
with or without either
of us.

no. 13

Ultramarine was imported to Europe in the fourteenth century and was so sought after it was worth as much as gold. It was so special artists reserved it for the holy and the royal, which is why we so often see the Virgin Mary in blue robes. It's believed that Michelangelo left his painting *The Entombment* unfinished because he couldn't afford enough ultramarine.

no. 14

Ultramarine means beyond the sea.

no. 15

Almost every blue we know is a synthetically created blue. Some of the most famous inventions were by accident, like Prussian blue. Johann Jacob Diesbach, a German dye-maker thought that by mixing his red pigment with animal blood, it would become redder. A chemical reaction turned it blue instead.

no. 16

Cobalt blue was used in Chinese porcelain beginning in the eighth century. Its chemical formula is Al_2CoO_4. It's lighter and less intense than Prussian blue. But then I read somewhere else that cobalt blue was invented by French chemist Louis-Jacques Thénard in 1802. This seems like a massive discrepancy. With further reading it appears both are true. While there is cobalt blue in Chinese porcelain dating back to the eighth century, the chemical formula of a purer alumina-based cobalt blue was discovered in 1802.

WHAT IT IS

Someone writes to me and reminds me that what I say holds weight. Although I sit here alone, I am never really alone. When my days inch by in peace, there is still something to be said. I have made my-self busy lately in taking inventory of the things simple and pleasing.

In the mornings, he gets up before I do, the room a mild darkness, a glow from behind the curtains. I forget where I am—still on a ship, still out to sea, still elsewhere always. In the mornings, there is warm tea and cold ocean air.

In a life I do not yet know, I will talk about this place. I do not know what I will say. Will I say I was hardly ever there? That I was just passing through?

I watch a video of you holding your daughter, and then I go for a walk around the block. I watch a video of puppies in the back of a pickup truck. I watch a video of someone making soufflé. There is an art to it really. Most people miss that, I think.

I take to the writing the way I take to working out, like both might make me a better person. Neither of them do.

Lately I've got the idea in my head that everything is getting better just because of the way I look at it. What I want to tell you is that everything gets better and it does not. We just get along and learn to live with it and then fall in love again. I am tired of being tired and sick of being sad and bored of being guilty.

I am looking forward to June. It is always an island, and I can barely say its name. Everything falls apart, and it comes back together again. There is something I am not saying, but I do not know what it is.

There are different kinds of hurt,
and still they always settle
somewhere in the body
and keep you up at night
as restless
and constant
as waves.

I GO NOWHERE

Most days I tell myself, get close to your hurt, braid its hair. I write letters to old lovers. I read them out loud. I watch for whales, count waves, read books. I go nowhere.

It is not easy to fall in love, but no one tells you that when you're young.

I take long drives to make myself feel like I'm getting somewhere. I take on insurmountable projects and lock myself away for the winter. I listen to music on the stereo, cook sweet potatoes, and cry in parking lots.

A few things there have never been enough of: coffee, time, and effort. I once said everything fails without consistent effort. But what I meant was, please stop the car so I can walk home. I'm mad at about things I can't even look at anymore.

All I want to do is go back to last summer and prove to myself I would not have done a single thing differently, even if given the chance to do it again.

I have never been good. And everything hangs on by a thread. I go nowhere.

Sometimes I wake in the dead of night and hear *come home* ringing in my ears.

TO BE SOFT

I thought I knew how to be soft until I saw you last night. Thought I knew what it meant to be light, to be passing by. I wonder always where you're going, where you've been, and why it takes me so long to see things clearly.

In a memory, I am standing outside of a fruit stand in Vienna. Or maybe it's just a photograph. All of Europe blends together as one long car ride and kissing near the Seine. One long lunch with white wine and playing cards in bars. If I think too much about you and I, in that way, I lose my footing and stumble. What I wouldn't give to be able to remember those things with ease. Do you ever think about the hotel room in Paris, or sleeping in the car along the river, or the time everything changed in that opera house?

When I wake in the morning, the sea is a moody grey-blue and the moon is full. The fog is thick, and I cannot see the horizon. On this day one year ago, I made big decisions that I couldn't sink my teeth into. If we trace it all back, on this day one year ago, things split into twos.

We are not allowed to go backward.

What I want to know is how the birds know to fly in a V. What I want to know is why the water is one day grey-blue and then next day aqua-eye-blue. What I want to know is why the wind swept me into another course entirely. What I am not saying is that I am learning a lot from where I stand. What I am never saying is that I am also happy.

I think now and then we have to be taught lessons we might otherwise shy from. We have to give up things we love. We have to get right by our own side. What I am learning is how to be soft and how to be good.

IT IS JUNE

A lake is nothing like the ocean. Silent and still, laced with ribbons of blue-green, a kind of chill that wakes you up in your sleep years later when you live far away. I think the lake could keep as many secrets as I'd let it. If I cannot be near the ocean, I find blue. I find a body of water and use it to measure my days against. I could slip under the water, watch the glimmer on the surface, forget there is even a world above.

We forget, and also we do not forget at all, where we come from. It fades into the periphery of a story you tell over dinner to someone you just met or a comment you make on a road trip when you swim in a lake in Nevada. How hot the air is in the summer, how cool the lake. I will grow old and my whole life will be stories, and I wonder then what you will say about me. What will be the epitaph attached to my name when you tell someone about me over dinner when you just met.

For three nights in a row, I sleep fitful and dream of Havana. I wake sweat-soaked and woven into the bedsheets, tied around my thighs and wrists—little worried knots made by someone while they dream. I wake myself up yelling for you. I swim in the lake in the middle of the night to cool down. Sneak out the back door and walk down the dock barefoot, slide my body in the cold still water, and never once think about what swims beneath me.

There is an island on the lake. Someone tells me one warm afternoon that in the middle of the wooded island is a field. That those who once owned this land gathered in the field before the winters came and swallowed everything whole. I imagine winter to be like a desert, the way it seems still and frozen and empty but is actually teeming with life, only no one stays long enough to learn it. But this is not my point.

The point is, it's June again, and I was almost afraid to say it, like I'd break the spell. June is an island. Something is coming, but I do not know what it is. I can feel it, though, sense its approach, wake up in the middle of the night screaming for someone who doesn't even say my name anymore.

But June is here, and I have said this before: there is nothing you can do in about June. You settle into it and let the rest of the world wait. Because there are no decisions made in June. June is a waiting space, everything else, a glimmer on the surface—a world you've already forgotten.

PART LUCK. PART YOU.

I have not been here in a long time. Or it feels like a long time. Because time can bend and stretch and fold depending on how you use it. In the summer it seems to heat up and slip between my fingers, sweet like honey, warm like silk. Is silk warm? I question everything these days, or always. Both are true.

I was on the road for weeks. Waking up in strange places is not strange to me. There is a familiarity to it that hurt at first, how much I missed that other life. But when the hurt fell away, something else came and took its place. A little voice reminding me it is my life and no one else's. The places I have been are mine, even if I share them with someone else.

Now I am home and the ocean is the same, but I am not. Someone asked me what shifted, what changed. I could not point at any one thing. A million small moments, and then you are somewhere else. Is that not how it always goes? But I will say this: you have to make room for those small moments to get it. It's part luck and part you, like everything else in life.

I am surprised lately how I often I talk of babies. Is it a reaction to other people or an authentic reflex of my own? I cannot tell yet. I feel divided in two and entirely alright with that. Building castles isn't easy and I am not done with this part just yet. Sometimes I miss the road. Sometimes I miss home. But I do not think it is true that they say you cannot miss both.

There is a list of things I remembered when I was on the road:
Life moves fast, but that's okay; you've got friends for that.
Mountains know how to glow just before the sunsets.
Rivers are the best kind of loud.

Dancing is real medicine for the body and the soul.

Love grows where you let it, just like wild poppies.

Everything comes and everything goes, it is not ours to decide when, how, or where.

Eat with your hands, food tastes better.

There is always time for naps, kissing, and cold beer.

This is all for now.

WHAT WE SAY

What we say is, I love you. What we say is, leave the windows open while we sleep. What we say is, the water is cold, but the sun is warm and is there still sand on your feet. Sometimes I don't feel lucky enough to be this lucky. Like it might run out if I look at it too hard or write about it too honestly.

All I do all summer is eat peaches and count words. Drink cold coffee and hot tea. Tell myself things will slow down soon and then secretly pray they will not. I have an idea that I will go to Vietnam in the winter and write. I have an idea my book will sell. I have an idea a year from now I will be very proud of the person I am being right now.

I think something happens when we aim to satisfy a later version of ourselves instead of the one we are caught up in right now. Somehow it makes the daily work easier if I am looking down the road. My hours are made up small things, and I do not think about you so much anymore.

I try to listen to the same advice I have given to so many other writers. Try to remember the things others have taught me. Stay in the room. Lean into the strange. Only write forward. Write in the mornings. Don't talk about it too much. Go for walks.

I am sure when I remember this summer, I will be surprised by how much I could do, how blue the ocean was, and what it meant to love good.

What will you remember
when you are no longer here?

A constant hush of water
glassy blue waves like moonshine
plants that droop
peaches that drip
music while we nap
lavender sky and dinner outside
counting steps
and sunrise
rug burns
house ferns
and the sound of your voice.

OF COURSE, WE ARE

I am never not thinking about it.
It stills and it stirs.
Rivers have undertows too.
They say if you ever get stuck, don't fight it.
You have to allow your body to go along because the water knows
things you don't.
And it will eventually send you back to the surface —
just somewhere else.

I wake up with the taste of river water in my mouth, like I've been
sucking pennies while I sleep. Copper fillings, fish food, driftwood.
Sometimes I dream dreams so tangible and real, my heart is changed
when I wake up. I dreamt about you all night. In the dream when
we met, I felt so clearly that of course, of course, we are friends.
Some unexplainable tether not of this life entirely but maybe carried
over on the shoulders of something and someone else. I know you
without knowing you.

It was so real I wondered if you had the same dream, and did you
too wake feeling closer to me than before? Saying to yourself, of
course, of course.

I do not know exactly how we weave our lives so they make such
pretty pictures. Unswum beaches and black-eyed Susans. I never
pretend to know anymore how other people feel. I try not to wonder
at it so much and read instead about how things grow and why the
winds change. We have to keep our minds busy, like swimming, lest
you get pulled into the undertow again.

no. 17

Cerulean blue was perfected in 1805 in Germany by Andreas Höpfner. By roasting cobalt and tin oxides, he made the sky-colored cerulean blue, but it wasn't available as an artist pigment until 1860.

no. 18

The word *cerulean* comes from the Latin *caeruleus*, meaning dark blue *caelum*, meaning heaven or sky.

no. 19

From space Earth appears as a blue planet.

no. 20

Indigo is a shade of blue, a blue appearing in abundance and used to dye textiles. It's one of the oldest dyes in the world, derived from a variety of plants, particularly called *Indigofera tinctoria*—it is the only instance I find in which the complicated history of blue feels simple. But of course, that's not true at all.

no. 21

Carol Mavor, in Blue Mythologies writes, "It is a myth that our blood is blue until it is oxygenated." I look down at my hand, blue veins like highways. It is another trick of the eye, a contract with the brain, a promise to see things as blue even or especially when they are not.

SOMETHING SO CLEAR

It slips through us. It's river water and empty paths and the smell of dried flowers in the hills up behind your house. I wonder if I will always be here, always still be there. Did I slip through a crack, see the future in a dream? Will we both wake up soon?

There is something so clear in this time of year. The way winds blow and force the planes to land backward, the way they kick up bad ideas like fire starters. Something is always burning somewhere. The horizon a brown ring. The last bit of sea before the horizon line is called the offing.

I imagine you taking her to see the sunset in the same kind of places and having the same kind of beer. Girls always look pretty near wildflowers. The question is, why do we care about what we care about? At least someone is watering the houseplants.

My mother calls the dog by the name of her boyfriend before my father, and I am struck by the sureness of how some things never leave us. Names we whisper when we are young are sewn into who we are. And someday we will both tell stories of the places we went and it won't hurt so much, and I will just be someone you loved when you were young.

I am not entirely sure what the key is, nor why it seems to allude me, nor where I buried it, nor why I dream of it. I wonder if others have it and slip easily into joy like they might a nightgown. I wonder how cold it is there in the mornings. I wonder, if I could, if I would go back in time. I wonder how she says your name.

There is something so clear in the air this time of year; it's pressing on me. It's waking me up in the night, and I go for a walk in the near dark. We are everywhere and nowhere. And it slips right through us.

IN NOVEMBER

All of November I am uneasy. A startling warm afternoon, a landslide somewhere nearby, a fire that is still burning. I wrote it once before, a foretelling of what would come. How uneasy I am in November. Everything feels nearly unlaced, threadbare, about to go bad.

A dead mouse in the walkway, a man calling for help over the sound of waves in the morning. Texts with bad news and sick dogs and the promise of something just about to break.

I read on the internet. I worry about things out of my control. Wait for something to step forward. Marie-Claire Bancquart says, "Exactly November. Everything in its place. And yet the unknown is nearby like an anxious bird." She is right.

I wrote this two years ago:

> There is a distinct feeling in November of having missed the party due to traffic, of having allowed the fruit to go to rot on the kitchen table. I keep on saying this. The two statements get after the same one feeling, and they cannot be separated. It has something to do with circumstances out of your control and being entirely at fault at the same time.

> Like I said, all divided up on the inside. You are always more than one thing at a time. I just want to sit here and think about it. I follow all of my thoughts by saying, perhaps it is the season. But that seems a strange thing to say in California.

In a contrast to the electricity in the air is a peace in my body. How can these things live in me at once? I am always asking the same questions, just under different circumstances. The sea glitters impossibly bright, and then sun sets and we say how lucky we are. But everything feels hanging on. As if we know things already that we cannot yet possibly know. They come to us in dreams of missed trains and awake at two a.m.

I cannot know now what it is. But it is always predicted by November.

GIVE ME

I do not know how to talk about the things I do not know how to talk about.

Someone on the internet asks me if I ever get tired of writing about myself. Truthfully it has never occurred to me to write about anything else. It is not because it is the subject I know the most about, but rather as the years go by, I am shown I am the thing I know the least about.

I study how to grow persimmons and the California aqueduct system, what makes the sea blue, and where one can go in the world to see the sun rise and set on the same beach. I takes notes on how to line dried octopus, and I board planes without knowing what I will find. I read books on French wars and breeding poodles and exotic aphrodisiacs in African jungles. I watch movies from the forties I listen to records from the seventies. I read early Old English poetry. Everything else has an end to it. Everything I study is fixed. Nothing changes the way I do.

Put me in a new climate, and I grow differently. I have something new to say or old to feel, either way. Give me a new lover, and I turn myself inside out. Give me a view. Give me time. Give me roses to grow.

Someone once told me not to worry so much about the things I couldn't write about or the ways I couldn't write. That all I needed was a few good approaches under my belt and I could ride those all the way home. The year is almost over, and I am only growing older. I do not know what I will be next.

What I do not tell anyone is that I do not know how to stop loving anyone.

LEARN THE STARS

In my dream last night, you want another girlfriend. I don't mind because I like her, only the conversation makes me aware I am getting older and I am less of some things and more of others. We make bargains with time, and it shows up in the strangest of places.

Lately everything feels like a negotiation. I am made to feel sorry more often than I like, and I wonder how one is supposed to decide where to place their energy and what sort of efforts we should let slide or throw out all together with the bathwater. What is that saying? How does one know which is the baby and which is the bathwater?

A bird comes to town, and we talk frankly for days on everything from motherhood to good men, and moving to why the sea is blue and whether or not those people swimming in the morning enjoy themselves. We eat oysters down by the bay and watch the boats tied to the dock bob in the water and go nowhere.

Life can be, in the same instance, incredibly simple and painfully complicated, and I've become convinced lately the two are not all that different from one another. We negotiate our way through loss the way one might find their way at sea with nothing but familiar stars to guide them. We move forward in some balancing act between the things we know to be true amidst all of the darkness of the unknown. The knowing and the not knowing, work together.

The end of the year always has the same feeling: sapped of its strength and also somehow pregnant with meaning. I am suspended but grateful, more sensitive, and yet sleep well knowing nothing can really ever be undone.

We learn, if we are lucky, how to see by the stars.

ON MAKING MARMALADE

If you want to show someone how much you love them, make them marmalade.

This year has only just begun, and I can already tell you one of the lessons it carries with it: anything worth doing well takes time, and anything you do is worth doing well. What we think will be quick, what we try and hurry, shows us there is only one way, and the way is through. With patience and grace and a steady hand.

If you're going to make marmalade, it's going to take you an entire day. You're going to go to the farmer's market early when they open so you can have your pick of the very ripe oranges from the bargain bucket.

Oranges, to me, feel so very California, a staple of my understanding of this place. They grow so frequently that sometimes you will a see a tree weighed down by unpicked fruit, so swollen it falls to the ground and rots. So much excess and so beautiful at once. Next to my sister's house there is an orange tree. I can see it out the kitchen window when I wash her dishes, and it reminds me of the few weeks I lived with her when I was very sad.

When you get home from the market, you will make tea and wash the oranges in a large metal pot that you fill with water and vinegar. Let the oranges sit for a little while, then scrub them clean because you use the entire orange. Something about this act will feel holy—the scrubbing, most likely.

The oranges will glow, and you will wonder which came first, the name of the color or the fruit. You have a vague memory of wondering this before and asking a friend over drinks in a dark bar. And they knew the answer, but now it escapes you—the answer, not the memory of the drinks.

Not everyone likes marmalade. It's a specific taste, a balance of the bitter and the sweet. Because you use the rind, you have to peel the oranges, save the rind, and then slice it into impossibly thin ribbons. About halfway through this process, you'll wish you had decided to do something else with your day. This can be made much simpler if you have a mandolin, in which case use that.

You'll spend the rest of the day cooking, watching, forgetting, floating around the house while you half do other things, but always still making marmalade. You cook the oranges and sliced rinds with a few cups of water. Cook them long enough so everything starts to wilt. This will take hours upon hours. The steam will be laced with citrus and tangle in your curls and make the house smell sweet and sticky. You fold laundry, and water plants, and let the dog out, and make more tea.

Once the oranges are cooked, you add sugar. More sugar than you'd think—pounds of sugar. You stir carefully as it spits and tries to burn you. This time you have to be more attentive; you have to wait and stir and let it boil but never burn. If it burns, it's all ruined. And then you stir some more. Eventually it thickens and cooks down, and you cross some kind of invisible threshold where everything you had starts to look like everything you want: the transference of effort into something entirely new. By this time it's late afternoon, and the sun in the house is different, and you have to put on a sweater, and the tea that you made and then forgot about has gone cold.

There are so many other things you are supposed to be doing today. So many things that need the same kind of tending to, the same care and attention, the same patience. But perhaps an act in one is an act in all. Perhaps some of it carries over like the sweet smell of the marmalade, perhaps not. Perhaps it's nothing at all.

You set the marmalade out on the counter to cool and thicken, and once it has you spoon it into jars that you've saved from store-bought sauerkraut and honey. You take some to your sister and some to your mother and store some in the fridge. And when he comes home, you feed him a spoonful. He kisses you with the bitter and the sweet on his lips, and he tells you it's delicious. Everything feels good and simple, and you remember that this too took time.

If you want to show someone how much you love them, make them marmalade.

REVISION BY REPETITION

My sister takes this photograph of me down on the beach, and I know right away it is the kind of picture I will look at when I am older and remember this stretch of sand and time and what it was like. It feels like the end of something, but I cannot tell of what. This happened to me once before, a tintype photograph taken in a motel room in Idaho. I still have it somewhere.

The early morning looks similar to the early evening, only the shades of blue are different. The mornings are soft like a children's blanket; it begs you into the day. The evenings are dramatic and heartsick and moody. Sunsets are for lovers. Sunrises are for the lonely.

I think so often of having a baby I am afraid I am going to will it into existence. The mind is a powerful thing. I wake up in my sleep whispering, *wait, wait, wait.* Ever since I was young, I've felt an acute awareness that I was losing time. I have always practiced in the permanence of things—first photographs and then language. One seemed to live longer than the other if you were good enough.

But how do we know if we are ever going to be good enough? I find myself worried about the things that do not matter as much as the words on the page or how I am going to talk about a dirt road. It is easy to get caught up in the business of life. We must remind ourselves to do the living.

I have a rattle in my lungs that feels like a promise. The waves are always larger in the winter; they roll slow and methodical. She writes me a letter and tells me they are a measure of time. This has not occurred to me, like this, until now—my entire life measured by the promise that another wave is coming. We take for granted the way the world works, the way our bodies work, when we aren't even trying.

I have begun to learn the different birds outside the window, and now I love more than just the albatross. I am very interested in the aerodynamic of the birds and why they fly in formation so close to the water you cannot tell where the bird ends and the shadow begins. Do they know this, or do they simply do it because they are birds?

All I do is rework the language and watch the waves come in and take my dog down to the water and drink tea. I read somewhere the only way to write better is to rewrite, so I do this for months. I rewrite like it's a religion. I pray all day at the altar of these waves, revision by repetition—the same sentences only different. Much like these days.

I cannot look at the ocean and not wonder at the color blue.
I cannot sleep at night and not think of you.
Like a bird navigating by unseen and yet so very real forces,
I am made to make my way somewhere new.

Everything feels circular, connected, and entirely on purpose.

THERE'S A WORD FOR IT

I become obsessed with diagnosing the issue. I plan trip to South America to take plant medicine and meet my soul parts. I listen to mediations on YouTube. I swim in the ocean at dawn. I take up tapping as a means to distract myself from myself. I make lemonade. I count the waves like sheep. I wonder what you're doing.

A therapist I see once tells me we mistake desire for happiness. Desire is actually the anticipation of happiness, and thus when it does not meet our expectations, we are left feeling lost and of want. Essentially what I hear is, life doesn't fill the whole order and it's okay to be hungry.

I count the seagulls in the morning and watch them swoop in circles about a grey, wanton sea. It's high tide, so everything is covered and smoothed over and made to look new again. I have a lot of editing to do, and my tea has grown cold, and I am not sure how I got here at all.

I'd like to be able to see straight and look around now and then. I suppose it would be easier for everyone if I could just get right and be happy. Someone tells me it's just my way of being; I shouldn't try to fix it but just make room at the table for all these parts of me who seems to rival one another.

I am not complaining. I am only nervous I am very near to ruining something that is otherwise perfectly well and good. I just don't know how to behave well. There is a word for all of this; I just don't know what it is.

ON THE SIMPLE

If it were simple, it would be simple. But the things that appear to happen like they are supposed to are anything but simple: a heartbeat, a bird's flight, table salt. The tide comes in, and we assume, because it is supposed to, that it will go back out.

Someone tells me, not deciding is also a decision. This feels personal to me.

I spend the weekend in San Diego and get a new tattoo on the inside of my right wrist that says, *okay*. As if to remind myself everything is okay, and will be okay, even when it isn't. While I am getting the tattoo, we joke about how we are only in this body for a moment, so whatever about forever, and it serves to solidify my understanding as of late, that I am only going to be alive for the tiniest amount of time.

When you cut down a tree, you can read the rings; they tell a story. Eucalyptus trees burn from the inside out, and avocado trees bleed red when they catch fire.

There has been now, for the past two weeks, a small brown bird with an iridescent red chest who sits on the railing outside my window. Today there are two birds.

Sometimes I think we can her each other's feelings.

The morning after the *okay* tattoo, I spend the day with an old lover whom I thought for years I would go to my grave still attached to. This was as simple a fact as my having two hands. My love for him and subsequent heartbreak was one of the most defining stories of my life. If I were tree, he would be the greatest of my rings.

But now, years later, a mild sun in San Diego warms the pavement as we walk and people stream around us. There are sixteen museums, and we don't go in any of them. We instead watch a street magician and then stroll through a greenhouse and read the binomial Latin names for plants brought here from islands in the Caribbean.

I am trying to pronounce one out loud, and he laughs with me. I see the moment from above as someone I used to be and am struck with simple plainness of the air between us. My body is just a body. And the story I had lived in and told myself for years was as foreign in my mouth as the words *Roystonea oleracea.*

Even the things about our lives we assume will never change eventually always do. At some point the air shifts, and the narrative develops, and everything is okay.

It is not simple, and yet it is. It happens just as it is supposed to.

We know, before we know, what we know.

ON THE CHANGE

I haven't written a single word since it started because I don't have anything to say. It feels like all of my twisting and horizon watching these past months manifested into something so much worse than what I could have imagined. No, I am not so self-idolizing to believe I could manifest something like this, but it is true when I say I knew something was coming. I just didn't know from where. I just could not have imagined this.

For someone who is admittedly nostalgic, ruminative, confused, and sometimes just plain sad, I am not a person of fear. And yet I find myself crying in the rain, afraid for my parents and my sister, and fearing the fever I imagine I have, but do not. The mind, I am learning more than ever, is a powerful thing. If I can think myself sick, can I think myself out of love?

Whatever I was worried about before seems small and far away now—questions I had are like trying to make echoes in a storm. They have nothing to catch, nothing to bounce off of. The landscape has so entirely changed, and we do not yet know the new rules. I read somewhere, *it won't always be like this*. And while that is true, it will also never be the same. There is also goodness in this.

I watch the waves come in pearly blue sets, whitewash that rolls and crawls toward the untouched sand. The beach remains empty, the streets quiet save for a lawn mower not too far away. The water is so constant I think sometimes I don't hear it anymore. I sit with my dog, who hears everything, and we both fit in the chair together. There used to be swimmers in the morning, but I haven't seen any this week.

I still do not have anything to say, just a recording, I suppose, that I am here. That we are all still here, even if this change feels abrupt and strange and wrong in so many ways. But it is not wrong. It is right. How do we know? Because it is happening. We have so much to learn—I think I'll pick up a guitar and try to remember the things I swore I would never forget.

INTO THE BLUR

It is one thing to say, *we take this for granted*. It is another thing to live in the knowing, to taste it, to have life so close you could reach out and touch it. If only…

The rest of my day is decided by how I spend my morning. I move carefully forward because if I slip, the entire day is lost to fog and worry and pacing the room so quickly I may wear the rug thin. If I make it through the morning hours without reading the news or asking why, then I know I can make it to sundown.

I keep myself busy by doing everything carefully. I untangle my hair in a hot shower. I make coffee slow and drink it even slower. I read poems to the dog and count the waves that come in. I am more grateful for this view than I have words for. We have so much more than we ever realize. I miss my mother. I set the table for no one.

I wonder what we will say about all of this later. I wonder sometimes if there is a later. How it will sound on our tongues, some strange fever dream we all slipped into? The lines are more blurred by the moment, night and day, day and night.

I name the days by the things that stand out. The day the bird flew inside. The day they took away the beaches. The day I slept fourteen hours. The day it rained so hard the windows rattled and blurred the horizon. The day you made a table. The day I learned to make bread.

Sometimes the fear is palpable, and I envy people I talk to who don't carry the weight like I am. I try to prioritize, narrow my focus, control my panic, but it does little. I open the windows. I cry at night. I worry there is no going back. I worry, even worse, that this is not the worst of it, that today will be something I covet in the weeks to come.

Everything that used to seem important feels like a forgone notion.

What I really want is to spend a summer in Maine and eat lobster, and drink white wine, and watch my daughter out the window in the yard of the house we rent for all of July. What I want is to be afraid of things like mosquito bites and too much salt in the salad and whether or not you still love me like you used to.

It's all a blur. Maybe we're there already. Maybe this is all a dream. Eventually we learn not just how to endure it but how to thrive and stay alive in it as well. We still have to make something out of all this.

no. 22

French artist Yves Klein dedicated his life and his work to the pursuit of the perfect color blue. He and a chemist friend created a matte version of ultramarine and called it International Klein Blue. He spent years between 1947 and 1957 painting objects with his color and once released 1,001 blue balloons over Paris. He wrote a letter to Eisenhower asking him to support his blue revolution.

no. 23

I listen to a podcast called *This Is Love*, in which they talk to a woman, Elena Palumbo-Mosca, who lived with Klein during those years in Paris where she worked as a dancer and swears they were not lovers. She was the model who painted her body blue and pressed it to canvas for his famous work, *Anthropometry of the Blue Period*, 1960. I wonder a lot about what the two of them said in private.

no. 24

Yves Klein died at the age of thirty-four from a heart attack. I think back on the note of the birds who can see ultraviolet light, blues we cannot see, and how very short their lives are.

no. 25

"Blue has no dimensions. It is beyond dimensions." —Yves Klein.

This is exactly what I feel when I stare out at the ocean and sky every day.

ON THE DRIFT—

I get good at going nowhere. I settle in. I keep a log of what this time is like on my island. I send letters to yours. Time was always measured by the tide, but now it's the days we count differently. I plant seeds in eggshells and water them in the windowsill. One sprouts the tiniest green, and I have an overwhelming sense of pride that I cannot say is akin to anything else I have done. I have narrowed my focus.

I once had a boyfriend who got a tattoo over his heart that read backward, *live an honest life*. This way, when he looked in the mirror, he could read it. He could remind himself daily how damaging a single lie can be. They grow like ivy and threaten to take the entire house down. I hated to admit back then how similar he and I were. How alike we were, growing up next to one another all those years, fed by the same waters.

Lately we talk about windows. We talk about what is outside your window and what I watch outside my window and how the world is the same right now even in different places. We get familiar with the square footage, the air ducts, the crack along the wall. We make peace and fret in the same moment. We are tongue tied, and tired, and restless. We are still here.

I am less desperate for something else. I feel like someone set out to sea — knowing we will arrive on another shore but not when. And we have little else besides the stars to guide us. I feel the rock of the boat, but it doesn't keep me up; rather, it now puts me to sleep.

I go for walks, and there is no one out. Early in the morning, a fog burns off and a car rolls by. A dog barks, a baby cries, and the wisteria hangs swollen and over-bloomed in the alleyways. Everything has an expiration. Even this. It's becoming clear we've got a lot to give up, and on the good days, I'm okay with this.

I MISS YOU

I am slowed. Stilled to the point that I watch seedlings grow and bread rise. I hear the bird nest near the window, my dog's wet paws on the kitchen floor. I smell rain even though it isn't here yet. The sea tosses and turns, but I am still.

Being restless is useless. Feeling cheated out of something we felt was rightfully ours is gone too. Anger like melted butter in the pan. The feelings go more than they come these days. We're settled in and stilled. In some ways, I've never been happier..

The world is narrowed to that of my windowsill. Whatever I worried about before seems to have left on the last tide. I have less and want less, and more than that, I am less afraid of what comes next. There is a kind of grace in knowing nothing will be the same. If not then, then what.

A friend tells me, maybe this is truly living. I tell her, I don't know anything.

Time has taken on an entirely other quality, thick like molasses some hours, thin like bath water for others. It slows and speeds up at its own will. Has it been days or weeks since we last spoke? Does it matter anymore?

We talk about where we will go next and orange trees and grapevines and skylights. We talk about what's for dinner and who won the last hand of cards. We talk about babies and green grass and the dog on the corner that barks when we take our evening walk. We talk about the weather like a house guest, and your mother, and that one time I took a trip to Spain.

I end every conversation with, I miss you.

STILL HERE

My days are scattered and semisweet like those honeysuckles we used to mouth the stems of when we were children. Everything feels less complicated today. Perhaps because the sun is out and the sea glitters, and this morning I reread an essay about the loneliest whale, and perhaps because for lunch I eat stale bread and goat cheese with my fingers and watch the dog stretch on the tile floor. Everything is reduced in these days, and today I am not upset about it.

Today there are two sailboats. I grow onions in the windowsill and promise myself that tomorrow I will get back to the good work, tomorrow I will make something of myself. But then again, maybe all of this undoing is just a different kind of making. Perhaps it is a good thing to go threadbare. To change one's course. To become something and someone other than what we had planned.

I used to dream about going backward in time, before time taught me how to stay still. Sometimes it feels like I am watching myself through the blur of a window. We are still here.

Summer slips by like an idea I forgot to write down,
a presence felt but nothing ever made manifest.
It's intangibility, something I can taste—
A mescal margarita in my kitchen
A pocket full of seashells
A book read in a single day.

The blue of the ocean shifts
almost imperceptibly overnight,
as if it is done putting on a show once the crowds leave.

I am left alone again,
and what I do not tell you, because you are not here,
is that September is my favorite month to be at the beach
like a secret.
And I would rather be alone for it.

no. 26

Some historians and scientists generally believe that humans didn't have a word for the color blue until they began producing it as a pigment. That to call the sea and sky blue was not something that occurred as a color; they just were. Color is as much an illusion as it is a fact.

no. 27

The wonder, then, if there was no word for blue, could humans not see blue? In the *Odyssey*, Homer describes the sea as "wine-dark." Not a single mention of the color blue, despite being out at sea for the majority of the epic poem. While there is a Greek word for the color blue now, it is missing from their ancient texts, furthering the idea that a word for the color didn't exist, because the color itself didn't exist.

no. 28

The Egyptians are thought to be the first with a word for the color blue. They were also the first to synthetically create a pigment. I am curious about the intersection of language and ownership and our ability to create and name something. We often do not have words, or the right words, for the way we feel. It does not mean that feeling is not real. Language often fails us.

no. 29

If I have a daughter I will name her Blue.

THE ORIGAMI OF TIME

I woke up with a familiar feeling from a long time ago—a small house I used to live in with my sister, where we always slept with the windows open and woke up late. A different time entirely, and yet the feeling was unmistakable. Like I'd fallen asleep here and woken up there: the glass door in my bedroom open, dappled light on the trees, and the sound of the water down below. Or maybe I was there, and I was waking up here.

I've become convinced lately of the origami qualities of time. How here is there and there is here. I look at a picture of my mother when she was just a few years older than me now, and life feels very quick. She hasn't left the house in weeks now—months, even. We bring her flowers and cookies and new books, and her joy reminds me of a child I don't yet have, and how good it feels to take care of other people.

My fear of life moving forward is reduced to ash. What a blessing to grow older. To love and lose and move on and live in different states, and have good enough things that it hurts to give them up. What a blessing to miss a part of your life. What a good life.

I have been so paralyzed by not wanting to lose anything, or change, or give up, or move on, that I had frozen myself, hung upside-down for years. I was unable to enjoy what I had and unable to let go of what I once enjoyed. Suffocating under the weight of my own guilt and indecision—or even worse, the decisions I did make but could never find peace with.

It all feels like such a waste of good time and youth and beauty and health and freedom and love and peace and all of the good things I have. There is no sense in not allowing yourself to enjoy the life you have in front of you. There is no sense in not making peace with your ghosts and letting the things you didn't do lay to rest like the dead. There is no sense in not sleeping in late and enjoying the way it feels to wake up naturally and forget where you are. There is no sense in it.

We hold tight to our narratives because these stories tell us who we are, but if we hold too tightly, there is no room for a story to happen and tell us who we are next. These ideas feel like tiny revolutions for me. Permission to be happy again, to be open to what comes next, and to allow life to surprise me. There is a lot of grace in letting go.

Because if time folds and bends and we all circle back in the end; if we are always with one another and nothing is ever really lost; if we are here and there and all at once, then what else is there?

We are still here. We are always still here.

MOVE THROUGH

We move through everything even when it seems we do not.

The red tide comes, and the water breaks slowly on the shore, thick and the color of red clay. I sit outside and watch the inky waters press forward until they reach me, stealing my blue away. At night when the dark falls, the waves light up neon green like blinking bar signs. It is a dangerous algae bloom that causes the bioluminescence.

Sometimes I wonder what we will say about all of this later. How I will talk about what I did or didn't do during this time, and how we watched it shift and shape and change like the red waters. Sometimes I am already there. Sometimes I have nothing to say at all.

I dream nightly about your daughter.

I worry I am growing used to all of this and that it will dull my senses to the dangers or make normal things that should not be normal. Our ability to acclimate is a curse and a blessing; we too soon forget the things we swore we would never forget. There is no going back.

In a different life, we bought a sailboat and spent a summer in Italy, like your father. I wrote poems no one ever heard, I grew out of my seasickness, and we taught our own daughter how to navigate by the stars.

All I really want is some land to call my own, olive trees, and good kissing in the afternoon. I want warm bread and a nightly breeze and to see my mother. I want poems that make my eyes weak, and I want sea grass, green glass, and tomato slices for lunch.

It takes olive trees five years to begin bearing fruit, others even longer.

TIDE COMES IN

I know nothing of what it means.

I wake up repeating this phrase to myself but do not know how to finish it. I say it anyway as I make black coffee then sit in my chair with the dog by the window and watch the swimmers in the cove swim past. I know nothing of what it means.

Whose words are these? Whose words are they when we wake up with the taste of another place in our mouth? Where do we go while we are sleeping?

I read your email over and over again. It has the sound of so many things deleted and unsaid, but I suppose that is exactly where we should be. It is a wonder I used to know you so well that I could measure how quickly you fell asleep. I know nothing of letting go gracefully.

For the first time in my life, I am disappointed, if only for a flaring second, when I get my period. I stare dumbly at the wall. The feeling lasts for the briefest of moments, almost undetected, but I see it and register it as something new.

Because of this, I try to remember the girl I was a few years back, with you, and the baby we didn't have. I pay her respect and acknowledge how much we grow, especially and because of the decisions we once made. I tell her don't worry, I'll take care of you next time.

It becomes clear to me how absurd I was in thinking I could go forward by going backward. How much we change and how nothing stays the same. Life is too short to be so sad all the time, and besides then you wouldn't have her small hands and I wouldn't have this view. I, too, have been holding myself hostage. I, too, have to lay down my promises and get on with things.

Because we make a life of decisions, and it is those very decisions that make our life. We know nothing of what they mean while we are making them. This is the agreement: to trust enough in the tide to discover where it takes us. A good friend told me recently, tide comes in, tide goes out. I would say this to you if I were saying anything at all.

I ask as if
there is an answer
as if there is
a method
to loss
to love
to why we wake up in the night

I ask as if
the waves will tell me
where they have been.

no. 30

I try to make a list of my own shades of blue by looking out at the
sea everyday:
be-soft-blue
sailboat-blue
moody-blue
home-blue
moon-blue
steel-blue
so-long-blue
still-up-blue
etch-blue
hewn-blue
barely-there-blue
gone-blue
low-tide-blue
horizon-bird-blue
heart-blue
sojourn-blue

no. 31

The ocean is controlled by the moon. This feels like a fantastical
fact, but so does everything else. The gravitational pull created by
the moon creates tidal force. The tide comes, tide goes out.

no. 32

There is a cycle I can count on. I watch the tide come and go, two high and two low. They are a promise I have come to rely on. I wait for low tide like a gift and collect seashells.

no. 33

Seashells are created by the organisms that inhabit them. They're mostly calcium carbonate with 2 percent proteins to make them stronger. They are not made of cells. I collect seashells in my pockets in the mooring at low tide and place them in a jar by the window.

no. 34

A pod of dolphins swim by. Dolphins "see" by interpreting sound waves. Sounds waves travel five times faster through water than they do through air.

LEFT ALONE

Most of what I want to say these days, I put in my letters. Morning magic saved for these alone. Sometimes, as a writer, I feel like I only have so much time in that place each day, and when it's gone, it's gone. It's a place I can only get to if I am left alone.

You tell me there is a tension between wanting to be a mother and being an artist. This touches something I have not been able to name. I feel this truth all the way down to the quiet places. It is the thing I do not want to admit, my fear of losing my solitude, that place where the magic gets in. What will happen to *me*? I ask you.

Everything has an iridescent timeless quality to it, like I'm dreaming or I've just woken up. I cannot tell which, and I do not think it matters. What I want is to drive north and lie naked sunning on the rocks at the slow bend in the river. I would follow you anywhere if we were still going places.

There is a tangle of balloons caught in the palm tree outside my apartment. The water today is a blue so clear I can see all the way to the bottom from my balcony. I wander from room to room and start three different projects. I make new coffee. I water the orange trees. I wait for something to happen.

I want to have a daughter and name her Blue. I say this out loud, iterations of the statement like an incantation. As if I say it enough, it will become true. I am always waiting for my heart to catch up with my body. I have said this before. This time, I think, I will tell it where we are going next.

I go outside and collect tomatoes off the vine. It is so bright that when I come back inside my eyes have to adjust. I think, this is what it felt like to fall in love with him. I suddenly couldn't see anything that I could see a moment before. It took me two years for my eyes to adjust.

I take my own picture in the mirror in the living room, like I have every day since the quarantine started. For lunch I make toast with olive oil and salt, thick tomato slices, and chunks of Humboldt Fog goat cheese. I sit naked on the tile floor and eat with my fingers and watch the waves come in and out. There is something feral about being left alone.

IT IS JUNE

A student from years ago reaches out to me and asks why I have not written anything in the month of June. Why I have not even once used the phrase "June is an island" which it is, now more than ever. This is one of my favorite phrases. For years now I have reckoned with this notion. I have been separated from myself, partly because of the world and partly because of my place in it, and partly because I think this happens from time to time.

If I can tell you anything about right now, it is that I am equally interested in a bird's ability to see the magnetic field of our earth as I am about the heat in Arizona. I spend a lot of time looking for seashells with small holes in them to string on fishing line. I read more than I talk to other people. I think a lot about having a baby. I think less about you having a baby. I grow tomatoes and am still wishing I could see my mother.

I do not know what happens next. I cut my finger open with a kitchen knife and got six stitches that still ache along my knuckle.

HOW WILL YOU REMEMBER?

I wonder what you will remember about me and what it is we remember about anyone at all. How is it some moments, some details, some way of movement, stick out in the shifting of the sand. Memories like land masses we measure ourselves against, how far we go from one another.

Everything this summer seemed to turn liquid and slip through my fingers. The tomato plants die, the ferns wilt, and nothing gets finished. I've made a life out of being idle and watching the horizon line. If I am taken away from the sea, I am restless, confused, and useless.

When it comes to remembering, if I think about my mother, it is the way her purse always smelled of cinnamon gum, how she folds toilet paper into squares, and the way she cuts celery for salads. Innocuous little actions, and yet the entire world is tied to them as if by string.

When I remember this place, what will it be? How an entire stretch of my life was kept in time by the tide or the feel of sand stuck to my feet inside? A tea kettle whistling or plants that always need to be watered? Will it be the night I drew a bath and then laid on the tile floor to break my fever? Will it be watching you swim?

How will you remember me here? Is it the way I walk to the window while I brush my teeth or the way I roll basil leaves and slice them into ribbons? Will it be the sound of the typewriter that doesn't work well or half-empty coffee cups leaving rings on my books? No, it will surely be things I do not even know that I do. Because that is how it goes. We remember others' unconscious acts more than anything else because they are tea leaf readings of who they truly are when they believe no one else is watching.

I wonder then, what do we imprint on the people we keep close? What do we accidentally do to one another? I have been in love too many times to tell the difference between what we take and what we leave. I know myself only in relative relation, like someone set out to sea. I measure my location by those very land masses. It is a virtue or a vice, depending, like everything else, on how you choose to read this.

I do know that someday, not so far from now, we will be somewhere else entirely. My life is a constant process of my heart trying to catch up with my body. My mother says, the lessons teach you how to learn them. I think it is a lot to remind ourselves that every single thing we do will one day be something we miss, even and especially the things you do not expect to. It is very easy to forget and hard to remember that nothing stays the same.

I go to the store and buy of flat of peaches knowing it might be the last of the season. They all ripen at once, and for days I eat nothing but peaches, refusing to waste a single one. The last sweetness of summer is something I refuse to go without. The world is a scary and ugly place, was it always this way? And what do these words matter—pretty sentences, like tying ribbons to telephone poles? I cannot tell if it does nothing or does everything.

THE BLUE OF IT

From here, I can see a line in the water shifting from blue to grey as the fog moves toward us. Then a line of birds. Then a line in the sand.

I have been working hard at a few things. It feels silly to list them out like a title promise, so I won't. But I will tell you I am working hard at understanding my own personal affliction so I might be able to better mitigate my response to life.

I tell my boyfriend, my fiancé, the man I'll spend the rest of my life with, that I wish he had known me before. That my real friends would never describe me as anything less than carefree. He laughs a little, and we keep on driving. I tell one of my oldest friends this, and she says, *I wonder what happened.*

I read an essay in which the author talks accurately of his dissociative disorder as an inability to be where he is. This makes sense to me. I listen to a YouTube video of a therapist talking about somatic healing and how our body will signal to the brain it is being threatened, even when it is not, if we have been unable to switch out of fight-or-flight mode. This also makes sense to me. I read about obsessive thinking and nervous disorders, and then reread *The Bell Jar*. My sister thinks I should medicate. My boyfriend thinks I should meditate. A friend tells me to move into it. Another one tells me to stay still and listen. All of this sounds right, and none of it feels like me.

Lately I wonder if the blue of this place is responsible for my state. That all of this blue all of the time has anchored within me an intense longing for something I cannot name and likely already have. The blue of longing. The blue of distance. I read these ideas from Rebecca Solnit religiously because this makes the most sense to me.

The fog arrives, obscuring the horizon. I get up and go inside, but by the time I sit down again to write, I do not remember what I wanted to say.

But I know you already understand this about me, that this affliction is the very thing that makes me. In a writing exercise, we are asked to choose a writer and identify in their body of work: *what is their ore?* What is the thing that runs through all of their work like veins? What is their big question? Or, best stated, what is the affliction from which they grapple with life?

It is only when I turn this exercise in on myself while compiling a book of prose poetry that I am asked to settle the debt. It is this or it is all the blue around here.

no. 35

Sitting on the beach, a friend reads to me facts about the ocean, and this one stands out: the waves are not the water. Waves transfer energy, not matter. The substance a wave moves through is called the medium; in this case, staring at the ocean, the water is the medium, the wave is the movement of the energy.

no. 36

A wave is a disturbance that moves energy from one place to another.

no. 37

Light waves are waves. Blue is a wave created by the energy of light as it travels through a medium called an electromagnetic field. But light waves are not water waves.

no. 38

The waves that reach my shore originate from wind, from gravitational attraction, from storms, from atmospheric pressure gradients, from you. The tide is considered a wave.

no. 39

I wonder if the same principles of waves apply to me and you—if an energy can come along and move us, change the way we see things, alter our course, create illusions, new colors, new places, new movements.

I want of nothing
but you—
Of cold drinks,
half-squeezed lemons,
and the sound of you
singing in the kitchen.

I love you so
I grow weary and
tired like the waves.
I walk circles
and pick seashells
and sleep in late.

Maybe I'll build
a house of seagrass
so you won't have to hold
my hand
my heart—

ON WHAT IS NEXT

The world is dissolved to the point of a pin. Of a heaving sigh. Of a shift in light. A grain of white rice. A drop of blood on the floor.

Everything rusts quickly here. It blooms overnight on the trash bin or guitar strings, the tea kettle, the watering can.

It's quiet when you leave, the kind of quiet I used to cherish. I could write an entire book on how well one person can waste a day. But space makes space. I think it's easy to forget when you are the one making it.

I count waves, count ounces of water, count words, count days. I buy a pair of overalls for a baby I do not have. I draw a new house in a notebook.

I am another year older, and I pass this mark by laying in the sand for days on end and then writing about laying in the sand for days on end. Something has come to an end, but I cannot quite touch my tongue to it.

A dear friend comes down to stay for the three days, and we read on the beach and drink in the afternoon, and when I tell her about my nerves, she says simply, you cannot live in the same moment forever. And like that, the matter is settled.

I wonder at what comes next, roll it over in my mouth and say it out loud. She takes a picture of me walking along the beach where I live, and when I see it, I tell her it will be the cover of my book. I want something I can hold in my hands. I want to hold these years in my hands. I've never been very good at letting go.

If I could be a bird
If I could know you
        the way
the albatross knows
   the way home.

I could loosen my grip
on this life
and let it glide.

Will myself to worry less
        sleep in late
in a sleeveless silk dress

Spend my love
on moontalk
   and the things
   that we both miss.

I can tell the summer is waning. It's in the slant of light and the chill in the morning.

We will not always be here.

Thank you.
I am sorry.
I love you.

Erin Rose Belair is a writer, from the coffee to the grave. For her, it's less of a vocation and more of a veneration. Belair received her MFA in fiction in 2010 when she wrote, *Vinegar*, her first collection of short stories. Stories from this collection have been widely published and won awards with *Glimmer Train* and *Narrative*. Author of *The Only Road Home*, and represented by Erin Harris at Folio Agency in NYC, Erin Rose Belair is a multi-genre writer exploring the boundaries of her craft.

She would like to thank Chance Welton for giving her the place and space to write what was necessary in these years, and in life.

CPSIA information can be obtained
at www.ICGtesting.com
Printed in the USA
BVHW011842230123
656884BV00039B/513

BRITAIN'S SE
DEFENC

BRITAIN'S SECRET DEFENCES

Civilian saboteurs, spies and assassins during the Second World War

ANDREW CHATTERTON

CASEMATE

Oxford & Philadelphia

Published in the United States of America and Great Britain in 2022 by
CASEMATE PUBLISHERS
The Old Music Hall, 106–108 Cowley Road, Oxford OX4 1JE, UK
and
1950 Lawrence Road, Havertown, PA 19083, USA

Hardback Edition: ISBN 978-1-63624-100-5
Digital Edition: ISBN 978-1-63624-101-2

A CIP record for this book is available from the British Library

Printed and bound in the United Kingdom by TJ Books

Typeset in India by Lapiz Digital Services, Chennai.

For a complete list of Casemate titles, please contact:

CASEMATE PUBLISHERS (UK)
Telephone (01865) 241249
Email: casemate-uk@casematepublishers.co.uk
www.casematepublishers.co.uk

CASEMATE PUBLISHERS (US)
Telephone (610) 853-9131
Fax (610) 853-9146
Email: casemate@casematepublishers.com
www.casematepublishers.com

Contents

Foreword

It's really quite remarkable to think that Britain was the only country in the Second World War to prepare a secret guerrilla and resistance movement before any enemy invasion had actually taken place. Nor did the enemy ever attempt to cross the English Channel. But in the summer of 1940 there were plenty of people who were convinced the threat of a German invasion was a very real one. Take Norman Field, for example, a young officer in the Royal Fusiliers, who had been wounded in the hand in France in May 1940 and was subsequently evacuated from Dunkirk. Despite his wound, he was itching to get back into action. 'God almighty!' he told me. 'To think those bloody Germans were going to come here!' So, I asked him, you really thought they were going to invade? 'Yes,' he replied, 'and so did everyone else.'

Of course, we now know what happened: that the RAF kept the Luftwaffe at bay, that the Royal Navy would have seen off any attempted German invasion in any case, that Germany then turned to the Soviet Union before it was ready and that the democracies, with their global reach, access to the world's resources and industrial muscle, were, along with the USSR, able to gradually grind down the Germans and defeat them five long years later. But men like Norman Field had no crystal ball and despite Britain's many advantages, both in terms of geography and material wealth, the strategic earthquake of the fall of France and the defeat of the British Expeditionary Force was such that an invasion of Britain by Nazi Germany really did seem both a very real threat and a highly probable one too. After all, France was, in modern terminology, a superpower with a vast army and yet it had fallen in just six weeks. Britain had the world's largest navy and merchant navy, a huge empire and immense global reach, but its army was small and had been defeated and humiliated, its weapons and equipment left on the sands of Dunkirk. This island nation, for all its assets, felt weakened, exposed and extremely vulnerable.

It was because of the dramatic events on the continent – and the defeat of France had seemed inevitable after just a few days of the German attack – that Anthony Eden, the Secretary of State for War, announced the immediate formation of the voluntary Local Defence Volunteers on 14 May 1940; if ever a decision demonstrated the profound shock and concern of the new Churchill government at events across the Channel, it was this: the raising of a volunteer army to defend Britain's shores in the event of an enemy invasion.

A few weeks later, after his return to England and having been discharged from hospital, Norman Field was recuperating at his mother and step-father's house in Ilminster, Somerset when he was visited by Peter Wilkinson, a friend and fellow officer in the Royal Fusiliers. Field had always suspected that Wilkinson was also working for the Secret Intelligence Service in some capacity; before the German attack had launched on 10 May 1940, his friend had on occasion mysteriously absented himself from the battalion on various 'courses' and 'assignments'. Neither Field nor his fellow officers had ever pressed Wilkinson about what he was up to – one simply didn't – but with defeat on the continent and Nazi Germany seemingly unstoppable, Field wanted to get an active post quickly and thought Wilkinson might be able to help.

'Peter,' he said to him, 'I don't know what you're doing and I'm not going to ask, but whatever it is, if there might be any opportunities for me, please do bear me in mind'. Wilkinson said nothing – there wasn't even a flicker of a response in his eye – but two days later, a telegram arrived asking Field to report to a place called Coleshill in Berkshire for an interview.

He duly reported as bidden and after waiting in a vast servants' hall, a small middle-aged man with a trim moustache appeared, introduced himself as Colonel Colin Gubbins, and told Field he had been given the job of setting up a top-secret underground operation in Britain to help deal with an invasion if and when it happened. The Auxiliary Units, as they were deliberately vaguely called, were a further organisation set up in the wake of the French defeat and threat of invasion. Not the Home Guard, but, as Andrew Chatterton describes it, 'a highly trained, ruthless, secret sabotage and guerrilla force'. Was Field prepared to join this organisation, Gubbins asked him? Yes, he replied, without hesitation, although had to admit he had still to be declared medically fit. This, Gubbins, assured him, was no impediment. Sure enough, within a couple of days, Field was sent for a special medical and immediately declared fit.

Even better, he was told he was skipping two ranks and being made a captain in the Auxiliary Units, a top-secret organisation. A few days later, he was sent to The Garth in Kent, where he was to become the intelligence officer for a key operational area and taking over command from Peter Fleming, brother of the Bond novelist Ian Fleming. In fact, it was Peter who was the better known at the time. A Guards officer and a highly renowned explorer, adventurer and author, he had been one of the brains behind the Auxiliary Units. It needed people with flair, drive, intelligence and imagination, characteristics Fleming had in abundance.

The Garth was a secluded farmhouse in the quiet village of Bilting, Kent. It was, perhaps, only natural that Kent should be one of the first places to recruit Auxiliary Units as it was the county closest to occupied France. Requisitioned by the army, it became the first regional training centre under Fleming. The growth of the Auxiliary Units meant Fleming was needed elsewhere and so Field was to shadow him for a fortnight and then take over.

What followed over Field's time at The Garth was the further growth of this extraordinary organisation, one in which secrecy and ingenuity were key watchwords. Everyone who joined had to sign the Official Secrets Act; they could not even tell their wives or closest family they were members. It was, and remained, an entirely deniable organisation, and until the end of the war and beyond, no one, other than those involved, knew of its existence. Recruits were warned that should the invasion come, it would more than likely become a suicide mission.

Cyanide pills were to be swallowed if capture looked certain. Ingenuity was key. Teams of eight men would operate together and, should an invasion occur, would base themselves in a hidden underground bunker equipped with supplies of food, weapons and ammunition to last a fortnight. How to hide the entrances to these bunkers prompted even greater imagination and ingenuity; Field devised an entranceway, for example, that was disguised as a sheep trough. Others were accessed through an outside privy.

The conversation I had with Norman Field was the first time I had ever gained more than a cursory insight into the workings of the Auxiliary Units. Although they were first written about in the late 1960s, they remained a shadowy wartime organisation about which much detail remained hidden. By the time I was talking to Field, his obligation to maintain the Official Secrets Act had long since passed, but his tales of operational bases and exploding fingers were purely his memories and nothing more, and related purely to his personal experience training and operating in Kent. To really bring clarity to our understanding of the Auxiliary Units, a great deal more work was needed: practical work, archaeology and a considerably greater amount of archival research – work that Andrew Chatterton has undertaken for *Britain's Secret Defences*, which vividly describes the vast network created around the country but also its evolution and development into something much more than a cadre of trained guerillas.

One of the reasons the Second World War, in all its vast reach and complexity, remains so enduringly fascinating to so many is because there is still so much to learn and understand. Andrew Chatterton has filled one particular hole with this important and timely book, a work born of immense knowledge, detailed and exhaustive study, and one which brings genuinely new and revelatory understanding to his subject matter.

Not only does he provide fascinating detail about the make-up, extent and detailed training of the Auxiliary Units, he has also investigated the development of civilian intelligence-gathering cells recruited by intelligence officers such as Norman Field, and who included housewives, teenagers, vicars and schoolmistresses amongst their numbers. Chatterton also sheds new light on further secret organisations that emerged, such as Section VII; his is the first work to cast significant detail on this. As he points out, the Auxiliary Units were an anti-invasion guerrilla force, but Section VII was designed to be more of a resistance cell had an invasion proved successful.

Yet as with so much of our ongoing interest in the war, at its heart it is about the people involved: in this case farmers, poachers, adventurers but also everyday folk, both men and women, who were prepared to make the ultimate sacrifice should it come to it. The Auxiliary Units, especially, were expected to display a level of tough ruthlessness not often associated with Britain's early war effort; what they learned, and the skills and techniques they developed, were also invaluable for the development of other, subsequent, special forces.

Many of these people have since gone to their graves with their secrets about the organisations they had joined and the training and preparations they undertook – roles which, thank goodness, they never needed to perform. *Britain's Secret Defences* brings many of them back to life and opens our eyes to an extraordinary and hitherto largely unknown organisation born at a time when many in Britain believed the country, and its freedoms, were dangerously imperilled. Our understanding of Britain's wartime past is greatly enriched as a result.

James Holland
April 2022

Acknowledgements

I first read *Last Ditch* by David Lampe in 2010. His story of a previously untold piece of British history from the Second World War naturally piqued my interest. Published in 1968, *Last Ditch* uncovered the potential role that thousands of men and women would have played had the Germans invaded and yet I and most others had never heard about it.

Further research brought me to the door of Tom Sykes, the founder of the Coleshill Auxiliary Research Team (CART) a group made of volunteer researchers who look into the activity and history of these groups Lampe first wrote about in the late 1960s. After a chat with Tom, and offering my services as a volunteer Press Officer, I was pretty much hooked.

CART has done an amazing job of researching, documenting and recording the highly secret groups of civilians that made up the Auxiliary Units and Special Duties Branch. Much of this information is included on the fantastic staybehinds.com website, but the group has also created the British Resistance Archive, an amazing collection of first- and second-hand accounts, documents and first-class research.

You will find references to the archive throughout the book and my thanks have to go to the entire team at CART. Tom Sykes, who has now stepped down, for taking my first call; Nina Hannaford, Chair of CART and researcher for Devon and Cornwall, for her continuing support (and cake); Martyn Allen for proofreading endlessly and his never-ending enthusiasm for this project; Dr Will Ward for his incredible knowledge of all things Aux; and everyone else at this fantastic organisation for their support, but more importantly for their continuing commitment to ensuring these civilians, most of whom have gone to their graves with their secrets, are remembered.

At the time of writing not all have gone. I have to thank Ken Welch, a 94-year-old in Mabe in Cornwall: one of, if not the last surviving Auxilier who had to put up with hours of questions from me when I visited at the end of 2021.

Also, thanks have to go to Joyce Harrison (as she was in 1940), who is currently 104 and living in Canada. In 1940 she was working at Country Hall in Chelmsford and would, without her family realising, sign up for the Special Duties Branch as a runner. Her memories have allowed us to understand much more about the training and role of this particularly secretive group.

My huge thanks go to the families of veterans of the various secret civilian organisations who have emailed, written, tweeted and DMed me over the past year with the stories their relatives told them.

The Second World War community on Twitter has been really supportive and many thanks go to Tony Pastor, Al Murray and James Holland at WeHaveWays for their support (and of course to James for writing the foreword). Thanks also to Malcolm Atkin and Austin J. Ruddy for their correspondence and permission to use their research (please check out their respective books too!).

Apologies and thanks to the number of people I have bored while talking endlessly about these groups. Sean Mills, Ian Stone, Stephen McCaffery in particular, but all of the Fat Dads' football team also.

Personally, I have to give credit for my passion and interest in the Second World War to my grandad, Tony. Endless summers as a child spent discussing the war, running around the garden with a shortened bean stick pole as a 'Sten', practising drill in the driveway. Thanks to my parents for their support and for reading the first manuscript.

Finally, a massive thank you to my family. My wife, Laura, for her understanding and unending support as I spent evening after evening tapping away on a laptop, and to my two daughters, Briar and Hettie, for putting up with me and accompanying me on trips around the country to search in woods for holes in the ground for hours on end!

Introduction

The story of Britain in the summer of 1940 is a well-told one. A country on its knees; old men joining the Local Defence Volunteers (LDV), later to become the Home Guard, armed with pitchforks and pikes. The regular army, although successfully evacuated from the beaches of Dunkirk, bereft of equipment, weapons and vehicles; and a population waiting for the inevitable invasion from the all-conquering German Army sitting just across the English Channel.

Britain was certainly in a less than ideal position in the summer of 1940. The British Expeditionary Force (BEF) was taken from Dunkirk and other ports, including Le Havre, as France fell. By 25 June, 368,491 British and French troops were brought off the beaches, of which a huge majority were British. This considerably bolstered the country's defensive capability, in terms of manpower at least. However, they had to leave much of their equipment, weapons, vehicles, artillery and tanks on the roads, in the countryside and on the beaches of France.

In an attempt to further bolster the defences of the country, the government turned to men in reserved occupations and those too old or too young to join up. The image of this newly formed LDV (and later the Home Guard) is another that adds to the perception of Britain in 1940. The response to Anthony Eden's broadcast on 14 May 1940 was remarkable. By 20 May, over 250,000 volunteers had come forward.[1] This response meant it was impossible to equip that number of men. Equipment was in short supply, but the government was also reluctant to issue rifles 'promiscuously to all volunteers unless special reasons exist'.[2] So initially at least, the LDV was issued with armbands and field service caps (not tin helmets), and they armed themselves with whatever 'weapons' they could get their hands on.

So, with Britain in this apparent state of weakness, the island (and with it the last vestige of democracy and humanity in Europe) seemed not only ripe for invasion but for defeat.

This is the narrative that has dominated all discussion of this period of British history since the end of the war. A vision of 'little' Britain hanging on 'alone' in the face of terror to save civilisation, is one that the country has become understandably proud of. This tale of reckless bravery combined with a lack of preparation has been backed up by TV shows such as *Dad's Army* and has, as a result, become an accepted part of history.

However, the perception of being ill prepared and weak does not reflect the reality. By the end of 1940 there were thousands of highly secret, highly trained civilian volunteers who would, in the event of an invasion, create havoc. Thousands of men in secret underground bunkers the length of the country were ready to come out at night and attack the invading army from behind. Thousands of men and women were trained in observing enemy troops and passing the information quickly via runners to other civilians operating wireless sets to get up-to-date, critical information to those in command.

Even the much-maligned Home Guard had secret guerrilla sections that were ready to take on the enemy. And if the worst happened and Britain was defeated militarily, there were other groups of civilians operating at even higher levels of secrecy that were to act as a post-occupation resistance.

In writing this book I aim to give a voice to these brave civilians, most of whom have gone to the grave without telling a soul of their roles. Britain was anything but weak and vulnerable. If the Germans had come, they would have been confronted by thousands of determined, highly trained and ruthless British civilians, all prepared to make the ultimate sacrifice for their country in its hour of need.

Part I

Anti-Invasion Civilian Forces:
Chaos and Sabotage

CHAPTER I

Birth of the Auxiliary Units

The idea of a civilian sabotage and guerrilla force that could cause havoc to an army invading Britain had first been discussed long before the summer of 1940 and even before the declaration of war itself.

In April 1938, the Secret Intelligence Service (SIS – later known as MI6) set up Section D. Going against its central role of information gathering and analysis, Section D was to give SIS more 'bite'. Described as the 'Fourth Arm', it was designed to weaken an enemy's infrastructure by sabotage and subterfuge, using clandestine civilian groups within its territory.

Major Laurence Grand of the Royal Engineers was appointed head of this new section and given pretty much a free hand in investigating how Britain could be more proactive against potential enemies and particularly the growing threat of Nazi Germany. Grand was a maverick, not full of tact and, more worryingly for others within SIS, not particularly discreet – not ideal traits for someone working in a secret service organisation.

A 'chain smoker, of thin build, with a black moustache, and always carefully dressed',[1] Grand had fought alongside Lawrence of Arabia in the First World War where he had built up an appreciation of the effectiveness of guerrilla warfare when fighting with the Bedouin irregular forces against the Turkish army. He certainly had determination, drive and the sort of persuasive powers that allowed him to convince superiors and staff alike that his way was best.

During late 1938 and early 1939, Grand sought to investigate ways to discredit Hitler's regime by secretly producing and distributing propaganda within Germany itself. Alongside this, and in contrast with the apparent approach of the appeasing British government, Grand was anxious to help prepare the countries that surrounded Germany and were likely to be the first targets of Hitler's aggression.

For example, even as the Munich crisis developed in 1938, Grand and his team had made their way over to Czechoslovakia and the Skoda armament plant. There, they discussed with the Czech intelligence service plans for future sabotage campaigns to be launched in the event of a German invasion.[2] Although the conversations with the Czechs came too late, throughout the very early part of the war Grand continued with Section D's efforts to organise resistance throughout Europe, whether it be propaganda or setting up sabotage cells within the local population.

The Home Defence Scheme – 'The finest body of men ever collected'

After the Blitzkrieg of 1940, when the Low Countries and France fell to the Germans in quick succession, SIS's main focus was no longer preparing other countries for invasion, but Britain itself. In May that year Grand, using some of the tactics and logistics garnered from his time in mainland Europe, constructed the Home Defence Scheme (HDS).

HDS was to play a crucial part in the formation of the Auxiliary Units. It was designed to be a short-term civilian sabotage and intelligence-gathering force, operating during the initial stages of an invasion of Britain. Although the British government had reluctantly agreed for efforts to be made abroad to set up civilian sabotage cells as part of Section D, it was much less keen about one being established on its own doorstep. This, at least in part, was due to the rules set out in The Hague Convention in 1907, which meant that non-uniformed civilian combatants did not come under the rules of war and were considered *francs-tireurs*, essentially meaning that, if captured, the enemy could do with them what they wanted. The prospect of the torture and mass execution of British civilians who had tried to fight back against the invasion did not sit well with the Chamberlain government, who refused to cooperate.

However, when Churchill became prime minister in May 1940, Grand suddenly had a potential ally at the very top of government. Writing directly to Churchill to ask for permission to start HDS in May, Grand received an enthusiastic yes. Churchill had witnessed the effectiveness of irregular forces and guerrilla warfare for himself in his time as a war correspondent in South Africa during the Boer War. Though ranged against the professional British Army, the Boer force – mainly made up of local farmers – had huge success and developed their own 'commando' system. The Boers would roam the veldt attacking supply chains, outposts and patrols and then disappearing before attacking again the next day. They would also attack transport; indeed, Churchill was taken prisoner during a Boer ambush on a train he was travelling on.

Despite being in the veldts of South Africa, these types of tactics could be replicated in the countryside of Britain. However, these were certainly not the tactics employed by the regular British Army in 1940. By recruiting British civilians to undertake what would have amounted to, in the eyes of an invading German Army, acts of terrorism, Grand had taken an unprecedented step. In his book *Churchill's Underground Army*, John Warwicker believed the 'proposition was revolutionary and set entire new standards in the British conduct of all-out war'.[3]

Time was of the essence. By appealing directly to Churchill, Grand was able to make quick progress and ensure he could get his hands on the large quantity of equipment required to arm a civilian sabotage force. Within weeks he had begun the task of distributing weapons and explosives across the vulnerable counties on the east coast including Sussex, Kent and Essex.

He sent Section D officers to these counties to recruit reliable, trustworthy civilians or 'key men'. This was highly secret and to date there is still very little known about the officers sent out to recruit volunteers. We do know that the civilians were to lead their own cells in their towns or villages in acts of sabotage, demolition and intelligence gathering. Grand suggested that such cells might be self-contained units of family groups, colleagues or estate workers. He later reported:

Recruiting went well. The qualifications were courage, intelligence, and discretion, and the bait was a certainty of execution if caught. The results were the finest body of men that have ever been collected. All classes and trades were represented, bankers and poachers, clergymen and burglars, farmers and lawyers, policemen and shopkeepers, every sort and kind of trade and interest, and the whole representing a cross section of England that would never submit to being ruled by an invader.[4]

The role of these key men and their cells was to live as normally as possible as the enemy entered their area. The key man was then to call upon individual cell members when specific targets were identified.

Alongside the recruitment of this covert civilian force, Grand and his team also began to distribute arms and explosives. These arms dumps consisted of different-sized containers and had everything that the civilians would need to cause as much havoc as possible. There were huge amounts of explosives (plastic and blasting gelignite), magnets for applying high explosives to steel surfaces, various fuse types, detonators and incendiary bombs, with some dumps also including weapons such as rifles, Colt revolvers and ammunition. These were distributed to cells in cardboard boxes called, rather confusingly, 'Auxiliary Units'. The name stems from the much feared and controversial 'Auxiliary Division' assassination squads that the British used in Ireland in 1920.

A MI5 report drafted just after HDS had ceased to exist, found little had been done to 'clean things up'. It found that Section D had 'left dumps of explosives all over East Anglia and the southern counties, some of which were known to police and all of which gave them cause for considerable anxiety'.[5] The secrecy surrounding the locations of the dumps meant that only the individual Section D officers knew exactly where they were – it is likely that some of the Second World War arms dumps that are still being found in the south-east corner of the UK are the result of Section D arms dumping.

However, by July 1940 HDS was being stood down. Grand certainly wasn't happy about it and made several efforts to continue HDS in some new form but without success. It might have been Grand's rather blasé approach to handing out weapons and explosives to civilians or the fact that non-uniformed civilians would be taking on an invading army, potentially being shot out of hand, that had been too much for those in command. According to Major Peter Wilkinson (later to be a senior staff member of the Auxiliary Units), General Edmund Ironside, head of GHQ Home Forces 'read the Riot Act' after he learnt about the way arms and explosives were being distributed to civilians by Grand and Section D. Ironside insisted that this should come under military control.[6]

HDS did not simply disappear though. Many of its civilian volunteers would be amalgamated into a new group, one combined with a similar force being set up under the auspices of Military Intelligence (Research).

Military Intelligence (Research)/XII Corps Observation Unit

Such is the irony of war that some of the inspiration for the Auxiliary Units appears to have come from Germany. Anthony Eden, Secretary of State for War, visited Lieutenant General Andrew Thorne, who was commanding XII Corps, a regular army group, in the Kent/Sussex area in June 1940. After a discussion about the seriousness of the situation in the area, Eden reported back to Churchill highlighting the lack of anti-tank guns, and by 30 June Thorne had been invited to lunch at Chequers to meet with Churchill. The lunch would have important consequences for the Auxiliary Units. During the conversation, it seems that Thorne discussed an idea he had first had during his time as a British military attaché in Berlin in the mid-1930s.

During his time in Germany, he had been introduced to the peasant militia that had existed since the 1700s. This militia would muster at times of danger to defend their lord's estate. They would not take on the invading force directly but, using hidden caches of weapons, engage in what would later be called guerrilla warfare. Although at a disadvantage in terms of numbers, the peasants' intimate knowledge of their local surroundings would have meant that they could have caused a much larger force a considerable problem. The idea of a civilian-based covert force was one that typically appealed to Churchill's sense of adventure and innovation. After his meeting with Thorne, he spoke to General 'Pug' Ismay, his chief of staff, who put him in touch with a branch of the army that had the personalities and means to get such a group off the ground.

Military Intelligence (Research) had been formed in 1936 initially to look at the defence of Great Britain. At first it consisted of one lonely officer and his typist but in the winter of 1938 another influential and important figure joined – Colonel John (Jo) Holland.

Holland, like Grand, was a Royal Engineer and had the same belief in the effectiveness of dirty tricks and irregular warfare. He had served with distinction during the First World War with the Royal Flying Corps, where he had been mentioned in despatches and awarded the Distinguished Flying Cross following a daring raid on the Bulgarian capital, Sofia. However, it was his time with the Royal Engineers fighting the Irish insurgency between the wars that began to persuade him of the effectiveness of guerrilla fighting. This experience made him the perfect man to start considering what such a force would look like.

Joan Bright-Astley, who worked for Section D but was seconded to MI(R) to be Holland's secretary, left a vivid description of her boss in her book, *The Inner Circle*. As well as describing him as a chain smoker who would hold 'in the smoke until the last wisp of nicotine had reached his boots', she thought he had '… an independent mind, an acute brain, a loving and poetic heart; he was quick, imaginative and of a fiery temper'.[7]

Holland had a man in mind within MI(R) who he considered the perfect fit to lead a prototype guerrilla band as envisaged by Thorne. This was another British Army officer who rubs somewhat against the grain of what is considered to be typical of the time.

The role of Peter Fleming

Peter Fleming was a Guards officer, an explorer, a journalist and an author, as well as being the brother of Ian, the creator of James Bond. Peter was a remarkable man in his own right. Born in 1907, and after being educated at Eton and Oxford, he left Britain in 1932 to explore the jungle rivers of central Brazil and to ascertain the fate of a Colonel

Percy Fawcett who had disappeared in the jungle in the 1920s. He also travelled extensively across Asia during the inter-war period and had, just before the outbreak of war, been asked to join Holland at MI(R). His role, initially at least, was to find ways, using his experience of travelling through the area, to assist Chinese guerrillas in their fight against the Japanese.

He had also fought as part of the prototype Independent Companies, one of the few success stories of Britain's intervention in the Norwegian campaign in early 1940. The Independent Companies were formed in early 1940 as part of a British Army plan to support Finland in its war with Russia. Under Holland at MI(R), these were groups of volunteers from Territorial Army divisions trained in guerrilla warfare. When Finland capitulated to the Russians, the troops changed their role to a raiding one on the Norwegian coast. After the launch of the German offensive against Norway, Nos 1,3,4 and 5 Independent Companies were sent to defend Bodø, Mo and Mosjøen. Here they had some success in using guerrilla tactics and ambushing German troops. Their successes were not replicated in the rest of what was generally perceived by those at home as a pretty disastrous campaign. The Independent Companies had further success during the withdrawal, but Norway would remain in Germany's hands until May 1945. On returning to Britain, the Independent Companies were disbanded, with men returning to their parent units and formations. Some did go on to be the first to join the new Commando units. Fleming's experience during his time in the Independent Companies and his pre-war activities meant he was considered the perfect man to see whether a British version of the German peasant militia was a viable option.

Fleming was based out of a house called The Garth in the village of Bilting in Kent. A secluded farmhouse, the building appears to have originally been a cottage, which had been enlarged about a century earlier. In the older wing the first floor had been removed, leaving the joists, beams and rafters exposed; the exceptional height and the two rows of leaded windows gave the look of a slightly impoverished and very old chapel.

At the beginning of the war, it had belonged to the Gowen family, however, the family had chosen to leave for the relative safety of

Scotland and had arranged for a Harry Sexton and his family to move in and look after the property. It was only a short period afterwards that the army took control of the house, with Fleming and his chosen men moving in. Initially, the Sextons moved to one end of the property with Fleming *et al.* at the other. Needless to say, this situation didn't last very long, with the army quickly taking complete control of the house and the surrounding outbuildings.

With this first regional training centre set up, Fleming began the process of pulling together the men needed for this new group. Attached to Thorne's XII Corps, this band of civilian volunteers was called the XII Corps Observation Unit.

The Garth was quickly transformed into a training HQ and storage facility for the huge amounts of explosives and weapons at Fleming's disposal. Those who visited him there found boxes of explosives being used as tables in front of roaring open fires. Once they had got over what would be considered today a health and safety nightmare, these civilian volunteers were given training in all aspects of guerrilla warfare.

Peter turned to another of his brothers, Richard, who was with the Lovat Scouts, to help provide instructors. Formed during the Boer War, the Lovat Scouts had proved themselves to be effective irregular fighters. They were the first to wear ghillie suits (camouflage suits designed to match the soldiers' surroundings) and were, by the First World War, the British Army's first sniper unit, nicknamed the 'Sharpshooters'. Richard, who shared his brother's belief in alternative ways of fighting, was to prove a useful addition to Fleming's group.

Peter also turned to another member of the Independent Companies, Mike Calvert, who went on to fight with distinction in the Far East with General Orde Wingate. Calvert, replicating the work of Grand at Section D, left dumps of weapons around Kent and Sussex and mined key bridges, port facilities and even houses likely to be taken as headquarters by the invading army. The plan was that as the Germans entered these areas, the civilian saboteurs of XII Corps Observation Unit would jump into action, cause as much chaos as possible and hold up the enemy's advance.

Fleming and his team recruited local civilians, usually men in reserved occupations who had an intimate knowledge of their local surroundings: farmers, farm workers, gamekeepers — men used to living off the land and handling weapons. These men would come to The Garth to learn dirty tricks and ways of sabotage and guerrilla fighting from Fleming, Calvert, the Lovat Scouts and other instructors, and soon their training was proven effective.

In *Last Ditch*, the first book written about the Auxiliary Units, published in the late 1960s, David Lampe describes how Fleming and Calvert had sought to prove to High Command the effectiveness of such a force. Creeping at night into General Montgomery's 3rd Division HQ in Steyning, they placed delayed-action charges inside a row of flowerpots around the terrace. The next day they explained to Monty what they had achieved, and, in typical fashion, he dismissed their claims, saying it was impossible and insisting that there was no chance of them having got past his guards and the high levels of security he had in place. Just as he finished his sentence the first of the delayed-action charges went off – destroying the flowerpots along with his initial derisory opinion of the guerrilla force (and also, presumably, his high opinion of his own security!). This was not the last time the Auxiliary Units would somewhat humiliate the regular army.[8]

Such stunts did much to raise the reputation of the XII Corps Observation Unit amongst senior regular army officers. Proving its effectiveness, the decision was taken to merge it with the civilians recruited by HDS (which was the final nail in the coffin for Grand's group by bringing them under military control and out of the hands of SIS) and extend the combined force to the most vulnerable counties in Britain. To achieve this, huge resources were needed. MI(R) was already stretched to capacity and this new organisation needed the logistical support and power of Britain's military. As a result, this newly combined group was transferred to GHQ Home Forces, under General Edmund Ironside.

Gubbins and the Auxiliary Units

The man brought in to manage the extension of this force was, like Grand, Fleming and Holland, an extraordinary figure. He was also very well placed to do the job. Not only was he already serving with MI(R), and a former comrade of Ironside, he had also written three booklets on guerrilla warfare.

Colin McVean Gubbins had been a gunner in the First World War and had been alongside Ironside during the Allied intervention during the Russian Revolution, where he had witnessed the effectiveness of Russian guerrilla fighters in and around Archangel. He had later been in Ireland (with Jo Holland) where he had experienced fighting a non-traditional force in the form of the IRA.

While serving with MI(R) he had written three booklets: *Partisan Leader's Handbook, The Art of Guerrilla Warfare* and *How to Use High Explosives.* His MI(R) role also saw him take three trips to mainland Europe as the threat of war increased. He visited the Danube and the Baltic to look into the possibility of raising anti-Nazi guerrilla cells in those areas. The third trip he made was on 25 August 1939, when he left London heading to Warsaw where he was to take up the post of Chief of Staff to the British Military Mission to the Polish Army – a mission headed by yet another colourful character, the remarkable General Sir Adrian Carton de Wiart VC.

Gubbins's role was, like Grand at Section D, to see whether he could help the Poles and the Czechs organise resistance movements before invasion. He had barely got his feet under his desk though when the Germans invaded Poland on 1 September 1939 and a quick exit was needed via Romania.

When he eventually returned to the UK, Gubbins, now a lieutenant colonel, was ordered to lead the group of the newly formed Independent Companies to Norway. On his return to Britain, Gubbins was informed that he was to head up yet another new organisation under the aegis of GHQ Home Forces. Only a week after returning from Norway, Gubbins was appointed head of this new combined covert group.

Utilising his connection with the Home Forces' Commander-in-Chief, Gubbins secured promises from Ironside that he would be guaranteed the equipment and supplies needed to make such a force viable. In return Ironside insisted that Gubbins provide a private and confidential weekly update report. Only two copies were to be produced each week: one for Ironside and one for Winston Churchill, who was growing increasingly enthusiastic at the prospect of a highly trained civilian guerrilla force. In each report Gubbins updated Ironside and Churchill on recruitment, supplies and training, ensuring that both parties were fully up-to-speed with the progress of the new unit.

With buy-in from the very top, Gubbins set about his task. He had all the personal traits to make this a success. Vera Long, who worked with Gubbins throughout the war, described him as having 'enormous energy. I have never met anyone in my life who had such energy.'[9] Gubbins needed all of this energy, as he worked against the clock to get a viable force in place across the country before the seemingly inevitable invasion started.

It was also at this stage in July 1940 that the name 'Auxiliary Units' started being used. This somewhat vague term was deliberately chosen, as it covered a multitude of possible uses and, if overheard by an enemy soldier, would not arouse immediate suspicion. The name might also originate from a division active in Ireland during the Irish War of Independence in the 1920s, which many of the senior officers in the Auxiliary Units would have witnessed. The Auxiliary Division of the Royal Irish Constabulary, known as Auxiliaries or Auxies, were made up of former British Army officers that had fought during the First World War. Its role was to conduct counter-insurgency operations against the IRA, acting as a mobile unit and raiding force. The group became notorious for the reprisals it took out on Irish civilians and property in revenge for IRA actions, most notably the infamous 'Burning of Cork' in December 1920, where, in revenge for an earlier IRA ambush, it set fire to the commercial centre of Cork causing millions of pounds worth of damage. Five civilians were also shot on the street. These Auxiliaries were disbanded in 1922 following the Anglo-Irish Treaty.

Whatever the origins of the name, it was now a force that had to be expanded quickly to be effective against an invasion. From his office in Whitehall Place, Gubbins began to take the prototype forces of HDS and the XII Corps Observation Unit, combine them and spread them to all vulnerable counties. To do this he turned to many of the men he had served with in the Independent Companies. Men, like him, with a belief in alternative ways of fighting an enemy and who were not frightened of using 'dirty trick' tactics to achieve results.

One of Gubbins's key appointments was Major Peter Wilkinson, who came in as deputy commander. Wilkinson was in charge of organisation, planning and liaison with SIS. Alongside him came Major Bill Beyts, who had been the training officer for the Independent Companies and was therefore the perfect choice to be head of operations and training for the Auxiliary Units. Beyts would later go on to join Force 136, the equivalent of the Special Operations Executive in the Far East.

With his senior team in place, Gubbins set out to recruit suitable members of the public to join the Auxiliary Units. Starting up new cells became the job of intelligence officers, also recruited by Gubbins and his senior team.

Intelligence Officers

Operational areas were run by Intelligence Officers (IOs) who, in turn, recruited the embryonic guerrilla cells. They would identify key points in their area where a patrol, made up of 6–8 men, could inflict real damage to the tail of an invading force.

The IOs themselves were recruited mainly through the 'old boys' network. Many were friends with Peter Wilkinson and had served in MI(R) or with the Independent Companies in Norway. Others were stand-out officers who had built themselves reputations during the fighting in France, with others appearing to be family friends of Gubbins.

However, what they all had in common was that they could be entirely trusted with such a secret mission and had the same mindset as Gubbins, Wilkinson and Beyts when it came to effective guerrilla warfare.

The first eight met (including Peter Fleming who had been appointed IO for Kent) at the Whitehall offices on 13 July[10] with others following quickly, getting the necessary promotion to captain if they were not already of that rank. The operational areas they were handed tended to be counties with which they had some affiliation, enabling them to immediately identify key areas in which to place patrols.

One of the first to be recruited was Captain Andrew Croft,[11] who was initially given the counties of Norfolk, Suffolk and Essex. Croft was typical of the type of IOs recruited. The son of a vicar, Croft had attended Oxford and went on to be awarded the Polar Medal for his part in the University's Arctic Expedition in 1935–1936. He had spent time in India as an aide to a young Maharajah and had been an early recruit in MI(R), leading the military mission to the Finnish Army, which would have seen the British Army fighting with the Finnish against the Soviet invasion. Before the men could arrive, the Finns and Russians had agreed terms and Croft ended up back in Norway. He was there as the Germans invaded and later joined up with the Independent Companies (with Gubbins). His experience with MI(R) and with Gubbins in Norway meant he would be a key man in the early stages of the Auxiliary Units. Croft was also later meant to be part of the 1953 Everest Expedition but had to drop out. Had he accompanied Edmund Hillary and Tenzing Norgay, his name would be somewhat better known than it is today!

Another of the early IOs was 45-year-old temporary captain Stuart Edmondson who, like many other IOs, would later go on to join the Special Operations Executive (SOE). Edmondson was the IO for both Devon and Cornwall and had owned a fertiliser business in Plymouth before the war. He had joined the Devon Royal Engineers Territorial Force in 1935 and just before Dunkirk he had, with his cohort of sappers, set up an assembly line in Plymouth, making Molotov cocktails for the newly formed LDV. His work made him another obvious recruit and Gubbins invited him to visit Fleming in Kent in July 1940 to see his prototype civilian cells in action and to replicate them in the West Country. Edmondson would go to the Far East to serve with Force 136 in December 1944. He also opened the only dedicated museum to the Auxiliary Units in Parham, Suffolk in 1997.

Nigel Oxenden, also 45, was given a temporary captaincy in July 1940. Oxenden was to remain with the Auxiliary Units for the rest of the war and made a considerable contribution, but at this early stage was recruited as IO for Norfolk. Oxenden had received the Military Cross for conspicuous gallantry in action during the First World War.[12] By November 1920 he had relinquished his commission and, perhaps showing something of his adventurous nature, had set up what was likely to be Europe's first surf club in Jersey in 1923. However, by November 1939, he was given an emergency commission and re-entered the army.

By the end of 1940 there were IOs covering Angus, Fife, Forth, Berwick and Northumberland, North Yorkshire, Lincolnshire, Norfolk, East Anglia, Kent, Sussex, Hampshire, Dorset, Somerset, Devon and Cornwall, Monmouthshire, Herefordshire and Worcestershire.

Patrol leaders and formation of patrols

From July 1940, each IO was making their way to their allocated county, with a Humber Snipe, a driver and pretty much free rein to set up the patrols when and where they wanted. The first task for all of them was to find suitable patrol leaders, much like the key men identified by Grand's HDS.

With an invasion seeming likely at any point, the usual recruitment 'red tape' was thrown out of the window. Gubbins told his IOs to look out for men 'who know the forests, the woods, the mines, the old closed shafts, the hills, the moors, the glens – people who know their local stuff'.[13]

Nigel Oxenden wrote a brief unpublished pamphlet about the Auxiliary Units in 1944. *Auxiliary Units History and Achievement* took a whistle stop tour of the Auxiliary Units from set-up to stand-down, including valuable glances into the thinking behind the Auxiliary Units and the challenges facing the IOs at this early stage in setting up the patrols.

When describing the beginning of the recruitment process, Oxenden mentions the type of men that they were looking for: '... IOs automatically looked for the gamekeeper or poacher type of recruit, as being already trained in everything but explosives. If these men were also last war veterans, so much the better; they were probably steady, and well aware of their own limitations.'[14]

He also discusses how some of the key men originally recruited by HDS remained in place and were useful leverage for the IOs coming to the recruitment process pretty cold: 'IOs were assisted by introductions to one or two men who had already been chosen by MI5 [*sic*, this is as written in the original source but was actually MI6], and equipped with bottles of sulphuric acid and little capsules of potassium chlorate and sugar, with which to make a crude and unreliable delay incendiary out of a bottle of petrol.'[15]

> The key man should be situated within a mile or two of key targets and should … be a man of good education – everything else comes with practice, provided the idea appeals to him. He should be given as long as possible to recruit from four to six men who he knows, and who will respect him. The local knowledge of this team will always give them an advantage over the enemy.[16]

Most potential recruits were approached about joining or leading a covert force completely out of the blue. Indeed, when a mysterious man came to the door of William Sage Ratford, a gamekeeper, in the village of Bentley in Suffolk, he told Ratford he was looking for six men: 'gamekeepers, poachers and burglars to form this group'.[17] Ratford would go on to be the patrol leader and sergeant of the Bentley Patrol.

Blacksmith Frank Dean in the village of Rodmell in Sussex was in his forge when 'a chap from the village poked his head over the railings. He said "I want you to come to Lewes, there's an army officer out here who wants you to come." I said "What's this in aid of Charlie?" "I don't know," he said. "I can't give you any details. But he's looking for seven men and he's one short."' Frank, still in his work clothes, left the forge and headed to the fields that surrounded Lewis where he met the officer, out in the open, in the middle of nowhere. The officer said he wanted to enlist small groups of men to cover the local area in the event of a German invasion.[18]

The type of men wanted for the Auxiliary Units were those that would have volunteered immediately for the LDV. Therefore, some of those joining the Auxiliary Units came directly from local LDV platoons.[i] The LDV was formed in the face of an increasing threat

---

i This has led to a misconception that has grown since the war that the Auxiliary Units were attached to the Home Guard in some way. Although it used the

of invasion as the Germans continued their domination of mainland
Europe. Even before Dunkirk, Anthony Eden, the then Secretary of
State for War had made a radio broadcast on 14 May 1940 appealing
for men between the ages of 17 and 65 to come forward to help with
the defence of the country. Seven days later 250,000 volunteers had
tried to sign up and by July 1940 this had increased to 1.5 million.
Initially, the numbers meant there were some issues with fully arming
and equipping the LDV but over the next few years, until stand-down
in December 1944, the LDV made up an important part of the British
Second World War effort, helping not only to defend against possible
attack, but also to free up regular soldiers to take the fight back to
Nazi Germany.

Reginald Clutterham was a farm worker in Ashill, Norfolk. He had
joined the LDV immediately after Anthony Eden had made his radio
appeal, but his career there was not to last very long. 'One day a man
came to interview me at my boss, Mr Broadhead's house at Burys
Hall. I was asked if I would like to do something more interesting
than the Home Guard.'[19]

Another Home Guard member, teenager Bob Millard, lived in the
village of Bathampton two miles east of Bath, on the banks of the
River Avon. He too had joined the LDV after Eden's appeal and found
himself on his first patrol as a newly enrolled member on the 'back
of a motorbike, civilian clothes, LDV armband. The chap driving the
motorbike had a shotgun across his back held with a cord, a piece of
string, and I was armed with a piece of pipe and a bayonet.'[20] Later
on Bob was approached by a friend who asked whether he wanted to
do something more interesting than the Home Guard. Bob indicated
that he was 'willing to try anything' and so they went to a house in
Bathwick Street where they met Jack Wyld (the future sergeant and
patrol leader of the Bathampton Patrol). Jack asked about Bob's and his
friends' families, about their knowledge of the surrounding areas and
their familiarity with weapons. Apparently satisfied with these initial

Home Guard as a cover for its activities, it was a separate organisation with very
different aims and objectives.

answers, Jack went away and a week later, having had his background checked, Bob was recruited into the patrol.

Meanwhile in Hockley, a village in Essex, Albert Cocks, a market gardener and early LDV recruit, was invited to attend a secret meeting at the residence of a local headmaster:

> I found that I was one of half a dozen lads of the village there. We were ushered into a room where we were introduced to two gentlemen in military uniform and by their bits and bobs it was obvious they were high ranking officers of the regular army. They soon put us at ease by explaining simply that they contemplated forming an underground resistance movement, a sort of private commando force. It would also be necessary for us to know every local hedge, ditch, culvert, drainage system; every inch of local moors, railway routes, bridges and all of this to cover a five-mile radius of one's place of residence.[21]

Later Albert was informed that he 'had been vetted by the local chief of police, as well as certain other sources which he preferred not to name. I must admit I went home that night wondering just what I had let myself in for and indeed, as the days passed and my involvement became more apparent, I was to realise the enormity of the task ahead should the balloon go up.'

The nature of the men leaving the LDV/Home Guard at this crucial point meant that many Home Guard local commanders were losing their best men to the Auxiliary Units. These were not the men portrayed in *Dad's Army*. They were fit, generally young, capable men in reserved occupations who were determined and willing to take on an invading army. It is not surprising then that Home Guard units in the areas the Auxiliary Units operated were not that happy when this type of recruit disappeared from their number.

Oxenden, is his review of the Auxiliary Units, refers to the issue of recruiting men from the Home Guard:

> Machinery did not exist for using the Home Guard from the top downwards to provide personnel. If a good man were located, and his enthusiasm aroused, he generally turned out to be already in the Home Guard, and the only possible officer for miles, so that the IO found himself at war with the local battalion commander, who was not 'in the picture' and knew us only as body-snatchers. Many of these feuds lasted for several years.[22]

It was not just the Home Guard who were losing men to the Auxiliary Units though. Some men, soon after signing the Official Secrets Act and joining the Auxiliary Units, were called up to the regular forces. James Batten, a head gardener in Cornwood, Devon, had initially joined the LDV. However, he was quickly 'poached' by the Cornwood Auxiliary Unit Patrol. Shortly afterwards, he was called up to the regular army and sent to Halifax for training.

A day or two later he was called in by his commanding officer who exclaimed, 'I don't know what the hell is going on but I have orders to send you home. I don't suppose you can tell me why?'

'I can't, sir,' said James. The commanding officer handed him a letter marked 'secret', for his eyes only. Jim opened it in front of the officer who asked to see its contents. Jim had to inform his superior he was not allowed to show him, which understandably irritated the officer even more. He was sent home to re-join his Auxiliary Unit having only missed one weekend's training.[23]

A member of the Pensford Patrol in Somerset had a similar experience. Having been called up, Jim Hooper found himself at Chepstow Racecourse as a recruit with the Royal Army Ordnance Corps. However, two days into his time with the RAOC he was told he could have his discharge papers whenever he wanted. 'I thought, now I'm in, I'm not sure I want to go home. But after a week, I didn't care for the sergeant, so I went back. Much later, my officer told me I was released because I was in the Auxiliary Units.'[24]

These remarkable stories relay two things: one, the Auxiliary Units were considered such a priority to the defence of the country that they took precedent over even the regular army (this will be further proven by the weapons made available to the Auxiliary Units), and two, the levels of secrecy that accompanied anyone who had joined were extraordinarily high.

Even when being asked to form a patrol, future recruits were told very little. Many recruits were asked whether they wanted to do something highly secret, a bit more interesting or dangerous than what they were doing in their current role and initially told very little else until they had signed the Official Secrets Act.

Dennis Blanchard, a farm worker in the village of Bewholme in Yorkshire, recalled his recruitment into the Auxiliary Units and the levels of secrecy involved.

> I arrived in the tent facing three officers across a trestle table. The officer in the middle was of some rank as he had scarlet tabs on his tunic and a scarlet band around his cap that was lying on the table with his cane. The person who took me in stood at one end of the table. The officer in the centre greeted me with a penetrating stare and after what seemed like an hour he reached forward and asked,
> 'Will you do a little job for me?'
> I replied, 'What kind of job?'
> His reply was, 'Oh I cannot tell you that.'
> He asked many questions about my private life but eventually I realised that he already knew a lot about me. He had done his homework well.
> His companion asked me, 'Will you be prepared to do intensive training of a secret and dangerous nature?'
> I replied with another question, 'What kind of training?'
> He replied, 'Oh, I cannot tell you that!'
> He immediately ordered the officer at the end of the table to take my name and address and to make the necessary arrangements. There was a short and serious lecture on security and the fire and brimstone that would occur if I breached the security. With that the Bewholme Patrol was born.[25]

Reginald Clutterham in Norfolk was told that 'I had been watched for a month to see the sort of people I mixed with and what we talked about. If I wanted to join this special organisation I was told that I would have to sign the Official Secrets Act.'[26]

In Queenborough, Kent, 16-year-old Jack Quaintance, too young to join the regular forces, had joined the Home Guard, combining it with his role as an ARP (Air Raid Precautions) messenger. Before the war he was also a member of the local small-bore shooting club and so was also very comfortable using a rifle. His enthusiasm and skills were soon recognised by the Auxiliary Units. 'I was approached by a local farmer, Lieutenant W. G. Johnson, who asked if I wanted to join some rough stuff. I signed the Official Secrets Act and reported to a farm at Cowstead Corner.'

Peter Boulden in Aldington, Kent sums up how most members of the Auxiliary Units felt. 'First thing we did was sign the Official Secrets Act. As far as we were concerned that was the end of talking about it ever. That was it.'[27] As a result, most veterans went to the grave without telling anyone their secret, not even their closest relatives and friends – a remarkable testament to the dedication that these men had for the Auxiliary Units and the secret they swore to keep.

Patrol leaders were recruited on the basis that they were trustworthy, the 'right sort of chap' and lived in an area that would benefit from having a patrol located in it. Once the Official Secrets Act was signed, the IO would leave it to the patrol leader to recruit the rest of his patrol and identify the best location in the local area to place their secret disguised underground base (Operational Base – to be discussed in Chapter Three). The IO would routinely look in on the patrol to check on the bunker and the progress the men were making with training.

Due to the nature of the role and the level of secrecy involved, the patrol leaders tended to recruit relatives, colleagues or friends of friends and trusted contacts, very similar to the advice Grand had given those forming the original HDS cells. What they all had to have in common though was a determination to fight the enemy army using whatever tactics would cause the most chaos, no matter the consequences to themselves. They also had to have an intimate knowledge of their local surroundings. The ability to travel silently at night across fields, ditches and rivers would give them a huge advantage over an invading force, who were in a strange country with little idea as to where they were or what was out there.

This required knowledge of the land meant that many Auxiliers (as members of Auxiliary Units were known) were farmers, farm workers, gamekeepers and estate workers. There are examples of gamekeepers recruiting poachers into their patrols, as they were confident that, in all likelihood, the poachers knew the land better than they did and could certainly handle weapons and set booby traps as well as having the ability to live off the land.

The patrol leader's recruitment of 'known faces' meant that multiple members of the same family, farm or business could be in the same patrol or a neighbouring patrol. A good example is of Bovey Patrol in East Devon. Leonard Pike (later sergeant of the patrol) was recruited by Edmondson (the Devon IO) in July 1940. Pike was an estate worker at Bovey House near Branscombe. Presumably Edmondson had chosen the area around Bovey because of the excellent targets. Just inland from the coast, so as not to get caught up in any invasion, the area also had the main road heading out of Exeter towards the east – very likely to be a main route for any invading army looking to break out of or move into the West Country. Bovey House itself was also another target, as it was a potential local HQ for the Germans. As with many patrol leaders, Leonard looked to relatives and colleagues – trusted men – to form the patrol. His brothers Harold and Eddie, also estate workers at Bovey House, joined him. Walter Denslow, another farm worker at Bovey House, joined as a corporal (second in command of the patrol), as did his brother Charles (Charlie) who was a dairyman on the Bovey estate. The rest of the patrol was made up of local farmer acquaintances.

A patrol in Icklesham, Sussex was made up of five cousins and a family friend – although good for keeping the secret before invasion, one might presume that the absence of so many in one family might well attract suspicion from the invading forces.[28]

Patrols of a similar make-up were being recruited along the length of the country and by the end of 1940 thousands of men were being trained in unarmed combat, explosives, sabotage, guerrilla warfare and assassination (although the nature of the units means it is hard to say for sure the exact number of patrols). Their role, were the Germans to invade, was a highly secret one, and one every member of the Auxiliary Units knew would probably end ultimately in their death.

CHAPTER 2

Role, Ruthlessness and Training

While being kept up to date with the progress the Auxiliary Units were making, Churchill wrote to Eden, the Secretary of State for War, on 25 September 1940.

> I have been following with much interest the growth and development of the new guerrilla formations … known as 'Auxiliary Units'. From what I hear these units are being organised with thoroughness and imagination and should, in the event of invasion, prove a useful addition to the regular forces.

What was the role Churchill had in mind? And how could the Auxiliary Units prove a useful addition to the regular forces? With patrols forming all over the country, thousands of men (after signing the Official Secrets Act) were learning what they had got themselves into. This was not, as they quickly discovered, a variation of the Home Guard but what was going to be a highly trained, ruthless, secret sabotage and guerrilla force.

The Auxiliary Units' role, as originally set out by Fleming and Grand in their own iterations and later carried on by Gubbins, was to be a literal underground force. The patrols were not taking on the invading army head on. Indeed, anything but − they were trained to avoid getting into running battles and instead to gain access to the target, destroy it and get back to their underground Operational Bases.

As has been stated these were not the old men of *Dad's Army*. Their age meant that, more often than not, they had young families. The level of secrecy surrounding the patrols meant that as the German Army entered their areas, they would simply disappear. Their families and friends would have no idea where they had gone or what they were up to.

Take a moment to consider this. There are very few situations in which a family is at more risk than when an enemy army enters their town or village. At this point, the Auxilier would have to leave. Leaving his family without telling them where he was going, whether he would be coming back and what he was up to. This was a huge sacrifice. It was also an action that was likely to shine a spotlight onto the family as the Germans searched for the missing man of the house. As we saw in occupied Europe throughout the war, there were often horrific consequences for relatives of suspected 'terrorists'.

Once the patrol was in the Operational Base (OB) they would wait for the invading army to, sometimes literally, pass over the top of them and then come out at night and cause as much mayhem as possible – destroying ammunition and fuel dumps, bridges, railways and trains, airfields and Luftwaffe aircraft, transport and convoys and German headquarters. Anything that would cause the invading army to have to pause. Stopping supplies and reinforcements from reaching the spearhead was their main role. By hitting behind the front line, the Auxiliary Units would also hope to cause panic to set in throughout the invading force.

To ensure this happened, there is also evidence of patrols being tasked with taking out German officials and even British collaborators. Accounts from Auxiliers make it clear that the patrols would have been completely ruthless in their role, with British civilians potentially being some of their first 'victims'. All of this was meant to ensure that the German Army did not get the free run that they had enjoyed during the Blitzkrieg in mainland Europe. Disrupting the supply chain would ensure that the main striking units would struggle to receive equipment, ammunition, food and fuel as well as reinforcements, giving the British regular forces time to recover and counter-attack where possible, or even to give enough time for help to come from the Empire or the United States.

However, such action was not going to be taken lightly by the Germans, and the patrols were under no illusion about what was in store for them once they had started their nightly attacks. Each patrol was given enough rations for two weeks. Many of the men recruited would have had the skills to live off the land after that period, but the fortnight's rations essentially represented the patrol's life expectancy after the Germans arrived in its part of the country. William Ratford of Bentley Patrol, Suffolk, was realistic about the role the Auxiliary Units would play and how long it was likely to last: 'Perhaps we would have been heroes for a bit. But it would have been suicidal, I should think.'[1]

Once the patrol had 'gone to ground', they would be on their own. No further instructions would be coming from their IOs. They would have, in preparation, identified key targets that should be destroyed in the days immediately following the German advance into their area. Geoff Devereux of the Samson Patrol in Worcestershire explains the types of targets that had been identified: 'Two of the potential vehicle laagers we had identified were Broad Green, about half a mile west of our OB, and Broadheath Common, about one and a half miles to the north-east. Laybys and wide road verges that could be used for vehicle parking were also noted.'[2] Devereux's patrol had also identified the railway between Worcester and Bromyard, which was likely to be used by the Germans to carry troops and equipment into the Midlands, as another key target.

Ken Welch, who at the time of writing is a sprightly 94-year-old living in Mabe in Cornwall, joined his local Mabe Patrol of which his father was the sergeant. It seems he had somehow got a glimpse of what his father was up to and in 1943, at the age of 16, was 'interested like a young teenage idiot'[3] in joining the patrol. His father, with presumably little choice, agreed. Ken remembers well the first target to be attacked had the Germans got to Cornwall. 'If we were invaded our first job would have been to blow up, or make inoperable, Penryn Viaduct, because that's the railway line up from Falmouth docks up to Truro.'[4]

After these initial targets had been destroyed, and if the patrol had survived, they would leave their OB each night and attempt to destroy a new objective, causing as much havoc as possible to the invading forces for as long as they could. During the day, the majority of the patrol would rest and plan the next night's mission. Geoff Devereux described how his patrol would also attempt to leave the bunker and identify new targets and how they gathered information: 'We had an old bicycle hidden in a wood so that one of us could ride around the area in overalls to locate possible targets. We often lay in wait outside local pubs to listen to the gossip after closing time as we felt this might prove a useful source of information.'[5]

A document in the Somerset County Archives designed for Auxiliary Units group commanders later in the war (September 1944) shows how, as the conflict was coming nearer to an end, the role of the Auxiliary Units had been thoroughly thought through. Each page is prominently marked 'Secret', emphasising the nature of the Auxiliary Units even at this late stage of the conflict. It gives a comprehensive overview of each aspect of the group's role. An introductory page on 'Patrols and Observation' gives a real indication of the importance of identifying targets and not having a night off.

> Patrols will never go out aimlessly but always as a result of something that has been observed. Generally speaking, the patrol will be undertaken in darkness or fog (but always on known ground) as a result of daylight observation.
> NO night can be missed. There MUST be a target every night.[6]

Nigel Oxenden outlined what a typical day might have been like for a successful patrol in wartime conditions:

> **1000hrs** Patrol wakes and eats.
> **1100hrs** As many as the Patrol Leader thinks necessary leave the OB to look for targets. All possible target sites and dispersal areas are known, and established routes are followed that enable a scout to observe each.
> **1700hrs** Observers return and report results. The Patrol eats.
> The men now rest while the Patrol Leader works out his orders. How long this rest can last will depend upon the time at which he proposes to attack. Before setting out, the men will have another meal, listen carefully to their leader's orders, prepare their charges and weapons, colour their faces and hands, and finally examine one another for articles that should be left behind.
> **2200hrs** The Patrol leaves the OB after waiting in the dark to get their night sight, and moves forward by bounds, at each of which the Patrol Leader assures himself that all his men are present, and anyone who may have lost touch with the man in front of him, is able to regain contact. The formation adopted is single file, at extreme visibility distance, following the Patrol Leader with a guide or runner.
> **2300hrs** The springboard is reached. This is a prearranged point, near the target, from which every man goes forward in slightly different directions to reconnoitre the defence for anything up to a couple of hours and returns to report to the

Patrol Leader who then decides on the safest line of entry into the target area. Before separating, the men start their time pencils so that these eventually fire more or less together, and not in a slow sequence.

0300hrs All men are clear of the target area. The correct time delay is that which will end about two hours after they have left it.

0430hrs The Patrol regains its OB having made the return journey with even more caution than the outward one. A meal is eaten.

0600hrs 'Lights out'[7]

Ruthlessness

With a limited number of nights to make an impact on the invading army, anything or anyone that was likely to reduce the time each patrol had to be effective would be dealt with quickly and efficiently. This included anyone who was asking too many questions or had stumbled across the OB. Charles 'George' Pellett, was a member of the Bridge Patrol in Kent. One evening in 1940 as the patrol moved towards their OB through a forest, Pellett spotted a local gamekeeper watching them from behind a tree. The patrol leader told them to keep moving right through the wood, before they circled and carefully made their way back, by which time the gamekeeper had disappeared. The gamekeeper had already seen too much though and obviously had his suspicions about the patrol. Pellett asked what they should do. The patrol leader was very clear: as soon as the balloon went up in their area, the gamekeeper would be the first shot; as Pellett put it, 'no messing about'.[8]

Auxilier Charlie Mason of the South Cave Patrol in Yorkshire remembered another particularly 'awkward' gamekeeper who refused orders to stay away from the area of the patrol's OB. On reluctantly leaving one evening, the gamekeeper told Charlie that he 'knew what was going on down there'. The patrol reported the facts and discussed what to do with the gamekeeper in the event of an invasion. It was decided 'That when the invasion comes, not if it comes, to get rid of him, to eliminate him, to booby-trap him, certainly to eliminate him! We would eliminate anyone who threatened our existence, put our hide or existence in jeopardy.'[9]

Ken Welch in Cornwall well remembers the first likely 'victims' of his Mabe Patrol.

> There was an old couple living in a little cottage on the road opposite our OB. They knew something was going on and so they sadly would have to say goodbye if the Germans came. Nobody, as far as I can remember, was named to do the task. I suspect we would have drawn straws to see which one of us would have taken them out.[10]

Some patrols were reportedly handed envelopes that were not to be opened until the Germans came. The envelopes contained the names of British targets that would have to be assassinated immediately. These might include the local head of police who would have checked the patrol's credentials to allow them into the Auxiliary Units in the first place. The police officer would have seen each of these names, and although he would not know what they were joining, he might well have let something slip to the invading army.

Other targets on the list would have likely included the intelligence officer who had first brought the patrol together. His knowledge of each individual patrol member, the location of all the OBs in his area and the potential targets was too much of a risk to allow him to fall into the hands of the enemy. Many IOs would have known or guessed that when the Germans came, they might well be a target for their own men. What action they would have taken is of course purely supposition, but it is unlikely that they would have allowed themselves to be captured.

Henry Hutchins of the West Dorset Scout Section Patrol was chosen as sniper. He was also handed a small brown envelope, inside of which he was told he would find a name. In the event of an invasion, and only in the event of an invasion, he was to open the envelope, read the name, find whoever it may be, and shoot him or her, as this was someone already marked down as a Nazi sympathiser.[11]

In East Devon, the Branscombe Patrol was located near the residence of Lucy Temple Cotton and her son, Rafe. Lucy was a close friend of Oswald Mosley, the leader of the British Union of Fascists (BUF) who was interned in May 1940 as a potential threat to Britain's war effort. In the late 1930s Rafe had been the lead organiser for Devon and a parliamentary candidate for the BUF, the 'Blackshirts'. It is known that the mother and son had made trips to Germany, had met with Hitler personally and been hosts to Joachim von Ribbentrop when he visited Devon during his time as the German ambassador in Britain during the late 1930s. Both Rafe and Lucy were arrested but quickly released and allowed home but kept under surveillance. However, in the event of an invasion, and the chaos that would inevitably come with it, the Cottons had the potential to be traitors in aiding and abetting the enemy.[i] By assassinating mother and son, the patrol would not only take away a potential ally of the invading army, but also make it clear that collaboration would not go unchecked, potentially removing support for the Germans in the local area.

The ruthlessness instilled in the men of the Auxiliary Units was not restricted to enemies or those who were asking too many questions though. It extended to the patrol itself. If a patrol member was injured during a mission and could not get back to the OB, the other members were obligated to shoot him. They could not risk him falling into the enemy's hands and potentially, under torture, giving away the location of their OB. Any threat that was likely to reduce the operational time of the patrol and their efforts to make as big an impact as possible would have to be dealt with, without question. Bob Millard recalls being told during training that 'the Patrol mattered more than the individual and that if someone was seriously injured and you couldn't get them any help they had to be shot. They would only be tortured and shot anyway.'[12]

Taking into account that many of the patrols were made up of family, friends and colleagues, the thought that you would have to shoot someone you knew and loved highlights the sheer ruthlessness that the patrols were expected to show in every aspect of their role.

When asked whether he could actually deliver the *coup de grâce* to an injured member of his patrol, Bob wasn't sure. 'That's a question

---

i   In 2005 the Cottons' house in Branscombe was being demolished. Under the floor, some newspapers were discovered. Multiple different copies of *Action* and *The Black Shirt* newspapers were found, both of which were British Union of Fascist publications.

I have been asked many times before. I simply don't know. Because we carried Mills bombs it was suggested that you used one of them to throw at the approaching Germans and used another to blow yourself up with. But fortunately, it's something that never, ever happened in real life.'[13]

Some patrols were provided with specific items to use in the event of capture or likely capture. Gilbert Smith of the Fritham Patrol in Hampshire was 'surprised to receive cyanide tablets for use in case capture seemed inevitable.'[14] Although cyanide was certainly not standard issue, Bert Verney of the Tawstock Patrol in north Devon also remembers 'having a phial of poison containing Potassium Cyanide for if captured or if someone from the village was held captive.'[15]

Taking cyanide to avoid capture is one thing, but Bert Verney's testimony indicating that they were also to use it on captured civilians takes it to a new level. It gives a real impression of just what these men were expected to do if the Germans had invaded.

Coleshill House

Gubbins knew that taking civilians and making them into ruthless and highly effective guerrilla fighters and saboteurs was going to be no easy task. During the early stages of its formation, Gubbins ran the Auxiliary Units from his office in Whitehall, central London. Practical and physical training tended to take place at the homes of IOs or in discreet places in and around the county they were stationed in. However, with the situation in London becoming increasingly dangerous with the threat of the German bombing, Gubbins found a suitably large and remote centre where men from all over the country could come and train and learn all the skills they would need to be the ruthless irregular force capable of holding up the invading German army.

Coleshill House was a Palladian manor house built by Sir Roger Pratt, with advice from Inigo Jones, in about 1652.[16] In 1940, the property was in the possession of the family of the Earl of Radnor, the Pleydell-Bouveries. In residence were two Pleydell-Bouverie sisters, Mary and Katherine who had agreed to hand over their house and estate for the war effort. The sisters were to remain at the house for the duration, alongside their dogs who Lampe describes as nervous animals before Gubbins and the Auxiliary Units arrived and even more frantic as the explosions started around the grounds (the sisters fed them on a diet of brandy and aspirin to try and calm them down). Things at the house had not changed considerably since it was built. Underground tunnels brought water to the house and even in 1940 there was no electricity, meaning one of the first jobs for the army was to install generators.

The house was set in the hamlet of Coleshill, near the market town of Highworth, near Swindon. It was well placed, as it was isolated with good links to the rest of the country (the nearest railway station was at Highworth). Initially the HQ staff came down from Whitehall Place every Friday to set up the training and catering at Coleshill, returning to London on the Sunday. The first course was held on 22 August 1940. However, quite early on in the Blitz, the offices at Whitehall were damaged and so the entire staff and contents were transferred to Coleshill.

Like everything associated with the Auxiliary Units, all aspects of what went on at Coleshill House was top secret. This was even to the extent that Auxiliers arriving from across the country had no idea as to the exact location of the training centre. Each patrol was sent a letter ordering one or two of the patrol to make their way to Highworth by train. Once there, they were to find the local post office and give a password to the postmistress, Mabel Stranks.

Mabel has been described as a somewhat cantankerous lady, but she took her role very seriously. On receipt of the correct password, Mabel would ring Coleshill House to let them know that another group had arrived, indicating that there were 'parcels' for them to collect. Coleshill would then send a truck to pick the men up and take them on a convoluted route back to the house, so by the time they arrived, the Auxiliers had no idea where they were. There is even a story that she kept General Montgomery, who was visiting Coleshill, waiting while she checked his credentials! Like all those involved in Auxiliary Units, Mabel's role meant that she too was likely to be questioned, tortured and eventually executed by the Germans had they successfully invaded. She died in 1971, aged 88, having never told anyone about her role. Even in the final three years of her life, after David Lampe's book *Last Ditch* had revealed her role to the world, she remained stoically silent.

Once they had arrived at Coleshill House, the recruits would take part in a weekend of training. Overseeing all aspects of training was Major 'Billy' Beyts. Having been an instructor to the Independent Companies in Norway, his role at Coleshill House was to ensure that the civilian volunteers were given the very best training possible, allowing them every chance of successfully holding up the German invasion. Each man was taught the effectiveness of operating at night. Beyts and his team emphasised the fact that anyone who is absolutely still in the dark is almost invisible. Therefore, moving slowly at night would be key for their success. Each Auxilier would be told, 'Time yourselves. If you have eight hours of darkness, then use four to reach your objective and four to get away again. Don't hurry and be killed.'[17]

Hundreds of men from all over Britain attended training at Coleshill House. Alongside Monty were other high-profile visitors, including future film star Anthony Quayle. Quayle had been given an emergency commission in January 1940 and by May had been posted to Gibraltar with the Coastal Artillery. Anxious to get a more 'hands-on role' Quayle was transferred back to the UK where he took up a role with the Auxiliary Units as IO for Northumberland, a post he held between March 1941 and November 1941. He too was ordered to attend training at Coleshill, and Lampe has recorded his memories of the type of training he undertook.

> On a course at Coleshill they told us to attack a wood in which they had a few old bits of metal and stuff pretending to be tanks in laager. I can remember coming up across a ploughed field in the middle of the night to attack this thing. Where the ploughing had finished, there was a piece of grass verge at the edge of the wood which the farmer hadn't ploughed up but left to walk on. They had some staff – some Lovat Scouts and people – walking around, simulating a perfectly ordinary German Patrol. They came round regularly and irregularly.

I'd crawled slowly all the way up the ploughed field in a furrow, I'd got denims on and I was absolutely caked with mud. I was cold and miserable, too, and as brown as the field. 'Well' I thought 'now here's where I get up to go across this grass verge before the sentry comes round.'

And – suddenly I heard him coming. He'd cut through the wood! Instead of going round he'd cut right through – and had come round again! I thought, 'Well here's where I lie still.'

And so I lay still. But my hands were up on the grass, poised to crawl over it. Brown and muddy, but there. And he came so close to me – he must have been within an inch of my fingers – that I felt the muddy ground give slightly under his foot.

He walked off and I lay there for a bit, and then I crawled in and tied the thing on that I'd got to tie on and went away.

He never saw me, and I asked him afterwards, 'Were you kidding that you didn't see me? Or did you really not see me?' And this fellow said, 'I didn't see anyone at all.'[18]

Whether Quayle's experience at Coleshill gave him any motivation for his later roles, particularly when he played a British Special Forces soldier on a mission behind enemy lines in the film *The Guns of Navarone*, is unknown.

Bob Millard of the Bathampton Patrol first visited Coleshill in February 1941.

Patrols from all over the country used to come to Coleshill, and when we went, we would arrive there on the Thursday evening and start almost immediately once you had been shown your bunk and that and given a cup of tea, been talked to, and we worked through until Monday, and leave on the Monday. The training was very comprehensive and was given by officers from different Army regiments. I don't know how many there were, I think four or five of them, and a number of Army personnel from the Lovat Scouts, who were a sort of commando unit.[19]

Millard also explained the training they received for the use of one of their key resources – explosives.

Training gave us more information on the use of explosives and explosive devices. We were shown TNT, gelignite and the plastic explosive which we had been issued with. We were told how to estimate the size charge that would be required for a certain job, shown the best place to place a charge to bring down a pylon or cut a railway line. We were also shown how to set up different types of booby traps, and techniques for disabling vehicles.[20]

Another key element of the training at Coleshill House was silent combat. This 'dirty' fighting was very much in contrast to the regular British Army training.

> Besides this sabotage training we were also given some training in personal defence. We were introduced to basic unarmed combat and shown how to use the garrotte and how to use the Fairbairn knife that we had been issued with. I can always remember being told to strike upwards and keep your thumb on the blade in case the knife twists. Fortunately, one didn't have to do that sort of thing.[21]

Geoffrey Bradford,[i] who was in the Braunton Patrol in north Devon and who seems to have been the last Auxiliary Units member recruited (on 1 July 1944), also remembers being taught how to use the Fairbairn-Sykes knife at Coleshill.

> We learnt detailed information about where to stick a knife in. The idea was that you used it from behind. It was a stabbing knife − the blade wasn't all that sharp. You wouldn't take anyone on from the front but hold them around the neck and in up through the ribs. It takes quite a time for die from a knife if you can't get it into the heart. You would have to stab them enough times and hang on there to see what happened.[22]

Major Bill Harston,[ii] a former prep schoolmaster, was, as well as being Motor Transport Officer at Coleshill, training officer in charge of silent killing. He made his new pupils pretend to be German sentries and would demonstrate how to approach silently and insert the knife before the German knew what was happening and could cry out. He was said to once remark that he was not sure how some of the Auxiliary Units members would react when forced to stab a live man's ribs. 'What I really need,' he said casually, 'is a body for them to practise on.'[23] He was apparently offered one by a contact who told him, 'I can let you have one old boy. Genuine German. It's in our

---

i   Geoffrey Bradford's brother, Roy, was also in the Auxiliary Units and later joined the SAS. Tragically, Roy was killed during Operation *Houndsworth* in France during 1944.

ii Harston was later an IO across a number of counties including Devon, Cornwall, South Wales, Worcestershire and Herefordshire during 1943 and 1944.

freezer. I'll have it put in your car.' Harston reportedly turned down this offer and stuck to straw-filled bags!

As well as silent killing, these civilian volunteers were taught stalking, how to use grenades and where to place explosives on German aircraft and tanks. There were mock OBs dug to give the recruits an idea of what it would be like to live underground for a period of time, as well as practice in the early days of where to locate them, how to dig and disguise them and how to approach the bunkers so as not to attract unwanted attention. They also undertook night exercises as Bob Millard describes.

> We did two-night exercises. We were shown first a plan of the area around the Coleshill House by the yard where vehicles would be parked. And then we were taken out some three or four miles in a van, dropped off and given a direction to set off in, and work in pairs to get back and try and get to one of these vehicles and put a chalk mark on it, to show that you had found it and put it up. As you did that there were one or two patrols out, patrolling the area which you had to cross, and you had to dodge these to get in. It was all good Boy Scout stuff, and it was quite fun provided it wasn't raining.[24]

Ken Welch visited Coleshill on one occasion. Apart from remembering it being bitterly cold, he also has a particular memory of a night exercise because of who his training partner was.

> On the Saturday night we went out on operations. I was with Colonel Douglas crawling through ditches! He was in front and I was behind. All of a sudden, he stopped. I didn't. You can guess what happened next![25]

The training at Coleshill was of the highest standard. Many of the instructors would later go on to train the emerging special forces including the Commandos, SAS, SOE and Chindits. Again, Millard describes what he thought of the times he visited Coleshill.[i]

> As you can see there was a lot covered and it was very well done. They had the training down to a tee. No time was wasted. Things were pushed home,

---

i   The Coleshill Estate now belongs to the National Trust, but tragically the house burnt down shortly after the war in 1952. However, the out-buildings where the Auxiliary Units members stayed, the practice OB as well as an excellent mock-up base are all there to see, with a number of open days held each year.

repeated, demonstrated and then left for you to practice. When you went back to the patrol you had all this in your head, and, of course, in the patrol you tried to practice it and work it out and go over it again and talk amongst yourselves about what had happened.[26]

There are some tantalising hints of what life would have been like at Coleshill House during one of the weekend courses. A document from the archives gives a full programme of activity for a group commanders' training weekend.

Friday
1930   Dinner
2030   Opening address Lt Col Douglas
        Subject: Role of Group Commanders
        In (i) Peace, (ii) Raids (iii) Invasion
2130   Syndicates discuss problems

Saturday
0830   Breakfast
0930   Lecture on the Observers Task and Training in it. Major Oxenden
1045   Explosives Captain Tallents
1300   Lunch
1430   Practical Lecture on Camouflage and OBs Major Oxenden
1600   Lecture on Administration Captain Wickham-Boynton
1700   Tea
1800   Care of Patrol Weapons Captain Lord Delamere
1845   Lecture on Security   Captain Fingland
1930   Dinner
2030   Syndicates give their solutions to problems

Sunday
0830   Breakfast
0930   Group Commanders state their views and experiences. General discussion. Brains Trust
1130   Snack Lunch[27]

Training away from Coleshill

With only two or three members of each Patrol attending Coleshill at any one time, it was up to those who did attend to pass on what they learnt when they got back to their patrol.

A number of solutions had been put in place to ensure that the training conducted at 'home' continued to be of the highest standard.

With the IO stretched across multiple patrols, and therefore unable to keep a regular eye on their level of training, it was important that other regular soldiers could also be available in each county to ensure this was happening. The first evidence we have of such units being set up is a 'war establishment'[i] dated 26 July 1940. The units, named Army Scout Sections, were created and drawn from the county regiments (although not necessarily local men). Each section consisted of an officer and 13 other ranks and transport (including a cook and a batman/driver for the officer). These were based on the regular soldiers of the Lovat Scouts that had originally helped Fleming in the early days of the XII Corps Observation Unit.

It was intended that after a couple of months' intensive training, the scout section would go on to train the patrols, with lectures, demonstrations and night exercises. By November 1940 there were scout sections in 14 areas (some counties had more than one scout section allocated).

Like the civilian volunteers, those regular soldiers who were picked to join the Auxiliary Units' scout sections tended to be, initially at least, young and physically tough. However, as Oxenden points out, this was a short-sighted approach, as scout section officers were often too young to take over from any IOs leaving the Auxiliary Units. Later recruits into the scout sections tended to be old enough to, if necessary, take over responsibility from the IO with the other ranks made up of men of higher educational standard, giving them the ability to more effectively lecture when required. Each scout section was supplied with an Austin two-seater car and a 15cwt lorry, both with Royal Army Service Corps drivers. The patrols also normally had a set of bicycles.

The scout sections often dug their own OBs and were the only patrols to be allocated wireless sets (No. 17 wireless sets) which would

---

i   A war establishment is the level of equipment and manning laid down for a military unit in wartime.

allow the IO to keep in contact with them (no 'ordinary' Auxiliary patrols had wireless sets provided).

As well as training and providing lectures for the Auxiliary patrols in the county, each of the scout sections would be expected to go into action with similar roles to their civilian counterparts had the Germans invaded. As such they were armed with the same weapons and explosives, but also had extra equipment including recce boats and assault boats.

The training that the scout sections gave the Auxiliary Units took place at a central location. For example, the regional headquarters for Devon was around Upton Pyne in the Pynes House estate where the section's OB was also located. Much of the training of Devon-based patrols took place in and around the neighbouring area of Thorverton, three miles west of Exeter. Being so close to the regional capital meant that the Devon scout section would, in all probability, target the rail network coming through Exeter. The destruction of key lines and bridges could potentially cut off the entire South West, from an invading army moving in either direction.

Walter Denslow, a corporal in the Bovey Patrol in East Devon, remembered visiting the Devon scout section in Thorverton and it being the most difficult training he faced during his time in the Auxiliary Units:

> The most difficult job I had to do, they picked us up one night in army trucks, we didn't know where we was going like. They took us down to a place called Thorverton I believe it was. There was a hall there, and seven Patrols met there, and when we got there, they gave us a map. And on the map, there was just North, South, East and West and just a red dot, and in the middle of the night we had to find that dot. Strange country, black. It was very different. I had to lead the Branscombe Patrol, not my own, and I led it where I thought I found it, but they only had about half of us found our targets.[28]

Aside from training with the scout sections, the IO and at Coleshill, patrols would train every weekend in their local area, practising using explosives and weapons, testing their skills and the defences of local army HQs, airfields and ammo dumps.

Getting used to handling explosives was a key, but dangerous part of each patrol's training. The point of a secret guerrilla force is to remain secret, therefore practising with explosives and grenades makes this somewhat of a difficult task, as Dennis Dyke of the Dinder Patrol in Somerset recalls: 'The local Home Guard didn't know what we were doing. We'd go out training and making explosions. They'd come tearing up looking for us, but they never found us.'[29]

Jack Chew of the Cheddar Patrol in Somerset remembers the dangers of practising with explosives:

> Our Cheddar Unit practised with explosives on the hill. It's a wonder we hadn't been killed. There was a big pile of boulders up behind Maskall's Wood. Arthur Pavey (Patrol Leader) said 'Let's put some plastic under there.' So, we put it in and tamped it all down and put the fuse on and got back a bit. Do you know, it went up nearly as high as the trees. There was rocks that big, coming down all around us and you couldn't run for fear you run into 'em.[30]

The nature of handling and detonating explosives meant, of course, that there were accidents. Peter Forbes, the IO for the Borders region, experienced one particularly tragic incident:

> Patrols would come to my HQ at the weekends and we'd practice explosives. Unfortunately, one day one of the Patrol members blew his hands off and he died. It was a terrible business, he had a wife and children. There was a terrible trouble getting a pension for her I think, I suppose because he was unofficial.[31]

The Auxiliary Units also tested the defences of local depots and HQs belonging to the regular army, much in the same vein as the XII Corps Observation Unit's 'attack' on Montgomery's HQ. These were likely to be used as HQs by the invading army and therefore potential targets. Herman Kindred of the Stratford St Andrew Patrol in Suffolk remembers being asked to test the HQ of a regiment nearby.

> We were asked to test their defences one night, I think it was the Tank Corps. We agreed and set off about one in the morning. Two of our chaps knew the caretaker of the hall (where the HQ was based) and may have cheated a little bit. They asked him to make sure that a bolt on a certain door wasn't in that particular night. They succeeded in getting in this door and they got all the way into the house and to the Commanding Officer's room, where he was sat at his desk doing some paperwork. He was most annoyed about it. Unfortunately, I was caught that night, but I was the decoy![32]

George Pellett, of Bridge Patrol in Kent, remembered targeting country houses near Canterbury in Kent. They practised on the likes of Bifrons Park and Charlton Park. It was an attack on Bourne Park though that George had particular memories of. Bourne Park was the home of Sir John Prestige who lived in one half of the house, with the other half requisitioned by the army. George had gained access to the grounds and then the house itself. 'We were taught how to open the door quietly. Touch the door handle, nothing, no electric shock, grab the door handle tightly, pull and then turn, ease the door slightly, peer round the door; and there was Sir John, sitting there reading a newspaper! So I backed out of there a bit sharp!'[33]

As well as manor houses, that were likely to be taken as HQs by the invading army, the Auxiliary Units would practise gaining access to other key targets they would have to destroy if the Germans invaded. Army bases were scattered around the country throughout the Second World War, giving patrols plenty of targets to practise on, as Peter Boulden, a member of the Aldington Patrol in Kent remembered: 'We attacked army posts. We told them we would be infiltrating them and that they wouldn't find us, sometimes they did, sometimes they didn't. But we did a tremendous lot of that. There were army camps all round here, so that was quite easy.'[34]

As in any invasion, it was anticipated that German forces would prioritise capturing airfields. For those patrols positioned near airfields, practising getting from the OB to the airfield, in the pitch dark across multiple routes was a common weekend activity.

They would also practise gaining access to the planes, as the Maiden Newton Patrol in Dorset did when 'attacking' a local airfield. They had to make their way across a number of water-meadows, through quarries and eventually onto the Warmwell airfield, practising multiple times to ensure that timings were right in order to get there, gain access and get away. Much like attacking a Luftwaffe-held airfield, the patrol had to breach the defences, avoid any patrols and reach the aircraft. Having successfully got to the aircraft, they had to 'mark' the aeroplanes to indicate that they had been reached and destroyed, which they did. On one occasion – perhaps highlighting the reality of the role they were to play in the event of an invasion – after successfully marking the planes, they were caught in the search lights. However, in this instance, instead of torture and death, they were given a cup of tea and sent on their way.

Not all patrols had such treatment after trying to gain access to a potential target held by the regular forces. For many patrols attacking a target without warning those guarding it gave them a good feel as to what it would have been like attacking if the balloon had gone up.

Jack French of Bridge Patrol in Kent led his patrol to attack a huge naval gun, which was to be used to shell the enemy as they crossed the Channel and was hidden in a railway tunnel.

> Well if you can imagine a foggy night in November, with no wind, no sound at all. Above the tunnel the gun crew lived in little huts and you could hear them, the guards, moving about. We thought that there would be a change of guard around 10pm and after half hour we were proved right.
>
> Once we got inside the tunnel, we had the great job, it was pitch black, of identifying where the gun was and climbing up to it to the various points we had decided to attack and stick our bits of plasticine that represented the charges. It was an 18inch First World War navel gun on a railway mounting and weighed about 250–300 tonnes, the gun plus carriage was about 150-foot long. It was a huge thing and it reached to the top of the tunnel within a couple of feet of the roof. And I was up there when unfortunately, we were surprised and the guard was called out and I'm afraid one or two of our number got duffed up. One of them was in hospital for a couple of days with suspected cracked ribs.[35]

As the war went on and the levels of secrecy were dropped a little, patrols would practise on each other too. Ken Welch remembers regularly undertaking exercises against neighbouring patrols. 'We would invade each other, to test each other's defences,' remembered Ken. 'We would try and blow up someone's barn in Constantine [the neighbouring patrol] and they would come and try do the same to us.'[36]

They also took part in exercises against regular Home Guard units. Frank Soames, a member of the Colyton Home Guard in East Devon, remembers an incident later in the war:

> A simulated effect attack came from the Special Services Home Guard.[i] They were mainly fit and strong farmers who were trained better than us. When they invaded the town, we weren't sure what we were supposed to do. I took one look at the size of them and thought discretion was the better part of valour. There wasn't any point in getting hurt for nothing. So, we capitulated.[37]

The patrols were also asked to take part in various demonstrations. In Scotland, for example, in the early part of 1941 Captain Maxwell, the IO for the Highlands, brought a number of regular officers to observe two patrols in action. After giving the officers a lecture, he took them outside to a high point and pointed out a convoy of 'German' trucks parking up in a laager (they were actually old British Army vehicles retrieved from scrap heaps) and a group of 'German' soldiers (British regulars) getting out. Asking the officers to imagine it was night, he pointed to a wood pile in a clearing nearby. Raising their binoculars, they saw to their amazement the wood pile swivel upwards and a dozen men (two patrols) emerge from the disguised OB. David Lampe takes up the story.

> The Resistance men moved like night animals, making not a sound. One by one they slithered easily under the barbed-wire concertinas and moved towards the parked vehicles. Surely the 'Germans' would see them. Or would they? The Resistance really did melt completely into the ground.[38]

Almost to the utter disbelief of the officers watching, not only did the Auxiliers gain access to the vehicles, they also managed to fix limpet mines to them, crimp the ends of the time pencils and without making a noise get back to their OB and inside. Maxwell, glancing at his watch, waited and then suddenly there was an explosion. The first truck went up in flames; the regular 'German' soldiers started firing wildly at an 'enemy' long gone. The total destruction of the convoy convinced all that witnessed it that the Auxiliary Units could play a vital role.

With practical training and demonstrations taking place across the country, each Auxiliary Units patrol was also provided with various

---

i   Auxiliary Units were known during and after the war by various different names, Special Services Home Guard being one.

training manuals backing up the physical training. Of course, like most things associated with this remarkable group, the training manuals were anything but ordinary.

To disguise these advanced training manuals from curious eyes at home and, more importantly, any enemy soldiers entering and looking for evidence of why the man of the house had disappeared, each of the various manuals looked like very innocent documents. The first of these disguised manuals produced was the work of Peter Wilkinson for MI(R) at the outbreak of war. It had a plain cover simply called 'Calendar 1937' and so, to the untrained eye, looked exactly that. Opening up the front cover, however, the reader is confronted by 'Notes on Incendiary Materials' with instructions on paraffin incendiaries. Later editions included the 'Calendar 1938' and finally, probably in 1942, 'The Countryman's Diary 1939' was published.

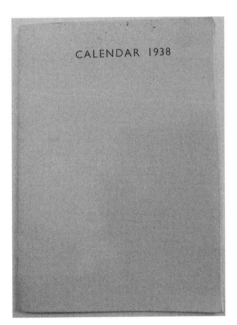
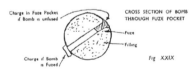

The front cover of the 'Calendar 1938'. Despite its plain exterior, the inside was full of training and tips on guerrilla warfare, sabotage and silent killing. (British Resistance Archive)

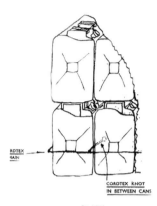

RDTEX
4AIN

CORDTEX KNOT
IN BETWEEN CANS

Fig. XXX.

III. AEROPLANES

he tail is the best part to attack. The following are two good methods:—

a) Place a unit charge *inside* the fuselage at the top of the tail wheel. (There is usually an opening so that the tail wheel can be drawn up during flight.)

b) Place a unit charge between the flat end of the elevator and the corresponding flat surface on the fuselage shown as XX in Fig. XXXI, or between the bottom of the rudder and the corresponding flat surface on the top of the fuselage shown as YY in Fig. XXXI.

35

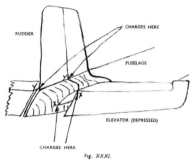

RUDDER

CHARGES HERE

FUSELAGE

ELEVATOR (DEPRESSED)

CHARGES HERE

Fig. XXXI.

IV. ARMOURED CARS

Armoured cars are of two types, those which are armoured underneath and those that are not. If they have no "belly" armour treat them in the same way as lorries. If they have "belly armour" attack the steering gear, the stub axles, or the king pins, with a unit charge.

V. SEMI-TRACKED VEHICLES

1 Fix a charge of 2 lb. primed Gelignite or 808 at any one of the following points:—

(a) Behind or on the driving sprocket

(b) Between the overlap of the idler and last bogey wheel.

(c) On the side of the engine.

VI. TRUCKS

1 Fix a unit charge at any of the following points:—

(a) Main frame at the point where the front shackle of the rear spring is attached

36

III. "GOLDEN RAIN"

4 A.W.'s

Cordtex

Trip wire

Pull
Switch

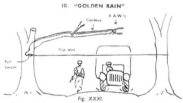

Fig. XXXI.

This can only be used when branches overhang a road. Fit the trip wire 7 ft. high, so that it won't catch a man. Connect to a Pull Switch firing 2-in. Orange Line, firing detonator. Cordtex leading to 4 A.W. Bottles suspended on a branch over centre of the road about 6 ft. ahead of the trip wire, so that the "rain" will fall on the lorry and not behind it.

IV. THE ROAD BLOCK

Trip Wire

Pull Switch

Charge

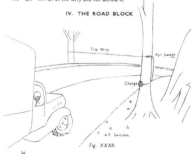

A.P. Switches

Fig. XXXII.

36

Choose a tree of about 9 in. to 12 in. diameter standing clear of others (so that entangled branches won't hold it up) on a stretch of road which lorries cannot leave easily.

Place a charge on side of the tree nearest the road and fit it up with a Pull Switch and trip wire as for "Golden Rain" (9-in. tree 1½ lb., 12-in. tree 2 lb. primed Gelignite).

Lay A.P. Switches in area where butt of tree is likely to fall. Sometimes it is worth setting "Golden Rain" within 20 ft. or so if conditions are suitable, with 1 ft. of Safety Fuze instead of 2-in. Orange Line. Now imagine what happens when an enemy convoy touches off the outfit!

V. FLESH CUTTER

Fig. XXXIII.

A piece of the thick steel wire is tightly stretched between two trees diagonally across a road frequented by lone enemy motor cyclists. Must be against a dark background if used by daylight, and at the height of the average man's neck whilst riding a motor cycle. If used at night you might lurk in the area and see if the motor cyclist has any dispatches. Even if you can't do anything with them, it might cause the enemy to change his plans if they disappear. If the wire is placed diagonally, the bicycle and rider slide off the road into the ditch leaving the road clear for another one.

37

Training and tips on guerrilla warfare, sabotage and silent killing from 'Calendar 1938'.

The diary, like the two 'calendars' looked innocuous. However, on the front cover the team at Coleshill had included an in-joke in the form of an apparent advertisement (see photo).

Each of the manuals has similar advice and training instructions. The 'Calendar 1938', for example, had a diagram showing the 'Flesh Cutter' which went into some detail about how effective a piece of wire tied between two trees across a road can be.

> A piece of the thick steel wire is tightly stretched between two trees diagonally across a road frequented by lone enemy motor cyclists. Just be against a dark background if used by daylight, and at the height of the average man's neck whilst riding a motor cycle. If used at night you might lurk in the area and see if the motor cyclist has any dispatches. Even if you can't do anything with them it might cause the enemy to change his plans if they disappear. If the wire is placed diagonally, the bicycle and rider slide off the road into the ditch leaving the road clear for another one.

The 'Countryman's Diary 1939' explains how to effectively destroy aeroplanes.

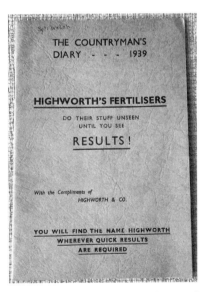

A later version of the Auxiliary Units training pamphlet was designed to put suspicious individuals off the scent. The front cover included in-jokes referring to the market town near to Coleshill House. (Ken Welch)

The tail is the best part to attack. The following are two good methods:–

(a) Place a unit charge inside the fuselage at the top of the tail wheel. (There is usually an opening so that the tail wheel can be drawn up during flight).

(b) Place a unit charge between the flat end of the elevator and the corresponding flat surface on the fuselage, or between the bottom of the rudder and the corresponding flat surface on the top of the fuselage.

Throughout each of the disguised manuals, advice is given on the use of explosives, where to place them on railway tracks and girders and, importantly, how they should be handled. For example, 'Don't handle unwrapped Gelignite in your bare hands, or you will get a headache.'

The patrols were expected to study these manuals and, alongside weekend trips to Coleshill, training in their own areas and liaising with their local scout section, they soon became some of the most highly trained troops in the country, certainly much better trained than the Home Guard and, in many cases, the regular army too. They also learnt to become accustomed to the conditions of living underground in their OBs.

CHAPTER 3

Bunkers, Equipment, Explosives and Weapons

Norman Field was commissioned into the Royal Fusiliers as a second lieutenant in 1937. After fighting in France with the BEF, by late May 1940 he was on the beaches of Dunkirk with a badly injured hand. As a casualty, Field was given priority and placed on board a minesweeper and after a treacherous route home (being dive-bombed by eight Stukas), he eventually made it back to Britain and was transferred to a hospital in Dartford, Kent.

While in hospital, Field was visited by Peter Wilkinson, an adjutant in the Royal Fusiliers, and by then one of the key men in Gubbins's senior staff in the Auxiliary Units. During Wilkinson's visit Field asked if there was any role for him within the 'undercover job' Field suspected Wilkinson to be a part of. A few days later Field was invited to Coleshill and then to The Garth where he was to take over from the departing Peter Fleming.

Field was appointed IO for Kent and, as a result, in early 1941 found himself escorting General Montgomery, who himself had just taken over command of XII Corps from Andrew Thorne, on his first tour of Auxiliary Units installations. While on Charing Hill, above the sleepy village of Charing, Field suggested to Montgomery that they rest on a sheep trough in a field and take in the spectacular views overlooking the English Channel. They both sat and after a while the general turned to say something to Field, only to realise that he had completely disappeared. The trough was no ordinary trough. It was the disguised entrance to the local patrol's OB. Only when Field stuck his head back through the rectangular entrance in the bottom of the trough did Monty fully grasp what he was sitting on!

This story highlights the level of ingenuity involved in the construction and camouflage of the secret underground bunkers the patrols were to rush to when the invading German forces entered their areas. Since the war, and because of the lack of official recognition for the Auxiliary Units, these Operational Bases have acted almost as monuments to the secret role the units were prepared to play in the country's 'darkest hours'. Some remain undiscovered; most are destroyed or collapsed, but those that do remain give an impression not only of the huge ingenuity involved within the Auxiliary Units, but also a very stark impression of what life would have been like for a patrol if the Germans had invaded.

During the early days of the XII Corps Observation Units in Kent, Fleming had quickly come to recognise that patrol members could not realistically be asked to sneak out of their houses at night, complete a mission and return before daybreak without attracting the attention of family members, potential informers or the Germans themselves. Therefore, the need for a secret, ideally underground, base for the patrols to occupy during the day in the fortnight they were expected to be active became a crucial element.

Fleming had quickly realised the importance of somewhere for the patrols to disappear to, using the 'aid of an imaginary Chinese general of the fifth century BC, to whom they attributed the maxim 'A guerrilla without a base is no better than a desperate straggler.'[1] The patrols dug rudimentary bunkers called 'hideouts', but this name was soon dropped, as it was considered too indicative of their activities, and the term Operational Bases (OBs) was adopted. As the patrols were extended across the country, more OBs were being dug. Oxenden, in his short official history of the Auxiliary Units, describes how many of these tended to be influenced by the memory of First World War 'dugouts', with barely enough sitting room for the patrol. As the number of patrol members grew, the problem became more acute and many original bases were scrapped.

Up until the winter of 1940, most patrols were digging their own OBs. Patrol members were given instruction at Coleshill about how to do this, but it seems that unless the patrol had a specific set of skills within it (construction, plumbing, etc.), on the whole, the OBs did not tend to be very effective. One of the major issues was the rather crucial ability to breathe underground. Oxenden describes the results of patrols attempting to dig and design their own OBs.

> Ventilation was a science of which little was known. The official teaching was that a pipe brought down to within a foot of the floor would provide an unfailing current of fresh air, but when the first 'stay-in' exercise was held, most of the earlier OBs soon drove their occupants into the open, sicker and wiser men.[2]

Patrols tended to locate their OBs five to six miles inland from the coast, to avoid being caught up in any initial stages of an invasion. Often on higher ground (although very rarely on the peak of a hill) and near a water supply, OBs were constructed near potential targets.

With many of the patrol members being farmers, farm or estate workers, gamekeepers or miners, they had access to lots of land on which they could dig and construct their OBs. Having access to a road or track somewhere near the potential site was a bonus, as it allowed for the delivery of building materials without attracting too much attention. Farmers and miners were, unlike the majority of the population, given access to petrol to keep tractors, other agricultural equipment and mining vehicles operating. Therefore, observing vehicles moving in and around farmland or mines could be fairly easily explained.

Less easily explained though was the large quantity of construction materials needed. Obviously, anything out of the ordinary in a rural setting is quite easily spotted. Therefore, various stories were often put about the local villages to explain anything anyone might have seen. Unexploded bombs, surveying a site for a potential anti–aircraft battery or even, in at least one case, holes being dug to store emergency food rations for the local population should the invasion come, were all used to put people off the scent and to attempt to keep them away from the area the OB was being constructed.

When it became clear that patrols digging their own OBs was not a good use of their time, or even particularly effective, the decision was made that responsibility for construction should be handed to the experts, the Pioneer Corps and the Royal Engineers. The level of secrecy that surrounded the Auxiliary Units meant that the number of people in the know was deliberately restricted. Bringing in men from other regiments was therefore a potential additional security risk, particularly in a worst-case scenario where the Germans invaded and caught the local Royal Engineer group who could then potentially take them directly to each OB. To try and mitigate this risk, those building the OBs were brought in from other parts of the country and once they had constructed their allocated bunkers they were sent immediately back home. They also built the OBs incredibly quickly to reduce the risk of catching the attention of locals, or potential spies.

Fred Clarkson of the 210 Pioneer Corps, based in Taunton, remembers just how quickly this could be achieved. Although he was not directly involved in building OBs, he knew the men that were. He remembered that all of the OBs in the Taunton area were built by this team. Further to this he knew that escape hatches were on sloping ground and had an angled exit with a camouflaged flap over them. He said that a 'section' constructing the OBs consisted of one sergeant, and, remarkably, 25 men. With such a big section, they aimed to build an OB in one day. Fred went on to help construct the forerunners of the Mulberry harbours in Southampton, before helping to set up Operation *PLUTO*. He then went to Dartmouth with 50 men at Slapton House and installed underground cabling to Plymouth.[3]

By the end of 1940 around 300 OBs were already in use throughout the country, another 61 by the spring of 1941, and by the end of that year there were some 534.[4]

Herman Kindred, the patrol leader of the Stratford St Andrew Patrol in Suffolk gave an account which provides some detail as to how the location of an OB was decided:

> At the end of October 1940, the engineers (Royal Engineers) were ready to build our hideout. I rather objected to the location they had chosen because I thought, if we dig down there will be a clay substance and we are going to have big water problems. They had another rethink and they asked me to have another look around the area and maybe make a suggestion as to where a better location could be found.[5]

This is a good example of how the use of local men with an intimate knowledge of their local surroundings could be hugely valuable. Herman did find a more suitable location and soon the Royal Engineers were digging:

> They put our shell down and very well done it was. The work and all the camouflaging was very quickly done. I think they said that if anything happened, that if anyone asked what was going on, to say that an emergency food supply store was going to be put up for the village. That was the tale given out by the Army at the time.[6]

Even after the Royal Engineers had been, some patrols were not happy with the design and layout of their OBs. John Thornton, a member of the Jacob Patrol in Herefordshire, remembered their first OB:

> The first was L-shaped and built of concrete blocks but it was too small. With six of us in there it was very claustrophobic, and we had problems with fumes. We asked for another to be built.[7]

The Royal Engineers came and built another, some distance from the original:

> It was at the top of the wood, near the reservoir and I believe that it was still there two years ago (*speaking in 2002*). It may still contain the bunks. It was built of thick corrugated iron with a brick, 20 feet long escape tunnel.[8]

There are examples of patrols, like those at Charing, using farm equipment to disguise the entrance to their OB. Others used the natural environment such as old badger sets or rabbit burrows. Some turned to ice houses, abandoned mines, quarries and even caverns behind waterfalls.

Although each OB was different due to the varying ground conditions and local geology, there was, once the Royal Engineers were constructing them, a common layout. The entrance tended to be a hatch, flush to the ground, deliberately covered in debris, ensuring that it was completely disguised. The importance of the entrance was not underestimated, as a training document from Somerset highlights: 'A poor OB with a good lid is a better fighting proposition than a good OB with a poor lid. But a good OB with a good lid is best of all.'[9]

Opening the hatch could be done in a variety of ways. From pulling what looked like a tree root to ring a bell in the bunker, alerting those inside of someone above and opening the hatch from beneath, to rolling a marble down what looked like a rabbit hole (each patrol member had a different coloured marble) to let those inside know who was on the surface waiting to be let in. Others used counter-weight systems that could be stepped on, allowing the hatch to rise and swivel open, some were as simple as a tray over the entrance covered by leaf litter to disguise it that could be pulled aside and quickly placed back over once the patrol was safely ensconced inside.

Once the hatch was opened, a ladder would take you down a vertical shaft (usually around 6–8 feet) into the OB. At the bottom of the ladder (or metal rungs set into the corner of the shaft at 45 degrees) you would be confronted by a blast wall, designed to protect the patrol if the Germans found the bunker, opened the hatch and dropped a grenade inside. Once past the blast wall you would enter the main chamber, which was the living quarters. Here would be half a dozen bunks for the patrol to rest on during the day, a table, chairs, a water tank (occasionally some were located outside the OB and fed to a tap inside) and some storage. Most patrols did not store their explosives in the OB, sensibly preferring to keep them away from the main living quarters in case of any accidents. The main chamber was constructed from concrete blocks and elephant iron (tough corrugated iron) and had the basic look of a very large Anderson shelter. This meant they could be relatively easily dug and built, and that those digging them did not have to stay in the area for any large amount of time, thus reducing the potential for attracting attention.

OBs were certainly not designed for comfort. Some had Elsan chemical toilets, while other patrols preferred the 'hole in the ground approach', perhaps preferring to take their chances rather than be caught emptying a toilet. Some had rudimentary kitchens. Cooking had the potential to attract enemy patrols because of the need to vent smoke out of the bunker. Again, Auxiliary Units ingenuity came to the rescue, with chimneys from the kitchen coming out of the bunker and funnelling up disguised hollow trees to allow the smoke to disperse above the tree line.

Located at the end of most OBs was an escape tunnel. Most stretched several metres away from the bunker, giving the patrol a chance to escape if the Germans found the site. However, most patrols realised that if their OB had been discovered, then successfully escaping the enemy would be almost impossible. Escape tunnels were mostly made of concrete drainage pipes, just big enough for a grown man to crawl through. Exits were as disguised as the entrance hatch. Some came out in walls, others emerged in hedgerows or banks often near a water source to aid in the patrol's getaway.

The problem of breathing underground had not gone away, but with the help of the Royal Engineers, solutions were implemented. Glazed earthenware pipes at the top and bottom of the OB brought fresh air in and took contaminated air away. This was further aided by hanging a Tilley lamp under the ceiling where the pipes converged. Warm air rose up through these vent pipes that drew in cool, fresh air from the pipes at a lower level. The pipes would thread their way underground across the roof and along the walls of the OB and would emerge, disguised on the surface. Some would be in small buried wooden boxes that had a wire mesh across the top allowing leaf debris to accumulate, aiding concealment while allowing air to flow. The pipes would also appear in other disguised places. Hollow tree stumps were utilised and, more commonly, they would break surface in a bank or holes reminiscent of rabbit burrow entrances. These days the pipes are usually one of the more obvious signs of an OB location, as they have not rusted or rotted away and are nearer the surface.

Although relatively 'safe' underground, the patrol would have been, during the day at least, blind to the actions and movement of the enemy, as well as any new potential targets. Therefore, Observation Posts (OPs) were set up by many patrols. These OPs were positioned up to half a mile away from the OB and were sometimes connected to the OB via a field telephone. This was the only outside contact those in the OB would have. The laying of the telephone wire was a matter of concern, as it could quite literally lead a German patrol from the OP to the OB. Advice was given on how to avoid this:

The telephone wire should not leave or enter the ground at the OB (and OP), but a small tunnel should be bored some five yards away, so that an enemy who may have picked up the wire will come to an abrupt halt a short distance away from the OB. The tugging of the wire will be noticeable at either end, and necessary drastic action can be taken at short range without delay. The tunnel can be bored by hammering piping in a downward direction from the earth's surface to about two feet above the floor level of the OB.[10]

The OP was not much more than a hole in the ground, just deep enough for a man to stand. The patrol members would take turns to be the observer in the OP and would, during the day, look out for enemy patrols. Precautions were made in case an enemy patrol had discovered the telephone in the OP: 'In case the enemy discovers the telephone, a password should precede the conversation.'[11] The observer would also be responsible for ensuring the entrance hatch of the OB was fully covered with foliage as well as any tracks made by the patrol making their way back to the bunker (patrols ensured that they had a myriad of ways to get back to the OB, to ensure that no tracks were created by consistent use of one route). From the often-excellent vantage point at which the OP would be located, the observer would be able to check for vehicle movements, new enemy positions, fuel and ammunition dumps and other potential targets for the following night. To assist with this and to avoid exposing the observer's location, methods of providing him with a good view of activity while keeping his head down were introduced. One document describes how 'It is hoped that periscopes may be provided. A hollowed-out tree stump allowing for the insertion of a periscope, could be planted on the Observers' OB (OP) lid, thereby giving the Observer a chance of seeing when the coast is clear for him to emerge.'[12] Having stayed up during the day to monitor enemy movement, he would not be expected to take part in the night attack.

Jacob Patrol in Herefordshire also armed their man in the OP with a .22 rifle. John Thornton remembers during training he much preferred to be positioned in the OP than the OB.

We stayed at the OB at weekends, from Friday to Sunday. After three days we would be getting on each other's nerves and would be ready to leave. I found it particularly difficult to stay there for any length of time and always preferred to be above ground. One man was always outside keeping watch armed with the Patrol's .22 rifle. The .22 was usually loaded with the long bullets but we also had short ammunition, too. There was a telephone in the OB connected via two wires to another hidden under a yew tree near the road. From there the observer could watch the common and give warning of anyone approaching.[13]

It was not just 'holes in the ground' that acted as OPs. Indeed, it seems some patrols set up the very opposite by planting spikes in trees, allowing them to climb and observe the invading army from a better perspective. A great example remains in a Scots pine in East Devon. Spikes make their way up the tree to a height of around 22 metres, giving the patrol member who presumably drew the short straw a fantastic view of the possible invasion beach some 5 miles away, a major route from the beach as well as lots of potential targets.

Later in the war, as the levels of secrecy were reduced with the diminishing threat of invasion, neighbouring patrols began communicating and training with each other. It also meant that the OP and its observer could act as a conduit between neighbouring patrols. This meant that information could be passed from one patrol to another without revealing the actual location of the main OB.

Another document discovered in the Somerset County archives gives advice to patrols on the tidiness of the OB. It also gives a really good impression of the huge amount of equipment patrols were storing in their bunkers.

> The inside of the OB should be as tidy and carefully arranged as a well-kept kitchen. The following is a guide to the items needed and the places for them. These will depend largely upon the size and shape of the space available.
> In Rack. Rifles
> In Storage. Rifle and TG ammunition, Mills Grenades, ST Grenades (less igniter sets), Jar of Rum, seven ration packs (if room), Tommy Gun (in box)
> In Kitchen, or part of OB used for cooking. On shelves or hanging – Primus, methylated spirit and prickers, kettle, saucepans, knives, tin opener, funnel
> On Floor – Paraffin and refuse bucket
> Personal Kit. In seven lockers, boxes or shelves: Mugs, plate, knife, fork and spoon. Washing things and razor. Change of clothing. Shoes for inside wear
> On Shelves. (Items that are affected by damp in glass jars). Candles, matches, revolver ammo, ST igniter sets, corks, water sterilization tablets, First Aid box, 'housewife', a few carpentry tools, 'small bits' from supplies, such as fuzes,

copper-tube igniters, time pencils and 'L' delays, pull and pressure switch caps, books, cards etc.

On Bunker. Paillasses, blankets and pillows, rolled or spread out as seats according to the construction. Kit bags could act as pillows.

Spade. Hanging near entrance

Water cans. In crawl tunnel. Buried tank outside filler if possible

Elsan closet. And spare Elsan fluid in special recess[14]

Not all patrols used their OB in the same way. Ken Welch of Mabe Patrol in Cornwall remembers using the bunker more as a store.

> We weren't going to live in the hideout, but at home. We were to receive orders [from his father, the patrol leader] to go and blow something up. We'd go to the hideout, collect the stuff, do our job and go home. There wasn't room for all seven of us in there anyway. The only time we were to stay, was if the Germans were in the area at the time we were collecting equipment.[15]

This approach might reflect Ken's date of joining the patrol (1943) when levels of secrecy had dropped a little and plans may have altered from the early days of 1940. It does, however, paint a picture of how things may have altered from county to county and patrol to patrol.

Equipment

The list of equipment in the OB only gives a very small impression of the true number of weapons, explosives and other materiel available to the Auxiliary Units. Even before the group was formed, Fleming's XII Corps Observation Unit and Grand's HDS had access to explosives and weapons that the LDV/Home Guard in particular and, in some cases, the regular army were crying out for.

Once the Auxiliary Units had formed from the combination of Fleming's and Grand's groups, Gubbins was able to immediately tap into his relationship with Ironside to ensure his new units would be fully armed as quickly as possible.

It was not just Ironside who was ensuring the Auxiliary Units were equipped with arms and explosives. Churchill, who was reading the updates sent by Gubbins to him and Ironside, also pushed for patrols to be extraordinarily armed. On one such update Churchill scribbled, 'These men must have revolvers.' With the premier placing his full support on the Auxiliary Units, the distribution of revolvers was soon underway. Four hundred .32 Colt automatics were issued at once, followed by a 100-percent issue of .38 revolvers. It was not until much later though that the .38s were followed by ammunition that actually fitted them.[16]

In these early days of the summer/autumn of 1940, most patrols took great pride in one of their principal weapons – hunting knives – which also proved to be a valuable recruiting draw. Compared with the Home Guard, which was still struggling with a severe lack of weapons, the priority placed on the Auxiliary Units meant that the knives 'enhanced a reputation for toughness that the unit was building up, as opposed to the "church parade" activities of the ill-equipped Home Guard proper.'[17]

It was, after all, the silent weapons that would allow the Auxiliary Units to be most effective in their role. They were trained to avoid a running battle with the invading army. Rather, their role would have been to, where possible, gain access to their target, destroy it and get away without even coming in contact with a German. Where this was impossible, their training allowed them to track and silently stalk guards and sentries, dispatch them without a sound and get to the target.

Therefore, silent weapons such as the Fairbairn-Sykes fighting knife, knuckle dusters, knobkerries, homemade knives, cheese cutter garrottes and truncheons were all key for the Auxiliary Units – anything that was quick and silent gave them the best chance to complete their mission without being killed or caught and allowed them to carry on the fight for at least one more night. Such was the emphasis on a silent approach that some patrols believed that they did not need other weapons. The Pelynt Patrol in Cornwall, for example, was said to refuse Tommy guns and other heavy weapons in the belief that theirs would be a silent conflict. They spent much of their time learning the skills of unarmed combat and the use of knives.[18]

The Fairbairn-Sykes fighting knife was held in particular high esteem by the patrols. William Fairbairn had served with the Royal

Marines Light Infantry in 1901, and by 1907 had joined the Shanghai Municipal Police. It was there that he met Eric Sykes and, together, they began to develop close-combat techniques and weapons that could be valuable in such fights. Fairbairn wrote the *All-In Fighting* handbook in 1942, providing an in-depth review into 'thuggery fighting'.

Their experience and expertise meant that the fighting knife they developed was the perfect weapon for 'up close and personal' fighting. As this type of warfare was not in the British Army's training handbook, Fairbairn and Sykes were critical in helping the Allies' special forces become the ultimate fighting units they proved and continue to be. Such was their influence on the special forces that the knife was for some time the symbol of the Commandos.

One other silent weapon that made an appearance in these early days, although seemingly restricted to Fleming's XII Corps Observation Units, was, remarkably, crossbows. Fleming was convinced of the weapon's effectiveness in silently taking out individual targets. He called the gathering of and training in such weapons 'Operation Agincourt'. However, the crossbow was, unsurprisingly, not to become a primary weapon of the Auxiliary Units.

Alongside the revolvers, Churchill insisted that the Auxiliary Units should receive other arms as a priority, certainly above the LDV/Home Guard and even the regular army. One such example was the Thompson sub-machine gun. From April 1940 some 107,000 were initially ordered from the US, rising to 300,000 (although it is reported many did not make it across, with some 100,000 lying on the bottom of the Atlantic having been sent there by U-boat attacks). These machine guns were given to the Auxiliary Units long before the Home Guard and the regular forces. Indeed, the Home Guard did not receive these weapons until 1941. Typically, the Auxiliary Units modified the weapon to make it more appropriate for their role. The round magazine, usually associated with the Thompson, was in many cases swapped for a straight one. The round version was perceived to make too much noise for the patrols' necessary 'stealth'.

By 1941, patrols were starting to receive Sten guns, replacing the Thompsons, which presumably were being passed to Home Guard units. By the time Ken Welch was joining his patrol, much of the transition from Thompsons to Stens had happened. He remembers that his patrol was happy with the change:

> Before I joined they all had Tommy guns. By the time I joined they had been changed for Stens. Stens were so much easier to carry, they didn't have that awkward round magazine.[19]

Patrols were also issued before the LDV and regular forces with the Browning automatic rifle (BAR), Enfield US rifle and the Winchester rifle (in varying models).

Another personal weapon was the Welrod pistol. With the silent approach in mind, the Welrod might well have proved to be an effective weapon in a night-time raid, especially in comparison with the Thompson sub-machine gun or even a Smith & Wesson. Major Nigel Oxenden was certainly unsure of the effectiveness of 'loud' personal weapons but thought the Welrod had potential.

> There are strong arguments against the carrying of firearms on night patrols. One shot could betray the presence of the Patrol and turn the attack into a headlong rout. The only weapon of this sort that could be used without wrecking the chances of the attackers is one that is silent and fitted with luminous sights. Such a pistol has been produced under the name of Welrod.[20]

The Welrod was specifically designed for dispatching sentries and assassinations. The soft click of the action of the Welrod have led to some comparing firing the weapon to the closing of a well-fitted door. It was considered perfect for engaging the enemy while allowing the assailant to get a good distance away, remaining undetected. Interestingly though, it seems the Welrod was only issued to specific scout sections rather than on a general basis to all Auxiliary Units patrols.

One of the more sinister firearms distributed to the Auxiliary Units was the sniper rifle, a special .22 rifle manufactured by a variety of companies including BSA, Winchester and Remington. In an update report from Duncan Sandys to the prime minister (Sandys was also Churchill's son-in-law) about the Auxiliary Units, Sandys made it clear that sniping would be in the Auxiliary Units' remit.[21] As well as being issued envelopes with potential British targets, patrols were also, as part of their role in causing as much chaos as possible, to target German officials. The rifles provided to the Auxiliary Units were fitted with a powerful telescopic sight (which actually proved ineffective, but it was too late to recall) and crucially, for remaining as secret as possible, a silencer or suppressor.

Don Handscombe had been a member of the Home Guard for three weeks when he was approached to join the Thundersley Patrol in Essex. He was in no doubt what the sniping rifles were to be used for.

> We knew of a list of people who might have collaborated with the enemy. But it was not produced to us. We were told that part of our duties may have been to deal with some of these people, but we didn't really know more than that. I would have felt justified in taking the lives of people we regarded as Quislings or collaborators. In the stand-down orders Colonel Douglas (then in November 1944 CO of the Auxiliary Units) wrote that he knew we would fight with orders or without. In my Patrol, we were all good shots. The .22 was passed round. We regarded it as an assassination weapon although it might have helped us to live off the land as well.[22]

Having gained access to the target, the main task for the patrol was obviously to destroy it. From the early days of Fleming and Grand, explosives were core to the role these groups were to play. As such, they were given a huge number and variety of explosives, fuses and grenades.

Grenades

Grenades, like firearms, were thought to be a last resort. Oxenden highlights the No. 77 grenade (an incendiary smoke grenade) because there 'is no indication of the point from which it is thrown, and there is no chance of taking cover from. It would always baffle pursuit.'[23] Patrols were also issued with No. 36 grenades (Mills bombs), ST grenades (sticky bombs) and AW bottles (phosphorous grenades manufactured by Albright and Wilson).

The phosphorous grenades were particularly gruesome and dangerous. The Nevern Patrol, in Pembrokeshire, South Wales positioned barrels containing a flammable liquid in the hedge leading up the steep hill from Nevern to Llwyngoras. Should the Germans be seen crossing the Nevern bridge the liquid would have been released and a phosphorous grenade thrown to create a wall of flame.[24]

There appears to have been frequent incidents in training patrol members to use the phosphorous grenade. Second Lieutenant Glenn W. Aitken was badly injured with phosphorous during training and had to be medically discharged from the Auxiliary Units in 1943.[25]

The phosphorous grenades also had a nasty habit of leaking, making them incredibly dangerous. Trevor Miners of the Perranporth Patrol in Cornwall remembered that a large number of phosphorous bombs had become dangerously unstable, so the patrol took them to a remote part of the cliff top near their OB where they stood the bombs on end. 'We fired at them with our .22 rifles, made a fantastic firework display. Some fell into the sea, but we had no other way of getting rid of them as they were so unstable.'[26]

As time went on the number of small arms and grenades grew to remarkable levels. By 1941 a fully manned patrol of seven men could expect to have:

7 x .38 revolvers (American)
2 x .30 rifles (American)
7 x fighting knives
3 x knobkerries
48 x No. 36 grenades (four-second fuses)
3 x cases of ST grenades (sticky bombs)
2 x cases of AW bottles (phosphorous grenades)
1 x .22 rifle (silenced) from various manufacturers
1 x .45 Thompson SMG (American)

There is a record of the weapons issued to the Langstone (Jonah) Patrol in Monmouthshire, Wales. Each man was issued with:

1 x Colt .38 six-chamber revolver
1 x Commando fighting knife (likely to be the Fairbairn-Sykes fighting knife)
1 x knuckle duster

The patrol as a whole was issued with:

1 x .45 Thompson sub-machine gun with 10 magazines
2 x Lee Enfield rifles .300-calibre
1 x .22 Remington rifle complete with silencer and telescopic sights
2 x Sten machine carbines MK3 with 10 magazines
100lb of explosives
150 grenades
150 phosphorous bottles with all the ancillary equipment to initiate demolition (explosives, booby traps, etc.)

For one patrol to have so much equipment is a true reflection of the priority placed on them by GHQ and those right at the top of government. Although by 1941 the Home Guard was in a very much better position than it had been in 1940, a Home Guard section made up of 7–12 men would have nowhere near the same level of weaponry provided to them; indeed, in many cases they still were sharing weapons and had limited amounts of ammunition.

Explosives

To effectively disrupt the invading army and stop supplies from reaching the spearhead units thrusting through the British countryside, the Auxiliary Units were provided with huge amounts of explosives. From the very start of the prototype patrols with Fleming and Grand, explosives were sought and, in many cases, successfully procured. This trend continued as the patrols expanded.

From July 1940, a plentiful supply of explosives and the accessories necessary for sabotage and booby-trapping were available. These explosives originated from a variety of sources, including the War Office, a continuing relationship with Section D and SIS and commercial suppliers. The first 'dumps' of explosives distributed to patrols were later called 'packs' and finally and rather confusingly 'Aux Units'. This term harks back to the early days of Grand and HDS distributing explosives to civilian cells in cardboard boxes called 'Auxiliary Units'. Oxenden was not hugely impressed by these early efforts.

> Aux Units Mark 1 were contained in cardboard boxes that disintegrated if buried or left out in the rain, and included, besides 10lbs of Plastic Explosive and a mass

of feeble and uncertain incendiaries, a hollow bronze casting of a lump of coal that could hold about two ounces of HE [High Explosive] and a detonator. This museum piece was a clue to our proposed activities in July 1940 – the crippling of our railway system, assumed to be in use by the enemy.[27]

By the summer of 1941 the Aux Units packs were being delivered in tin boxes and were provided a better selection of explosives. As Oxenden put it, 'The funny little incendiaries of 1940 were gone, and plastic was no longer issued, gelignite taking its place.'[28] As Oxenden alludes to, there was a huge variety of explosives available, including Nobel 808, dynamite, ammonal, gelignite and still in some cases plastic. Just a few pounds of high explosives in the wrong hands could have destroyed entire buildings and killed dozens of people. The average patrol had upwards of half-a-ton!

Time pencils were provided in huge numbers too. Designed to set the explosives off after a particular length of time, the time pencils with detonators were a crucial element of a patrol's inventory. Oxenden recommended: 'Extreme time pencils are never needed. Two delays, of about 1.5 hours and 4 hours, will suit all occasions.'[29]

Practising with the use of explosives and detonators was an important but difficult task. As a highly secret organisation, loud explosions had the tendency to give one away, but patrols practised nonetheless. A good example of this comes from the Fritham Patrol in Hampshire. Patrol member Gilbert Smith recalled an initial period of intensive training, mostly in explosives, as the patrol members were already crack shots and familiar with camouflage. As part of this training his patrol was ordered to launch a mock attack on a local army camp, with the aim being to leave time pencils (with detonators, but no explosives) on the differentials of the parked Bren carriers. The camp was told that the patrol would come on one of three nights, although the camp only knew it was a test and not who would be trying to get through their defences. The patrol went on the second night, when there was heavy rain. Within seven minutes the patrol was in and out of the camp having set their time pencils, 30 in all. Twenty minutes later the time pencils went off. The patrol had brought the colonel of the target unit from his headquarters at Minstead Hall as an independent witness of their success. When the charges went off, he was left rather red faced. Gilbert reported that the colonel angrily commented, 'I think I've got a lot of rotten troops and, I don't know for sure, but I think you are the biggest rotters I've ever met!'[30]

A fantastic demonstration of the huge number of explosives and booby traps available to patrols was the amount that area commander Captain Reg Sennitt had in his possession at the end of the war. Reg was a farmer who commanded the Dengie group of patrols in Essex. After waiting 20 years for the army to come and collect the ordnance his patrols had left behind in his milking shed at stand-down, he eventually told the local police. After seeing the sheer amount of highly dangerous ordinance, they rather quickly called the army who retrieved:

14,738 rounds of ammunition
1,205lb of explosives
3,742 feet of delayed-action fusing
930 feet of safety fuse
144 time pencils
1,207 L-Delay switches
1,272 detonators
719 booby-trap switches
314 paraffin bombs
131 fog signals
121 smoke bombs
36 slabs of gun cotton
33 time pencils and booby-trap switches attached to made-up charges

Medical kits

Patrols were supplied with medical kits as well. The kit included items such as amputation knives, bandages, splints, antiseptic creams, ligatures and, in some cases, morphine. The Langstone (Jonah) Patrol did have morphine in their kit. The instructions given on its administration were as follows:

- If a man was badly injured but expected to live, he could be administered with a quarter of a grain of morphine

- If he was potentially fatally injured, he could be administered with a half a grain and it would not affect any recovery he may make

- If the man was most definitely not expected to live, a whole grain could be administered[31]

This last case would no doubt hasten death.

Clothing

In the early days of the Auxiliary Units patrols, much like their LDV/Home Guard contemporaries, were dressed purely in civilian clothing, with a denim suit provided to protect day-to-day shirts and trousers. Unlike the LDV, no armbands or insignia were issued to the Auxiliary Units at all during 1940 and 1941. The armbands provided to the LDV were meant to give the volunteers a veneer of an official armed force, hoping that in the event of capture it might be enough to persuade the invading forces not to execute them as *francs-tireurs*. The very nature of the activities being undertaken by the Auxiliary Units would mean their execution (after torture) whether they were wearing uniform or not, and so initially at least there was little effort to provide them with any.

As many of the Auxiliers were farmers, farm workers, miners and gamekeepers, hard-wearing 'appropriate' clothing was more readily available. As Oxenden points out: 'Rubber agricultural boots are comfortable and silent; and the only special clothing that is indicated is some form of jacket that can combine plenty of pockets with warmth.'[32]

As the war went on, the threat of invasion diminished, and some levels of secrecy were dropped. The Auxiliary Units were brought increasingly under regular army conditions. This meant more traditional training, formations and even 'square bashing'. At the same time, more uniform and insignia was being provided. In 1942 the Auxiliary Units had been split into three Battalions: 201 Scotland, 202 Wales and England north of the Thames and 203 England south of the Thames.

Battalion flashes and some Home Guard badges (to continue some level of secrecy and mislead other units) were introduced with the newly delivered battledress, with units also receiving military greatcoats and side caps. This was very different to the vision set out by the likes of Fleming, Wilkinson and Grand of an underground, irregular guerrilla force and was more of a reflection of the men coming in after them.

Another item that all Auxiliary Units had were rum jars. Patrols were issued with a sealed gallon of rum, each with strict instructions that they should only be opened in the event of a German invasion. Of course, the Germans never came but many patrols took no notice of this and successfully filtered the rum from the jar, drank it and filled the jar back up with other liquids, all without breaking the seal!

With the rum consumed and Hitler launching Operation *Barbarossa* in June 1941, the men of the Auxiliary Units understood that threat of invasion, at least for the duration of any war on the Eastern front, was considerably diminished. By the end of 1941 it was becoming clear that the fighting in the east was not going to be over quickly and by the end of December the industrial and increasing military might of the United States of America was now part of the fight against Nazi Germany.

However, despite the reduced threat, the Auxiliary Units kept up training most weeknights and every weekend, honing their key skills to disrupt any invasion, no matter how unlikely that was. Their role was to change over the course of the rest of the war. Some would go on to take the fight directly to the Germans in occupied Europe, with a few of these brave men losing their lives in the process.

CHAPTER 4

Changing Role and Stand-down

As the threat of invasion diminished, the role of the Auxiliary Units changed. Some went on to take the fight directly to the enemy, their role morphing from a defensive to an offensive one. However, most still had their reserved occupations and so continued their training in Britain. There was still a role for the Auxiliary Units to play. The prospect of localised enemy raids remained a real consideration, and patrols also had a part to play in the Allies' plans for the liberation of occupied Europe.

When Hitler turned his attention to Russia in June 1941 the immediate threat of invasion looked to be over for the time being. However, those at the top of the Auxiliary Units recognised the huge potential the force had and so were determined to ensure that patrols were not dissolved. By the end of 1941, it was clear that the units 'must either go on or go under.'[1] Coleshill House did such an extraordinary job of making sure that the units 'went on' that they were actually expanded. The War Office bought into the argument that patrols continued to be a real asset to the wider war effort and agreed to the creation of about 100 new patrols, to include the untouched areas in parts of the Borders, Northumberland and Durham.

Anything haphazard about the initial recruitment and arming of the patrols had now gone, with IOs having access to an embarrassment of riches when it came to weapons, explosives and other supplies. Indeed, some of these 'new' patrols were much better equipped than those which had been set up the year before.

However, it was not all good news for the Auxiliary Units. With the immediate threat of a full-scale German invasion gone and the need for Britain to become more proactive in taking the fight to the German forces occupying much of Europe, many of the leading lights of the Auxiliary Units were leaving. Most left to join other, new organisations that were helping the fledging resistance forces in mainland Europe, taking with them the experience and knowledge that they had built up with their time in the Auxiliary Units.

Gubbins left the Auxiliary Units in October 1940. He was appointed war substantive lieutenant colonel as Director of Operations and Training, SOE. By 1943 he had been promoted to temporary major general and Executive Head of SOE.

As Gubbins left for SOE, he took Fleming with him as well (with Norman Field arriving to take over in Kent). Peter Wilkinson (later Sir Peter Wilkinson) stayed with the Auxiliary Units until 1942, when he too left to join Gubbins in the SOE. It was Wilkinson who was to head up the Czech section of SOE and who provided the weapons and training to the two Czech SOE agents that assassinated Reinhard Heydrich in the summer of 1942.

'Billy' Beyts who had done so much to design and implement the high levels of training within the Auxiliary Units also lasted in the organisation until 1942. He too joined SOE, but not the European branch. Beyts was sent to India as Chief of Staff to Colin McKenzie to help him set up SOE in the Far East (later to be known as Force 136).

Losing these core individuals, who had indelibly left some of their own personality and beliefs at the core of the Auxiliary Units, was always going to be a hit to the organisation.

Indeed, even at the end of the war, Oxenden seemed to still be dreadfully upset at losing Billy Beyts. He includes the following in his report on the Auxiliary Units.

> On July 2nd, two years to the day after his appointment as GSO 2, Lt–Col GHB Beyts MBE, MC left the unit. He had probably done more than anyone else towards shaping its policy, formulating its aims and methods, coining its phrases and building up an almost unique spirit of enthusiasm and friendliness, and his departure was felt as a personal loss from one end of Britain to the other.[2]

Those who immediately followed these huge personalities had big boots to fill and it was pretty clear from the start that they did not appear to be of the same standard or, indeed, believe in or understand the role of the Auxiliary Units.

Taking over from Gubbins was Colonel C. R. Major of the Royal Irish Fusiliers who was appointed in November 1940. Major had previously been GSO (General Staff Officer) in Eastern Command. His first appearance as head of the Auxiliary Units was not perhaps as one might expect.

> Colonel Major made his debut at a weekend course (at Coleshill House), disguised as a Home Guard, both to learn much that he probably didn't know, and to see the unit from a viewpoint that would never again be accessible to him. The IOs present on the course, however, were introduced to him upon their arrival.[3]

It quickly became apparent, however, that Major's experience as an 'undercover' patrol member did not give him a full impression of what the Auxiliary Units were designed to be about, or if it did, he did not agree with the fundamentals.

As John Warwicker put it: 'Under Gubbins, there was no time for nominal rolls or formal administration. Records were in the minds of the IOs or, at best, scribbled on the back of an envelope. This was tight security. Colonel Major set about standing all of this on its head.'[4]

Uniforms were issued and under Colonel Major they were required to be worn during training and during periods of 'stand-to'. A closer affiliation with the Home Guard, something up to that point that had been considered an absolute 'no-go', was also introduced. Joint training and even church parades were suggested, which did not go down too well with the hardened and highly trained guerrilla and sabotage fighters of the Auxiliary Units.

However, the most 'dangerous' change made during Major's two years as CO was the introduction of a 'group system'. This saw joint training between patrols at a given location under one group commander (GC). The GC tended to be a liaison officer with a commission from the Home Guard and a veteran soldier with experience during the First World War. It was intended that the GC would 'go to ground' with one of the patrols in the event of a German invasion, but it quickly became clear that spending any time underground, particularly during the hard winters, would not suit their age and often their physique. As such they were relegated to a more administrative role. The damage had been done though. As each GC knew the location of each patrol and who was in them, the creation of the role had formed another possible weakness in the cell network. Throughout the country the names of GCs were likely being added to the lists of 'first targets' that patrols would have to take out immediately in the event of the German invasion.

Oxenden, in his own style, was not backwards in coming forwards with his own criticism of the group system when commenting on Major's replacement (Lord Glanusk) arrival in 1942.

> The greatest service that Lord Glanusk did for the unit was to throw doubt upon the wisdom of the elaboration, both in essentials and details that had grown up. Once the matter was seriously questioned it became increasingly obvious that the Auxilier had been in some respects over-rated, and that such a policy would inevitably mean confusion and inefficiency in action.
>
> Tests of cross-sections of the unit here and there showed that, after two years training, less was known about the use of explosives than in 1940, and that many of the 'toys' since issued would never, and could never successfully be used, and that liaison between Patrols was little more than wishful thinking, and of questionable use at that. At one stroke our policy had been cleared of much hampering undergrowth. From now on the Patrol was self-contained and would fight alone; from now on the rank and file would not be asked to think.[5]

Glanusk did bring the Auxiliary Units back to near their original purpose by scrapping the group system, but not at all in other ways. The Right Honourable Sir Wilfred Russell Baily, DSO was the third Baron Glanusk, known as Lord Glanusk. He had fought during the First World War with the Grenadier Guards and was awarded the DSO and Croix de guerre. His Guards mentality followed him into his Auxiliary Units role though, with drill being introduced to the training schedule at Coleshill. He left the Auxiliary Units in 1943 and had tragically died of a heart attack by 1948.

Competitions

As part of the group training, inter-unit competitions became a part of the training of Auxiliary Units. This took away some of the security protocols set out when the units were put together. The first competition to find the 'champion' of Great Britain started to bear fruit in the winter of 1941–42. All the counties were given several months to decide which patrol would represent them. This was through regional competitions, with patrols making their way through to national semi-finals, five or six at a time, at Coleshill House. The four winning teams would return for the finals.

The finals were set up around the key activities the patrols were expected to undertake in the event of an invasion. The principal event was, according to Oxenden, 'a night patrol, in which there was inevitably a string element of luck, but others, night-firing, grenade throwing, an efficiency race and explosive problems, were a good test of knowledge and skills.'[6]

One of the outcomes of the competition was that it highlighted a difference between the younger and older men of the patrols. The younger men, probably because of the nature of the tests, showed their older comrades up. As a result, IOs looking to recruit or replace patrol members tended to look for younger men. This in the long term had a detrimental impact, because as these younger men were called up, replacing them became harder and harder.

The second competition took place in the summer of 1942. It differed only very slightly from the first competition with an explosives element added but the same element of luck was included in the main event – the night patrol.

A third competition was arranged in 1943, at the earliest possible date after harvest (highlighting the fact that many of the patrol continued to be men of the country). This final competition aimed to take out the element of luck, with the principal event moving from night patrols to daytime reconnaissance. It seems it was this third competition that the Crowle Patrol from Worcestershire took part in. Jim Holt of the patrol remembered being at Coleshill where their objective in the competition was to placed magnets on a lorry parked behind a high wall. The patrol was allowed to recce their target during the day and then had to attack it the following night. One member of the patrol managed to reach the target by crawling in the pitch black along the high wall. Unfortunately Jim, who had been trying to reach the same target by crawling in the ruts of a cart track, was trodden on by one of the guards and captured. Since Jim had been caught, his patrol finished second.[7] The competitions added little to the experience or skill sets of patrol members, but rather was a new way of practising what they had already learnt. The regional heats and national finals also added new breaks in the level of security surrounding the units and really marked the beginning of the end.

Anti-raiding role

Realistically, by 1941 the threat of an all-out invasion had passed. However, the threat of German coastal raids was now considered a very real and dangerous one. Commando-like raids to gather information, destroy key infrastructure, disrupt the early preparations of an Allied invasion of occupied Europe and the taking of prisoners were all considered at the time very real possibilities.

As such, by the summer of 1942, the Auxiliary Units, like their Home Guard cousins, were preparing for local raids. This role meant patrols taking on a more counter-attacking responsibility rather than sitting and waiting for the Germans to move over the top of them.

This new role did, however, provide a 'gift' for IOs as Oxenden explains.

> This warning was a gift to IOs for although no universally applicable directive could be issued from HQ, they were able to formulate their own in conjunction with their local military commander, and the rumour of a renewed threat to our shires was a wonderful tonic for fading enthusiasm in the ranks.[8]

For those coastal patrols engaged in this new raid role, a special issue of Stens was delivered and the .300 rifle came into its own.

A trip to the seaside

As the war was drawing to an end the justification for keeping the Auxiliary Units going was getting increasingly harder. However, even as far into the war as D-day in June 1944, patrols were being utilised for their skills. For example, patrols from all over the country were sent to defend the Isle of Wight in the weeks prior to and during the D-day landings and initial Normandy operations. Despite there being a number of established Auxiliary Unit patrols on the island the need to organise a 24/7 defence meant that other patrols, from all over the country, were sent to boost the defences and protect it from a potential German counter-attack. The Isle of Wight was critical for the success of the D-day landings, with communications and the highly secret PLUTO pipeline running through it.

Samuel Gilling of the Sandford Levvy Patrol in Somerset, who had twice been sent home from joining the army because of his Auxiliary Units role, remembers being called up to head over to the Isle of Wight with other members of his patrol.

> I was working for the War Agricultural Committee and I just had to tell them I was called up. Nothing was said where we were going or what we were doing. Of course, we thought we were off to France.
>
> We got picked up and taken to Bishops Lydeard (HQ) and fitted out overnight. We left the next morning about half past seven and it wasn't until we got to Southampton that we knew where we were off to. We got on this boat and were taken over to the Isle of Wight into Parkhurst Prison. There were ack-ack sites on the Isle of Wight and we were stationed on one of them. They thought the Germans might send paratroops over. The invasion communications went through the Isle of Wight, and there was PLUTO, the big oil line. That's what we were guarding.
>
> We were all Auxiliers, no Home Guard. We were on duty all night and used to go back to the camp and have breakfast, a good clean up and a couple of hours sleep.
>
> We had to recce the likely German landing points. Then we selected the best defensive positions to stop them. That was all until a fortnight after D-Day. Then we went home again. It was all very secret.[9]

A document ordering men from patrols in Essex, to join other Auxiliers on the Isle of Wight to protect it from possible German counter-attack gives a really good impression of just how secret the mission was.

Gordon Drake who was Group Commander of Group 3 in Essex kept a large number of documents and orders including one entitled, 'Seaside Training Course'. This was the codename he had allocated for the guarding role the men chosen were to undertake during their time on the Isle of Wight. Nothing on the document outlined where they were going exactly, or what they were expected to do, but it did outline what they should bring including their denims, first field dressing and respirator.

The document also orders that: 'All personnel will take Sten + 3 mags, if not possible take rifle. No ammunition for the above weapons will be taken. Pistols + 36 rounds .38amn will be carried by Officers only.'[10]

It was also very specific about other areas:

You will NOT, repeat NOT, bring
1. Explosives
2. Any weapons except those enumerated above

You will take this letter when reporting for duty
You will fill in the enclosed form, have it signed by your employer and return it forthwith. You will be compensated up to £3. 18. 6 for loss of earnings for one week + 1 day's compensation of 13/1
You will NOT, repeat NOT, discuss the above with anybody outside Auxiliary Units[11]

Len Escott of the Langstone (Jonah) Patrol in South Wales was sent to Freshwater on the island.

While at Freshwater, we had a constant rota of patrols, day and night – beach patrols, cliff patrols, and patrols inland, with a system of signals to call on re-inforcements, if needed. It was quite hectic and we had very little rest. To hear all the accents, from the north of Scotland to Dorset, from Wales to Norfolk, was quite an experience.

When our period of duty was up, we were relieved by others from Auxiliary Units. We gathered, at the time, that the island had been virtually stripped of troops to send to Normandy, but intelligence got wind of a mass of German paratroops across the water, and it was suspected that they might be dropped to the island, in order to disrupt the sailing of convoys and cause trouble. So, they called in our thugs from all over Britain to replace the Regulars.[12]

Patrols were sent from as far away as Northumberland to garrison the Isle of Wight during the D-day operations – the Choppington Patrol in Northumberland was sent the 350-odd miles to take its turn guarding key infrastructure on the island. The support around D-day was not the only time that patrols were expected to serve away from their locality though.

A royal duty

A role that perhaps reflects more than anything the level of training and belief that those in high command had in the Auxiliary Units' ability, was the one they played in guarding the royal family.

Throughout the war, various members of the royal family would spend time at Balmoral in Scotland. Although their determination to stay in London during the Blitz meant that they spent less time at their Scottish retreat than in peacetime, George VI and his family did spend some time there and, as a result, needed the utmost protection from potential German paratroopers or Nazi sympathisers.

The nature of the Auxiliary Units' training and skills meant that they were perfectly suited to the role. They were more than capable of blending into the surrounding woods and countryside and not attracting attention while keeping an eye out for potential kidnappers and assassins. Patrols in Scotland and Northumberland were taken to Balmoral during the periods when members of the royal family were in residence. Often, they were issued with new uniforms and Glengarry hats for when they attended Crathy Church (the church the royal family attend when staying at Balmoral).

Len Crackett, a patrol leader of the Acklington Patrol in Northumberland, later told his son, Ken, about the times he spent at Balmoral: 'I was also told he and others would on occasions go to Balmoral and live rough in the grounds when the Royal Family were there. He told me that the Queen (then Princess Elizabeth) and Princess Margaret would play a game of trying to find them. Once discovered they would have to re-locate.'[13]

A rumour also exists that the princesses called the men of the Auxiliary Units that they encountered on the Balmoral estate the 'Fighting Farmers'. Each man that spent time on patrol at Balmoral was awarded a citation from the king, thanking them for their services.

Taking the fight to the Germans

Whilst patrols were getting used to new roles within Britain, some Auxiliers took the fight directly to the enemy by joining some of the newly founded special forces that were taking on the Axis powers, often behind enemy lines.

The level of training and experience in handling the weapons and explosives that were so effectively utilised by special forces during the Second World War meant that patrol members were perfectly suited for roles within these groups.

The Special Air Service (SAS) was founded in the summer of 1941 by Lieutenant David Stirling of the Scots Guards. By early 1944 the SAS needed to expand to effectively support the forthcoming invasion of occupied Europe. Needing men that were trained in fighting behind enemy lines, the men of the Auxiliary Units were a ready source of recruits.

By 1944 the slow discontinuation of the Auxiliary Units had begun. Although most civilian volunteers would stay on until stand-down in November of that year, many of the Regulars involved, particularly those in the scout sections, had left and returned to their units. The fact that there were highly trained saboteurs and assassins lurking in the midst of 'regular' regiments soon came to the attention of the legendary SAS commander Colonel Blair 'Paddy' Mayne.

In early 1944, Mayne invited the ex-Auxiliary Unit Regulars to London where they watched a film on the SAS and were given information on the regiment, the role they were being invited to undertake and asked to volunteer. One scout section officer who had led a section in Dorset believed that around 130 men joined from Auxiliary Units. The official history of airborne forces (*Airborne Forces of the Second World War 1939–1945*, written by Lieutenant-Colonel T. B. H. Otway in 1951), however, quotes the figure of nearly 300 men recruited from a 'special auxiliary force' disbanding at the time.

Around 30 Auxiliary Units officers were included in that number. Major Peter Forbes recalled attending the Curzon cinema with Major Dick Bond, the training officer. Forbes later volunteered for the SAS but was turned down, as a pre-war accident meant that his arm was fixed at the elbow, making parachuting almost impossible. However, many of his Auxiliary contemporaries did join up, mainly from the Regulars making up the scout sections, but also some civilian volunteers, whose reserved occupation no longer restricted them joining up as D-day approached. Figures from the British Resistance Archive suggest that nearly 50 ex-members of the Auxiliary Units joined up to the SAS, including 11 civilian volunteers. A remarkable 15 joined up from the Dorset scout sections alone.

Several county IOs entered SAS service including the Somerset IO Ian Fenwick, and Sussex IO Roy Bradford. Brigadier Mike Calvert who had helped set up the Auxiliary Units in Kent would go on to command a SAS brigade at the end of the war. Most of the men of the Auxiliary Units joined 1 SAS Regiment and were involved in the regiment's operations in France in 1944 and later in Germany.

The ex-Somerset IO, Fenwick, was a particularly interesting character. He was a noted cartoonist for *Punch* magazine and a friend of David Niven. Fenwick was IO in Somerset from November 1940 to September 1942, at which point, like many Regulars, he joined Gubbins at SOE. However, by February 1944 he had joined 1 SAS, commanding D Squadron.

On 14 June 1944, Fenwick dropped into France around Orléans with 58 others including fellow ex-Auxiliers Cecil Riding (a scout section commander in the Scottish Highlands) and Thomas Varey (ex-scout section member in the Scottish Highlands).

The operation's purpose was to sabotage the rail links running through the area and prevent German supplies passing through – a mission that those in the Auxiliary Units would have been very familiar with. The operation ran between 14 June and 19 August and although effective in hitting supplies and tying down German forces in the area, it came at a cost.

Captain Ian Fenwick was killed leading a patrol into action on 11 August 1944. Despite being warned by an elderly Frenchman about a German ambush ahead, Fenwick insisted that they would advance anyway. Leading from the front, at the wheel of his jeep and the twin Vickers machine guns blasting everything in sight, a German machine-gun nest was put out of action quickly. Tragically though, a 20mm cannon shell passed through Fenwick's head, very quickly ending the life of former Somerset Auxiliary Unit's IO. His fellow ex-Auxilier Cecil Riding took command of the squadron.

Just days before, on 8 August 1944, Thomas Varey had also been killed. Varey had parachuted into France in early July 1944, but the landing site had been compromised by the Germans who stood waiting disguised as French Resistance. He was wounded immediately and captured by the Germans. He was given morphine by a comrade but not taken to hospital. They were immediately told to change into civilian clothing, on the grounds that they were being marched to Switzerland as part of an exchange of prisoners. However, after stopping in wood, they were lined up and told that they would be shot. This was presumably part of Hitler's 'Commando Order' issued in October 1942 that stated all Allied Commandos encountered should be shot immediately without trial, even if they were in uniform and trying to surrender. When it became very clear what was happening, the group broke for the dense wood, with two making it away. Unfortunately, Varey, hampered by his wound, could not escape and was shot.

The most recent research has found that around 12 ex-members of the Auxiliary Units lost their lives in the service of the SAS. Eight of these deaths occurred during Operation *Bulbasket*. Taking place between D-day and 24 July 1944, *Bulbasket* was designed to allow the SAS to cause as much chaos as possible for the occupying German forces around Poitiers. Unfortunately, their base location was betrayed and the Germans attacked it, taking 34 SAS prisoners (and a US Army Air Force pilot and seven French Resistance fighters), who again under Hitler's Commando Order were executed without trial.

Stand-down

For those Auxiliers who did not join the SAS, or were called up to the regular forces, the patrols carried on for a surprisingly long time after the invasion of Europe. It was not until November 1944 that they were finally stood down.

Peter Fleming was instrumental in the first prototype of the Auxiliary Units and would later become the first IO for Kent. (The Peter Fleming Estate)

Coleshill House where the Auxiliary Units established their HQ and training centre. The main house would later burn to the ground. (British Resistance Archive)

The Garth in Kent where Fleming organised the initial Auxiliary Units patrols under the guise of XII Corps Observation Unit. (British Resistance Archive)

One of the best examples of an Auxiliary Units patrol – Warsash Patrol in Hampshire. These were not the old men of *Dad's Army*. (British Resistance Archive, colour by RJM)

Spetisbury Patrol in Dorset. Another good example showing the type of men recruited into the Auxiliary Units. (British Resistance Archive)

A rare image from inside an OB. Sandford Levvy's OB was in an abandoned mine. (British Resistance Archive)

Another rare photograph of a patrol in an Operational Base, this time the Admiralty 5 Patrol in Somerset. (Estate of Eric Dwane)

The secrecy surrounding the Auxiliary Units mean pictures are very rare. This is the Sandford Levvy Patrol again, 'training' near to their OB. (British Resistance Archive)

As the threat of invasion diminished, the Auxiliary Units' role changed. Patrols from Scotland and the North of England were sent to Balmoral to guard the Royal family. (Estate of Sergeant Matt Aitchison)

A group shot of the combined Cornish Auxiliary Units. (Groups 1–4). There were more of these pictures at stand-down as patrols split up. (British Resistance Archive)

Ken Welch (second from the right, without cigarette) and his father (sergeant, far left) inspecting Ken's Webley pistol. (Ken Welch)

Ken Welch in October 2021. (Author's collection)

A model Operational Base in the British Resistance Organisation Museum at Parham, Suffolk. (British Resistance Archive)

The stand-down lapel badge. The only recognition the Auxiliary Units members received for their service. (British Resistance Archive)

Collapsed OB in Dorset. Recent clearing of undergrowth by CART led to the discovery of a number of items. (Nik Brown)

Communication wire that would enable the OP to talk directly to those in the OB. (British Resistance Archive)

Possible hatch release mechanism found in the sh of the OB. (British Resistance Archive)

A rare intact Operational Base in East Devon. An escape tunnel seems to have begun to be dug but not completed. (British Resistance Archive)

Not all OBs were the classic elephant iron shelter – this example of the Moffat Patrol in Scotland was in a cave. (British Resistance Archive)

A recently 'discovered' intact OB in Dorset. These are, understandably, becoming rarer, as the main chambers rust and collapse after 80 years. (British Resistance Archive)

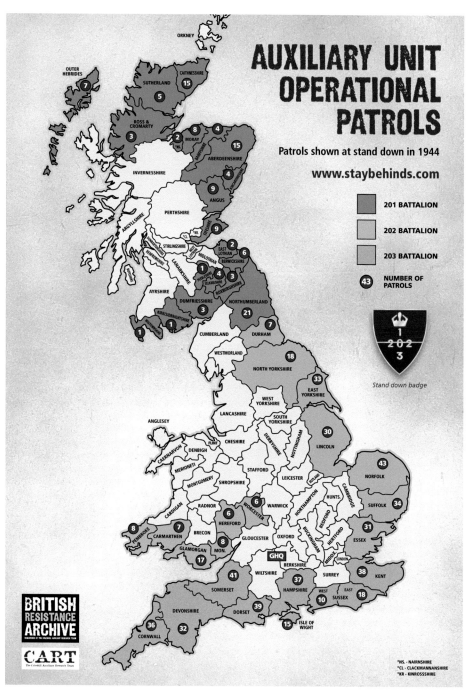

Map of the known Auxiliary Unit patrols showing the numbers in each county. The map also splits into the three battalions the patrols were divided into later in the war. (British Resistance Archive)

On 18 November 1944, the then commander-in-chief of the Home Forces, General Sir Harold Franklyn, sent a letter to Coleshill House informing them of the understandable decision to stand-down the patrols.

> In view of the improved war situation, it has been decided by the War Office that the Operational Branch of Auxiliary Units shall stand down, and the time has now come to put an end to an organisation which would have been of inestimable value to this country in the event of invasion.
>
> All ranks under your command are aware of the secret nature of their duties. For that reason, it has not been possible for them to receive publicity, nor will it be possible even now. So far from considering this to be a misfortune, I should like all members of Auxiliary Units to regard it as a matter of special pride.

With the process of stand-down underway and with many of the regular soldiers having already made their way back to their regiments or the special forces, the final commander of the Auxiliary Units, Colonel Douglas, sent a letter to IOs and patrol leaders on 30 November 1944.

> I realize what joining the Auxiliary Units has meant to you; so do the officers under my command. You were invited to do a job which would require more skill and coolness, more hard work and greater danger, than was demanded of any other voluntary organisation.

He went on to say.

> It now falls to me to tell you that your work has been appreciated and well carried out, and that your contract, **for the moment**, is at an end. I am grateful to you for the way you have trained in the last four years. So is the Regular army. It was due to you that core divisions left this country to fight the battle of France; and it was due to your reputation for skill and determination that extra risk was taken – successfully as it turned out – in the defence arrangements of this country during that vital period. I congratulate you on this reputation and thank you for this voluntary effort.
>
> In view of the fact that your lives depended on secrecy no public recognition will be possible. But those in the most responsible positions at General Headquarters, Home Forces, know what was done; and what would have been done had you been called upon. They know it well, as is emphasized in the attached letter from the Commander-in-Chief. It will not be forgotten.

So, with no public recognition possible due to the ongoing secrecy surrounding the Auxiliary Units, patrol members were expected to simply go back to their day jobs and say nothing to friends or family. And most did.

This secrecy meant that, unlike the Home Guard, the Auxiliary Units were denied the Defence Medal, unless they had spent the requisite amount of time in the Home Guard as well. The only recognition offered was a small lapel badge. As early as July 1944, plans were already in place for the manufacture and distribution of the badge. In a recently discovered document[14] sent to all group commanders in East Anglia (and presumably the rest of the areas in the country where the Auxiliary Units were operating) it is outlined what this lapel badge would look like:

> It is believed that at the end of the war most, if not all, Auxiliers would like to possess a token of service with Auxiliary Units. For this purpose a buttonhole badge, in the form of a shield in GHQ colours (red and blue) with figures 201-2-3 embodied is being produced and will be available almost immediately

It also describes the distribution process, with group commanders sending in the maximum number of badges they needed to send out to patrol members. Tellingly, the level of secrecy remains in place.

> Final distribution of badges will be left to Group Commanders who will also be responsible for:–
> (a) Seeing that they do not fall into the hands of men not entitled to wear them
> (b) That all concerned are notified that in no circumstances will they be worn until the end of the war with Germany i.e. cessation of hostilities in Europe

It also makes clear who is paying for them: 'As there are no Army funds from which the cost can be met it will be necessary to make a charge of 6d each.'

These small lapel badges, now worth a small fortune, were sent across the country, with group commanders asked to 'remember men who have ceased to be Auxiliers for valid reasons such as call-up, but not if men were sacked or returned to Home Guard as useless.'[15]

So, with a letter thanking them, but offering no public recognition, and a small lapel badge, the members of the Auxiliary Units disappeared back to 'normal' life.

What came of the OBs and equipment? As already mentioned, there was a huge amount of equipment, weapons and explosives that was not collected at the end of the war, giving the police and the army several nasty shocks in the 1960s and 1970s.

However, much of the left-over explosives were used, some of it by the farming members of Auxiliary Units to get rid of the pesky trees in the middle of fields that got in the way of ploughing, some of it in a more celebratory fashion.

The Bruton Patrol in Somerset put on such an impressive display of explosions for the local community on VE Day that they managed to deafen the local and rather unfortunate piano tuner.[16]

The Langstone (Jonah) Patrol in South Wales also helped out on VE Day. Leslie Bulley, a patrol member, had a hidden supply of phosphorous bombs buried in sand in the cellar of his house in Newport. On VE night, the bonfire for the local street party was damp and refused to light. Leslie went to his cellar and, without being seen, tucked one of the bombs into the bonfire as a propellant. The result, perhaps somewhat predictably, was a horrific stream of melting tarmac and because it was phosphorous, things only got worse when unsuspecting locals tried to put it out with water! Leslie, it seems, was never caught as the man who had added the propellant, and he rather quickly removed the detonators and in the dead of night tipped the remainder of his secret stash over Newport Bridge.[17]

Most patrols simply walked away from their OBs. Some sealed the entrances and escape tunnels; most did not. Others stored the left-over weapons and equipment in them, thinking that the underground base would be safe enough. The authorities thought these bases too dangerous to be left though, with thoughts of children discovering them and hurting themselves. Indeed, many of the clues researchers rely on for the location of Operational Bases come from people who as children played in 'big Anderson shelters' in the woods during the 50s and 60s. With many bunkers on farmland, the prospect of livestock getting trapped or vehicles falling into them was a real concern for farmers. Some farmers who moved onto the land post war only found out about the existence of OBs when one of their cows had fallen through the rusting roof of a bunker or had fallen in themselves whilst driving across it in their tractor. The authorities were also concerned about the potential use of OBs as hideouts by criminals on the run.

All this meant that teams of Royal Engineer demolitions experts were sent across the country to destroy them.

Of course, the nature of a highly secret, highly disguised underground bunker means that they are hard to find and with most of the patrol members having returned to civilian life and still constrained by their signing of the Official Secrets Act, it is perhaps no surprise that the demolition teams were not particularly successful in their task. Many bunkers survived into the following decades and were often the reason for mystery family walks into woodlands as former patrol members checked on their condition.

Over the years most have collapsed, the elephant iron simply rusting away with inevitable consequences. Some remain intact though and serve as a reminder of what these remarkable civilian volunteers were willing to do for their country.

Post-war meetings

As the years passed, some patrols set up annual reunions to keep in touch and talk about things they could mention to no one else. Some patrols produced menus or invites with in-jokes that only those in the 'know' would understand. At the end of the war there were also small articles in regional newspapers talking about the 'British Maquis', with some detail on this mysterious underground resistance army. Where these articles originated from is still unknown and must have been shut down pretty quickly, as the story was not picked up by the national newspapers.

As a whole, though the secrecy surrounding the Auxiliary Units was maintained. Most Auxiliers went to the grave without telling a soul of their role. Ken Welch, the Auxilier from Mabe in Cornwall, told no one of his wartime role until the early 2000s. He did, however, wear his stand-down lapel badge for a few years after the war, leading to one unusual, unintentional meeting.

> I wore my badge for a few years afterwards. I remember being at a hotel at some point after the war and I went to go and 'point Percy at the porcelain'. Someone walked in and recognised the badge, because he was wearing one too. We exchanged a couple of words whilst we were standing up there and then went our separate ways.[18]

A menu from the Monmouthshire/Worcestershire reunion a month after stand-down. Like the training pamphlets, the menu has plenty of 'in-jokes'. (British Resistance Archive)

A picture of the Monmouthshire/Worcestershire reunion at the Greyhound pub in Llantrisant. (British Resistance Archive)

To this day, Ken does not know who the other Auxilier was, but the meeting perhaps exemplifies how many Auxiliers got on with their daily lives and never really considered their role again. Opened in August 1997, Parham Museum is the only dedicated museum to the Auxiliary Units and Special Duties Branch. Stuart Edmundson (IO for Devon and Cornwall) was at the opening, as were many other

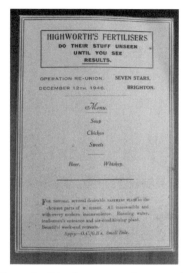

Another reunion menu. Group 3 of the Sussex patrols met at the Seven Stars in Brighton. The top has a reminder of the training pamphlet and the bottom a hint of the OBs.

Auxiliers. In the reunions that took place at the museum in the early 2000s, many of the Auxiliers turning up were shocked at how many patrols there had been. Arthur Dunford, a farmer's son, joined the Abbotsbury Patrol in Dorset in early 1942. By October 1943, he had been released to join the RAF. In December 1943, his brother Gerald joined the same patrol as Arthur's replacement. It was not until the early 2000's that they spoke about their roles to each other for the first time, and as a result realised that, not only were they both in the Auxiliary Units, but had been part of the same patrol![19] There are also stories of sons replacing their fathers in a patrol but only finding out it was their father they had replaced decades later, as neither had spoken about it at all during or after the war.

It was not until 2013 that Auxiliary Unit veterans were first given permission to march past the Cenotaph on Remembrance Sunday (with the Home Guard, Bevin Boys and Land Army all marching for a number of years before). Michael Gubbins (grandson of Major General Colin Gubbins) led the contingent on that first march, with Auxiliary Unit veterans Trevor Miners (Perranporth Patrol) and Dillwyn Rhys Thomas (Margam Patrol) also taking part. Apart from this, there remains no 'official' recognition from the British government that the Auxiliary Units even existed despite years of lobbying on behalf of veterans and their families.

What was the reasoning behind such a high level of secrecy? Another question is, why were lists of names and some addresses of Auxiliary Units members taken in the latter part of the war and now sit in the National Archives? (See the Appendix for more details on this). For a secret organisation, even when the threat of invasion had diminished, the recording of the names and addresses of thousands of men seems somewhat ridiculous.

Could this and the levels of secrecy after the war be the actions of a government unsure of what the future may hold in terms of other conflicts? Churchill had very obvious misgivings about the Soviet Union's intentions after the defeat of Germany and having access to thousands of highly trained guerrilla fighters and saboteurs might be a very handy thing to have (especially if a future enemy had no idea they existed). There were certainly very similar units operating in West Germany during the Cold War, with regular British and American forces trained to go underground if the Soviets had invaded and wait to come out at night to disrupt the invading forces.

The early 1950s also saw the re-establishment of the Home Guard to combat a possible invasion threat. Was it also the intention of the government to bring back the Auxiliary Units? This, again, could explain why they needed the list of men and for the level of secrecy to be kept, even after the war. However, there is no hard evidence that the reestablishment of the Auxiliary Units ever occurred after stand-down.

Whatever the reason, the enduring secrecy surrounding the Auxiliary Units has added to their reputation of stealth, cunning and ruthlessness. They were, of course, thank goodness, never called upon to defend Britain from an invasion. Their commitment to their role and the potential sacrifice they were prepared to make should not be forgotten though, nor should the organisation's impact on the wider war. The training and experiments that were undertaken with and by the patrols had a direct influence on how other irregular forces would later take the war to the enemy. The likes of the SAS and SOE were not only recruited directly from the Auxiliary Units but took much of their approach too, which was then put into direct action against the enemy.

The success of irregular tactics in occupied Europe points to how successful the Auxiliary Units might have been had the Germans come. They would have delivered a short, sharp snap at the heels of an invading force, attempting to prevent the Blitzkrieg impact that had so badly hit the Low Countries and France. There was no thought of a prolonged campaign – every member knew that this was essentially a suicide mission. The consequences of a patrol's actions on the local communities, their own community, would have likely been horrific but, as we have seen, most Auxiliers seemed to have seen the bigger picture and would have carried out their activity until the inevitable end.

It is hard to argue with Peter Fleming, the man who started the prototype patrols in Kent, and his summary of the likely success of Auxiliary Units if the worst had happened.

> ... even assuming that the British resistance movement would have melted away in the white heat of German ruthlessness, it might have struck some useful blows before doing so; and within a bridgehead under heavy counter-attack its divisionary activities would have had a value wholly disproportionate to the number of guerrillas involved.[20]

CHAPTER 5

'Unofficial' Auxiliary Units and Home Guard Guerrillas

The idea of a secret, hidden group of well-trained, well equipped guerrilla fighters and saboteurs, ready to take on an invading army is obviously a good one. The Auxiliary Units by their very nature were highly secret and so could not pass on their experience and expertise to other elements of the British defences.

However, some of those involved in the setting up of the Auxiliary Units would later go on to join other areas of Britain's defences or to other parts of the country where the Auxiliary Units were not active.

One very good example of this is Lieutenant General Andrew Thorne, who had been so instrumental in some of the original thinking behind the Auxiliary Units. In April 1941, Thorne was sent to command Home Forces in Scotland, with Bernard Montgomery taking over at XII Corps based in Royal Tunbridge Wells.

While in Scotland, Thorne looked to organise his defences and, having been a key part in the set-up of XII Corps Observation Unit with Peter Fleming in Kent, it is no surprise that he would have looked to replicate this in his new area of influence.

With Auxiliary Units already established along the eastern coast of Scotland, Thorne looked to areas that had no such cover from underground forces. To help set up these units, Thorne turned to an already established Auxiliary Units scout section commander.

Lieutenant John 'Tim' Iredale joined The Argyll and Sutherland Highlanders in October 1940, but by December 1941 had been appointed scout section commander in Fife and Angus. As with other scout sections, his patrol's role was twofold: firstly, to offer training to local Auxiliary Units patrols and secondly, in the event of an invasion, to act as a patrol itself and undertake sabotage and guerrilla warfare.

It appears that Thorne approached Iredale to set up patrols, including OBs, in the Shetlands and may have turned to him for his previous experience on the islands. The background of Iredale and the Shetlands comes from David Lampe in his book *Last Ditch*.

The story starts with a shepherd on the Shetlands, out at night during the lambing season, hearing a rather strange humming sound from a cove nearby. After hearing the noise on a few occasions, he took a look over the cliff edge and, in the twilight, managed to make out the silhouette of a submarine, running its engines to charge the batteries. The shepherd reported his sighting to the local police who, in turn, informed the HQ Scottish Command. It was quickly established that it was not a British submarine, and a scheme was put together to try and destroy it should it return.

It was then that Iredale was sent to Coleshill House. At six-and-a-half-foot tall, strong and an excellent swimmer, Iredale was the perfect candidate for a highly dangerous mission such as this, but as he arrived at Highworth train station, he had no idea why he was being sent there. Over the course of the next week, he learnt how to set time pencils, handle plastic explosives and place limpet mines.

Like the patrol members who attended the training course, he was also taken out to the surrounding woodland, where the derelict tanks and traction engines were located for practising sabotage and shown how to pierce various thicknesses of metal and armour. After his time at Coleshill, he went to 'Station 12' at Aston House, Knebworth, Hertfordshire, which was the Military Intelligence (Research) sabotage college where he studied a scale model of a U-boat.

He then travelled up to the Shetlands and waited for the U-boat to reappear. When observers identified the submarine had entered the cove again, Iredale made his way there, stripped off, strapped a limpet mine to his chest, checked a couple of time pencils, attached them to the mine and set them to go off after he had left the area. He then waded out to sea and swam out stealthily to the U-boat. Treading water, he attached the limpet mine to the submarine, just below the waterline and swam back. According to reports, the submarine was never seen in the cove again.

This seems an unlikely story – Lampe suggests that it might be a bit too remarkable, saying that German naval historians doubted that a U-boat would have risked charging its batteries in sight of the British coastline. However, Auxiliary Units officers insisted to Lampe that it did take place, and considering that Iredale served with the Auxiliary Units, SOE and later SAS, the tale might have more truth to it that it first appears.

So, Iredale, with his time with the scout sections and his possible direct experience on the Shetland Islands would seem the perfect candidate to act as an IO there. With Thorne not taking over in Scotland until 1941, any 'unofficial' Auxiliary Units set up would have been from mid-1941 onwards. Researchers have found evidence of several underground bunkers on the Shetlands. The structures are very similar to other OBs in other parts of the country, with disguised entrances and in some cases, escape tunnels as well.

There has been some speculation that they were used by the local Home Guard units, but with no Home Guard veterans known to have spoken about using the bases, as well as the design of the bunkers and local rumours of a 'secret resistance', everything points to Auxiliary-like Units, being based on the islands.

There appears to have been at least one patrol in the Scalloway area, with an associated OB, and researchers have names that seem to have been in the patrol, including John George Nicolson, Andrew Irvine and Angus Craig. There is some evidence of another two or three patrols on the islands, although none of this, at time of writing, is concrete. There is no mention of the Shetlands in any of the records available to researchers and therefore these patrols must have been acting outside of Coleshill's command, reporting directly to Thorne.

Another 'unofficial' unit operating very much like the Auxiliary Units appears to have been located in Leicestershire. Historian Austin Ruddy has investigated a group of regulars in the Charnwood Forest area. Samuel Hall, a regular soldier, had been instructed to form an underground resistance group in the event of an invasion.[1]

Prior to the war, Hall had been a miner but had signed up in 1932, joining the Leicestershire Regiment, and was soon on his way to the

North-West Frontier. By the outbreak of war, the regiment was back in Britain and Hall was now a 29-year-old sergeant. It was at this stage that he was instructed to form a resistance group. It was made up of 6–8 men of the regular forces so very much in line with the scout sections of the Auxiliary Units. The group set up in the caves in Charnwood Forest and used the nearby Mount St Bernard's Abbey as a contact point.

This group had a seemingly large operational area. In preparation for an invasion, the group had, according to Ruddy:

> Placed charges under the metal footbridge alongside Trent Bridge in Nottingham and were told to detonate them in the event of invasion. It was only in 1947 while the footbridge was being repainted that the explosive charges were discovered, forgotten for two years after the war had ended![2]

Interestingly, there are also reports of a large exercise in the run-up to and just after D-day taking place around Charnwood Forest involving 300 Jedburgh trainees and the Home Guard. The trainees had the task of 'contacting resistance groups in Charnwood Forest and direct attacks on railway communications and vulnerable points'.[3] This might be a pure coincidence, but the role that the regular Auxiliary Units played, even in the latter part of the war, suggests that these 'unofficial' groups may still have been operating too and used their skills and training to act as the 'French Resistance' in this exercise.

The Home Guard and guerrilla fighting

Like the 'unofficial' Auxiliary Units, the idea of the Home Guard having their own guerrilla-like units is a good one and one that was certainly suggested by a number of Home Guard units across the country throughout the war. *Dad's Army* has distorted our view on who made up the Home Guard; undoubtedly, veterans from the First World War (and beyond) played an important role but, equally, like those in the operational patrols of the Auxiliary Units, younger, fit men in reserved occupations also contributed significantly.

As soon as the LDV was formed, a debate started on how and where they were to be used. Initially, at least, they were to be in a static observing role, keeping their eyes peeled for the much-feared parachute landings. Like other units involved in Britain's home defences, as the war went on, their role changed and discussions around possible guerrilla-like activity were continuous throughout the conflict.

There is even an episode of *Dad's Army* where the prospect of raising a guerrilla/Commando unit is mentioned. In Series 5, Episode 10, a discussion takes place about a training major wanting to form a 'Home Guard Commando unit out of the younger fitter chaps – a striking force to operate behind the enemy lines to winkle out petrol dumps'. Incidentally, Private Pike was sent to join this new unit but didn't get in, as he couldn't find HQ! It seems that Jimmy Perry, one of the writers behind *Dad's Army*, was in a Commando section of the Home Guard himself, which would explain the inclusion of this plot. Although not 'secret', he was part of a unit made up of younger members expected to undertake 'Commando-like' roles in the event of an invasion.

Some Home Guard units were determined that a form of guerrilla warfare should be undertaken by at least some of their number. By mid-1941 this was coming from the top of the Home Guard command chain. Lord Bridgeman took over as Director-General Home Guard in the summer of 1941. In August 1941, while discussing the Home Guard with the press, Bridgeman commented:

> The Russians have laid stress on the importance of sabotage and similar activities behind the enemy lines. This is a task for which, if invasion comes, the Home Guard will be particularly suitable. They will be able to undertake those harassing enterprises which interfere with the enemy's communications and keep him looking over his shoulder. The Russian campaign is extending our knowledge of what can be done.[4]

This could be the very description of the role the operational patrols of the Auxiliary Units were to undertake and as if to unconsciously back this up, Bridgeman would later go on to describe how the fight against the invading German Army should be undertaken.

> Don't let us forget that this is a cad's war. There are no rules, except to kill any German who lands in this country by any available means; and the more lowbrow the battle is, the greater the likelihood of achieving the essential ingredient of

victory, namely surprise, by which the Home Guard, if it uses it rightly, can discount whatever advantages of training and equipment the enemy may possess.[5]

Again, this could have been taken out of the operational patrols' training pamphlets. This enthusiasm dripped down into individual units across the country. An Edinburgh company commander, for example, 'worked strenuously to turn his men into a body of first-class guerrillas or 'banditti' rather than second-class regular soldiers'.[6] Maurice Petherick MP wrote a letter to the war minister to express his concerns about Home Guard units in the south Midlands. He describes how they 'have got it into their heads that, if attacked by a superior force of Germans, they should hide and perhaps indulge in a bit of genteel harassing'.[7]

Of course, Petherick's joint role as MP and commander of the Auxiliary Units Special Duties Branch gave him the advantage of knowing what was already secretly in place. However, he was certainly not alone in his concerns about the Home Guard's move towards guerrilla warfare tactics. The nature of this reluctance replicated some of the same arguments that were brought against the formation of the operational patrols of the Auxiliary Units. Fears that random Home Guards roaming around the countryside could be treated as *francs-tireurs* and shot out of hand by the invading army were heightened. This was a fear about the Home Guard in general and explains the relatively quick production and distribution of LDV arm bands to try and get some form of uniform to the volunteers to legitimise their role.

There was also concern about how these Home Guard 'guerrillas' were to impact other defences if they were to come into action during an invasion period. Even for those who were ardent believers in the Home Guard's role being restricted to fighting from fixed positions, defending strategic points, there was an acceptance that if these positions became indefensible, units should escape where possible and continue the fight elsewhere. However, this did not necessarily mean disappearing into the woods and undergrowth and fighting a guerrilla war but taking new positions at nodal points. Indeed, in August 1941 a draft instruction leaflet for the Home Guard, written by Lieutenant Colonel Short of the Directorate of Military Training, highlighted how Home Guard units could be more effective in fixed positions than roaming the countryside in small bands: 'Blind imitation of Russian guerrilla tactics by local Home Guard units without the authority of the local commander will hinder, not help, our defence plans.'[8]

However, the determination of Home Guard units to expand their role seems to have continued throughout 1942 much to the dismay of GHQ. Lieutenant General Sir Bernard Paget, Commander-in-Chief of Home Forces, seemed particularly concerned at this constant pushing from individual Home Guard units. In 1942, instructions were issued by Paget clearly trying to stop any further discussion around guerrilla-like units in the Home Guard.

> There has been a good deal of pressure lately, encouraged by the Press, for Home Guards to become guerrillas. This is unsound; they are not trained or equipped for that sort of fighting and they would be a menace to the Field Army. It must not be allowed except in sparsely populated areas where there are no nodal points, and the country is particularly suitable for it. Instructions issued must not detract from the overriding principle that there will be no withdrawal from nodal points while there are any men left to defend it.[9]

This continuing determination of Home Guard commanders to introduce guerrilla warfare tactics obviously also impacted the actual GHQ guerrilla force, the Auxiliary Units. Paget mentions that guerrilla Home Guard forces might be acceptable in areas of the country where it is suitable; it might be that he is also referencing areas where there are no Auxiliary Units already operating. In areas where operational patrols had been established, the potential for, at best, a doubling-up of role and, at worst, a severe leak in the security surrounding the Auxiliary Units, meant that there had to be better management of the situation.

This did not always happen, as can be seen from a letter from an Auxiliary Units officer to GHQ Home Forces in October 1942. He complains that Home Guard commanders, especially it seems in the eastern counties had 'laid down a policy of guerrilla warfare for their people and say quite openly that they are going to take to the woods'. He was not impressed by their effort and believed they 'will not function at all in the face of some Boche attack pressed home. In my humble opinion, they will run like stink without firing a shot.'[10]

Wintringham and Osterley Park

It is obvious that there was nervousness across GHQ about the guerrilla role that the 'ordinary' Home Guard wanted to play. Some of this might have originated with the concern that ran through the GHQ and other quarters when Tom Wintringham, a veteran of the Spanish Civil War, had set up a private 'school' for Home Guard personnel.

Wintringham was born in 1898 and, during the First World War, had served as a mechanic and motorcycle dispatch rider in the Royal Flying Corps. It was in the inter-war years that he found his place on the left wing, joining the newly formed Communist Party of Great Britain in 1923. It was his political leaning that meant, during the Spanish Civil War, he left Great Britain heading to Barcelona as a journalist for the *Daily Worker*. This role did not last very long though, as he moved from journalist to joining the British Battalion of the International Brigades.

It was his experiences during the Spanish Civil War that led him to offering an alternative view of how future battles against Germany may be fought. After he returned from Spain, he was appointed as war correspondent for the *Picture Post*, where he began campaigning for a 'People's Army' as early as 1938, made up of civilians ready to take on an invading army.

Along with other British veterans of the Spanish Civil War, and heavily advertised in the *Picture Post* and the *Daily Mirror*, Wintringham set up a Home Guard training school at Osterley Park in West London, after gaining permission from the owner, the Earl of Jersey (who said yes on the proviso that the house itself was not destroyed). The school was designed to circumvent some of the frustrations of perceived lack of urgency from the War Office in the training of the Home Guard.

Wintringham and a small number of his former Spanish Civil War comrades were able to provide first-hand experiences of not only fighting fascist forces but the likely tone and nature of the battles the Home Guard would fight if the Germans came.

Amongst the training at Osterley, Home Guard members were taught similar tactics to those the Auxiliary Units would receive at Coleshill House. Wintringham promoted the course as a weekend programme of 'ungentlemanly warfare' and on 10 July 1940 the first course took place. Those attending were taught hand-to-hand combat, demolition, anti-tank tactics, sabotage and hit-and-run raids. Over the next few weeks these courses became increasingly popular.

Alongside the courses and his articles in the *Picture Post* and *Daily Mirror*, Wintringham also produced a booklet, *New Ways of War*, published in August 1940. The booklet combines Wintringham's thoughts on the nature of the Nazi threat, what lessons could be learnt from the invasion of the Low Countries and France, tactics to counter the threat and some hint of his frustration with the British government and armed forces.

He highlights three areas that needed to be addressed in order to meet the Nazi tactics:

1. Understand the tactics of infiltration and train our troops in them, and in the methods of meeting them

2. Realise the connection between those tactics and the trench deadlock; for defensive purposes realise that these tactics make linear defence and passive defence no longer valuable, and make counter-attack the only basis for successful defence

3. Clear out of our army remnants of the past – ideas, methods of training and organisation and the men who cannot change – and revive in the army the qualities necessary for carrying out and meeting infiltration; qualities of initiative, independence, the spirit of attack and counter-attack[11]

A lot of this makes sense with the benefit of hindsight and, indeed, was being encouraged throughout the ranks of the Auxiliary Units, but to the authorities already worried about Wintringham and his colleagues' allegiances, it looked like he was trying to undermine the regular army. The language he uses to describe civilians taking part in local defence seems to reflect his left-wing leanings. This is particularly the case in chapter five, in which he talks of a 'People's Army' and the role that the half a million or so ex-servicemen who served in the First World War could play in local defence and training others.

The Local Defence Volunteers are the beginnings of such a force. They have been given too little to do, and often the wrong things to do; their organisation and leadership is not yet that of a People's Army. But the force is growing and developing; it can grow until the real eagerness of our people to defend their homes finds full expression within it.[12]

Indeed, the further into the pamphlet you go, the more you feel he is actively targeting the ruling classes. He gives specific instructions on how to make home-made grenades and discusses the idea that if 'we can produce a single ton of potatoes more by doing so, we should abolish private property in land'.[13] He goes further to say, 'On men and arms and food, this conclusion is inescapable: that since we need socialist measures for victory, these measures will best be carried out by socialists'.[14]

Charles Graves, in his book *The Home Guard of Britain*, sums up the concerns of the War Office.

> Unfortunately, some of its sponsors, notably Tom Wintringham and Edward Hulton, seemed inclined to make a political issue of their admirable enterprise, and the War Office could scarcely be expected to accept the criticisms levelled at it in Picture Post and approve of Osterley in its entirety.[15]

Graves's book has a foreword written by Paget, so it will have an obvious lean towards the establishment. However, it highlights that the authorities were keen to keep a handle on the activity being taught at Osterley. Despite the very real threat of the far right, the traditional fears of a Bolshevik far left revolution taking place in Britain remained heightened. So, while training in many of the areas that Wintringham highlighted were getting going at Coleshill House, the War Office was quietly taking more control of activity at Osterley. Media outlets were discouraged from further promoting the courses and by September 1940, in return for 'official sanction and material aid',[16] the military had taken over the running of the school. Wintringham and his colleagues were kept on in some capacity, but eventually it was moved to a smaller venue and became very much in line with the more traditional training methods being taught across the country. However, before Osterley closed, Wintringham had taught 4,940 officers and men of the Home Guard.[17]

Much of what Wintringham suggested, certainly in terms of tactics at least, would be later brought on board by the regular forces, but despite their hugely relevant experience, Wintringham and the other teachers at Osterley could not even join the ranks of the men they had taught because of their affiliation with the Communist Party. Later in the war, Wintringham would form the Common Wealth Party with Richard Acland and J. B. Priestley. However, by 1949 he would be dead after suffering a fatal heart attack.

Secret Home Guard guerrillas

What Osterley Park and Wintringham show though is the realisation, across the country, that any German invasion would have to be countered very differently to traditional British Army tactics. As a result, it seems that some Home Guard units, while officially continuing with their 'square bashing' and church parades, also created secret guerrilla and saboteur groups that would have acted very similarly to the Auxiliary Units. These groups, unlike the Shetlands example, were not set up by ex-Auxiliary Units officers but by forward-looking officers and individuals, perhaps influenced by Wintringham, who saw the need for an alternative, ruthless reaction to a German invasion. Other groups took this role to another level, with secrecy being the difference between these units and others being set up in plain sight.

Despite the secrecy, there is evidence of these units across the country; very few men have come forward, but those who have tell a story that those in the 'official' Auxiliary Units might well have recognised.

Instead of using the phrase 'guerrilla', like the Auxiliary Units, these Home Guard units seem to have picked alternative names for themselves to differentiate themselves. In Leicestershire, for example, the term 'shock squads' has been used for these units. In 1940 Allan Hopcroft was in a reserved occupation, working as a wages clerk at a factory which made webbing side-packs, straps and backpacks for the regular forces. He had joined his local Quorn (Leicestershire) Home Guard unit as one of the younger members. However, in the late summer of 1941 a mysterious Lieutenant Whitford came to his unit and invited them for a 'chat' about joining a 'special section'. Whitford informed them that:

> We don't want to spread it around, but we are looking for some young, active men. He did not tell us what it was about until we got into it. He said he wanted to form a 'shock section' in 'dirty tricks'. They wanted a silent section: if the Jerries had come, we'd have gone about in civilian clothes to raise havoc.[18]

Whitford was clear that it was the young men of the unit he was interested in. While the older men of the Home Guard were useful for guarding bridges and other fixed points, it was the younger men he wanted to go out and do some damage. They remained in Home Guard uniform, with nothing to tell them apart other than the knife in their belts that all shock squad members carried.

Whitford also appears to have provided the training. Born in 1899, Richard (Dick) Whitford had a long military career. During the First World War he had served in the Merchant Navy as a third officer on SS *Shirley*. However, by the 1920s he was in the Palestine Police Force (and presumably having a similar experience to Fairbairn and Sykes in the Shanghai Municipal Police). By the late 1930s, however, Whitford had joined the wireless interception service at Chatham and by 1941 had joined the Y-Service, which coincidentally, or not, was also where a number of recruits for the Special Duties Branch had originated. It was while with Y-Service at Beaumanor Hall that he served as the head of the Y-Station's Home Guard. It is likely that Whitford became a trainer and recruitment officer (much like the role the IOs played in the Auxiliary Units).

A partially deleted record of the Quorn Home Guard found by Austin Ruddy shows that there was also a Second Lieutenant Leavseley involved in the Shock Squad. He was originally a sergeant in the Quorn Home Guard and so, like the chain of command in the Auxiliary Units patrols, may have been the patrol leader. Leavseley's daughter told Ruddy that her father's involvement in a guerrilla squad of the Home Guard would make sense: 'He kept mentioning Bull-in-the-Hollow farm and training on the railway beside it. After his forays there he often came home muddy.'[19]

Hopcroft also remembers what this section would be expected to do in the event of an invasion:

> When invasion came, we'd carry on at work until we got the message from our sergeant or officer. We'd then go and do whatever we were supposed to. There was talk about secret message holes but it never really got down to that.[20]

Unlike the Home Guard, this group had no uniform and knew what that meant for them in the event of being captured:

> We'd go on operations in civilian clothing. At night, you had your face blacked, that was all. We knew it was against the Geneva Convention, but we weren't worried.[21]

Their role was, very much like the Auxiliary Units, to hit the enemy's infrastructure and logistical support. 'Because there was only ten of us, we weren't meant to get into a big battle, 'cos we wouldn't have stood a chance.'[22] Hopcroft mentioned that the Shock Squad's role would also include some ruthlessness towards their own population:

> Traitors in the village? I thought we would have collaborators in this country: spivs and wide boys out on the make. Whitford told us to give them the chop.[23]

A mock sabotage mission during the winter of 1941 also reflected much of what was being done with the Auxiliary Units. Hopcroft remembers an attack on Beaumanor, home of the Y-Service. Whitford had told the regulars guarding there that they were to be attacked by a Home Guard unit and to be on the look-out. Blacked-up, in the freezing cold and in the face of driving snow, the Shock Squad also wore white sheets to blend into the quickly changing landscape. Faced with a six-foot wire fence, the squad would hold a rifle between two men, with a third jumping onto it to be rolled over to the other side. They were armed with just dummy grenades and black powder to ensure there was a 'noise'. After 'dealing' with the sentry and knowing the Beaumanor's grounds like the back of their hands, the squad were soon about their job taking out various key objectives. Generators were marked 'destroyed' by small bags of chalk being placed on top. The squad successfully extricated themselves without being caught and reported back to Whitford. A similar exercise is said to have taken place at a searchlight unit at Woodhouse Eaves. This mock attack has huge similarities to those undertaken by Auxiliary patrols.

There is also some tantalising evidence that these Home Guard guerrilla units had underground bunkers, similar to those used by the Auxiliary Units.

> In a copse at Bull-in-the-Hollow Farm, I think, was an underground base. You'd go through a lot of little pathways to find it. You'd pull the hatch down and cover everything up. It wasn't a doorway, just a hatchway down. Inside were bunks, explosives, ammunition and medical equipment. I don't know for certain but I believe that there was a number of them all over the place.[24]

Unlike the Auxiliary Units though, there were plans for the shock squads to carry on, even if the Germans occupied the area. Although there seems to have been a realisation that as amateurs their life expectancy would have been very low had the invasion come.

Over the course of 80 years or so, it is obvious that memories become distorted; people prefer to 'remember' an exaggerated role they would have played and, in the years since, had read about the Auxiliary Units *et al.* However, Hopcroft's testimony and the documentation found by researchers point to Home Guard shock squads being a reality. Indeed, Hopcroft also mentioned other similar squads based in nearby Rothley and Barrow-on-Soar. Certainly, there were no Auxiliary Units in the Leicestershire area and so whatever Hopcroft was in, it was a different organisation. The fragments of paperwork suggest that it was connected to the local Home Guard units, but the secretive nature of the shock squads suggest that this was more than 'just' a Home Guard guerrilla section.

It is not only in Leicestershire that alternative local groups of civilians were being trained in alternative combat methods, away from the traditional training most Home Guard units were receiving. Throughout the country, and in counties where the existing Auxiliary Units did not already exist, secret Home Guard guerrilla sections were being formed, trained and armed.

The son of Second Lieutenant George W. Manning in Bedfordshire certainly believes his father was in such a unit. As he was working for Igranic Electric in Bedford, George's role was a reserved occupation, so he joined the Home Guard, commanding the No. 2 Platoon in Bedford.

His son Derek told researchers that in the early 1950s his father had taken him and his brother to the site of a bunker.

> We were walking in the open country to the south of Mile Road, Bedford and along a stream bank on the edge of Elstow Moor when my father told us to wait for a moment and he would show us something. He picked up a solid stick from a hedgerow and began scraping the earth behind some bushes near to the stream. He had to try the same near to other bushes before finding a metal ring covered by bushes. With some effort and much clearing of earth he eventually raised a trapdoor and descended down a steel ladder into an underground chamber.
>
> I well remember his words when he got to the bottom of the ladder. 'Good God – everything is still here – I must get onto the army and have all this stuff removed straight away.' He would not let us go down in case some of the explosives were dangerous.[25]

After showing his sons the bunker, George went on to explain what his and his section's role would have been.

> He told us that during the war if the Germans had invaded, he and some of his men were going to hide in a bunker and that they would come out at night and kill as many Germans and blow up as many vehicles etc. as they could.[26]

Both the bunker and his section's aim seem to suggest a role very much in line with the Auxiliary Units. Even the explosives left inside the bunker at the end of the war tell a familiar tale. However, it is a tale told outside of where the Auxiliary Units were operating and seems, like the case in Leicestershire, associated very closely to the Home Guard.

In Lancashire there are several examples of guerrilla-like formations being set up outside of but linked to the traditional Home Guard formations. Ron Freethy, in his book *Lancashire 1939–1945 – The Secret War*, identified Major Roger Fleetwood-Hesketh (later Lieutenant Colonel) as one personality organising such groups. He lived at Meols Hall in Churchtown, Southport. It was there that Fleetwood-Hesketh seems to have set up his own private secret guerrilla unit, designed to take on an invading army from behind the lines. He gathered a nucleus of local men he could trust and trained and armed them in and around the grounds of Meols Hall. Once the threat of invasion diminished, Fleetwood-Hesketh did not disband his unit but took some of them to his next role.

Fleetwood-Hesketh was a key element of Operation *Fortitude*, the campaign designed to put the German Army off the scent of where the Allied forces were planning to land on D-day. One member of his guerrilla unit, 18-year-old Alan Potts of Southport, worked with Fleetwood-Hesketh on the secret maps compiled during the build-up to the invasion.

Another group was set up by Nevill Alexander Drummond Armstrong. Born in London in 1874, by the turn of the century he had made his way to the remote Yukon region of Canada, big-game hunting and gold prospecting. During the First World War he had joined Canadian Expeditionary Forces and by 1916 had been promoted and, using his experience as a big-game hunter, was Commandant of the Canadian Corps Sniping School in France. Mentioned in dispatches multiple times, he was awarded the OBE in 1919.

During the inter-war years, Armstrong returned to Canada and embarked on a number of big-game hunting expeditions to the wilds of the Yukon, writing two books on his adventures in the late 1930s. By the time the Second World War had started, Armstrong had returned to Britain and was again utilising his skills as a hunter and sniper as he acted as colonel and commandant of the Royal Marines Sniping School, 1942–1945. At some point before this though, and after his return to Britain, Armstrong spent time in Lancashire, training a group of younger Home Guard 'lads' in the art of unarmed combat, marksmanship, camouflage and other non-traditional military tactics. One member of the 'Armstrong Brigade' was Peter Ainsworth who lived in Chorley.

> We were trained in the grounds of Worden Hall, near Leyland but we travelled all over with the Major to demonstrate our military skills under his direction. At first we felt stupid blacking our faces and weaving vegetation into our uniform until we saw some of our members walking away from us and then blending so well into the landscape that they seemed to disappear. We learned to crawl properly and shoot straight.[27]

Such was the success of this 'brigade' that by 1942 Armstrong had published a book, *Fieldcraft, Sniping and Intelligence*. What role the Armstrong Brigade would play in the event of an invasion is uncertain, but it goes again to highlight that the Home Guard was not just about old men guarding nodal points. This was a very different organisation to the narrative surrounding it over the past 80 years.

No matter where they were in the country, these groups appear to have had access to caches of weapons hidden in houses or secret locations in their towns or villages. Allan Hopcroft, of the Quorn Home Guard Shock Squad in Leicestershire, remembers:

> You'd know where you could get a rifle and what to do. We had stashes here and there. We knew various houses in Quorn where you could get ammunition or supplies.[28]

A discovery in 1993 in a manor house in Newark, Nottinghamshire, of Lee Enfield rifles and revolvers, points to similar groups of secretive civilian units working away from regular Home Guard battalions. The Defence of Britain archive, which recorded the find, describes the discovery of 30 x Lee Enfield rifles with Enfield revolvers found clipped to roof beams in the loft of Grassthorpe Manor in Newark. A Defence of Britain report[29] speculated that the evidence pointed to rifles being hidden for recovery in an emergency, rather than stacked for immediate Home Guard use.

Indeed, this many Lee Enfield rifles (which were of a type that was in use in 1940–1941) would have been hugely valuable to the regular Home Guard at this point in the war and would not have been hidden in an attic. Nor would they be stored there after being replaced by other weapons later in the war. The Defence of Britain team thought that all of this added up to an Auxiliary Unit's arms cache, part of a possible operational base. However, like Leicestershire, there were no 'official' Auxiliary Units operating in Nottinghamshire and so there has to be an alternative explanation for such a cache to be kept in the house and then seemingly forgotten about for the next 50 years.

The house was owned by a 'respectable, forthright spinster'[30] called Emily Richardson who lived there throughout the war. Emily's great nephew certainly thinks that she was made of the right 'stuff' to be associated with a 'resistance'-like organisation and, indeed, the choice of recruiting formidable spinsters to secret organisations in Britain

(Mabel Stranks and the sisters at Coleshill House amongst others) fits the bill. The manor house itself is located close to the River Trent but is relatively isolated, the perfect choice for a weapons dump. There is little other evidence to point to where the weapons might have come from, but it offers a tantalising view of what could have been happening throughout the country.

Industrial saboteurs in towns and cities

Another key secretive role that the Home Guard would have played was a crucial one, demonstrating some of the lessons learnt from the invasion of France and the Low Countries.

The Home Guard, as well as protecting towns and villages, were also set up in individual factories and workshops. These 'works units' were tasked with defending the critical locations where important supplies for the British forces were being prepared. However, equally, the factories, in the hands of an occupying force could provide the same for the enemy. As such, as well as taking on the enemy in the streets surrounding the factories, these Home Guard units were trained to disable (but crucially not fully destroy) key machinery if it looked like the invading forces were going to take the building. However, there is further evidence that there were other plans in place to completely destroy factories had the German's successfully occupied them.

The industrial Midlands seems, understandably, to have been the core area for these saboteurs. An article in the *Leicester Mercury* in the 1960s suggested that something very similar was happening in that city too. Referring to them as 'industrial key holders', the article describes their role.

> There was, for example, a shoe machinery works doing research and experimental work of a highly secret nature. So secretive in fact that at a time when we were a high invasion risk, certain Leicester people were given 'sabotage' keys. These would give them access to works where war research and classified weapons were being produced. The job of the sabotage key holders was to put the plant beyond the use of the enemy.[31]

Much of this seems very similar to the work that SIS's Section D and Military Intelligence (Research) were up to in the late 1930s in the countries surrounding Nazi Germany. The conversations taking place with the Skoda factory in Czechoslovakia, for example, about how the factory could be put out of service if the Germans had invaded and occupied were happening too late to ensure it took place, but in Britain, SIS had the opportunity to better prepare.

In 1940 both MI5 and SIS undertook a survey of all key industrial assets with factories, sending back specific plans on how they would deal with the threat of the invading army taking over – very much in line with what they were doing in mainland Europe. Historian Malcolm Atkin has found evidence that Home Guard commanders were given a highly secret list of key factories in their areas from which they would take vital components to take them out of action had the Germans arrived.[32] These appear to be the 'key holders' described in the *Leicester Mercury*.

These key holders seem to be instructed to 'hide' components rather than to destroy infrastructure. The same went for fuel stations. In France, as the panzers sped through villages and towns, they simply filled up at local petrol stations, as there had been no thought to put them out of action. Atkin has also found evidence of secret 'Pump Destruction Squads' made up of Home Guard members, who would only act once the Germans had broken through (of course on the assumption that they had survived the initial German attack). These squads were to dismantle the parts of the machinery of petrol pumps just before the Germans overran, denying them access to a potentially crucial supply of fuel (especially if the Auxiliary Units were successful in their attacks on the German's own supply chain). However, the key to this was that the parts were not destroyed and could be put back into place to assist any British counter-attack.

Throughout the country, but particularly in the Midlands, plans were in place to make factories unusable for an occupying force. Harold Goodwin & Company, a motor servicing company in Worcestershire, had a secret team of three men responsible for immobilising the vehicles, battery charging equipment, tools and other machinery and hiding spare tyres.[33]

In Birmingham a corporal (who wished to remain anonymous) in a works Home Guard unit was introduced to a lieutenant who asked whether he'd be interested in joining 'Branch X' which would 'require extra training and for me to go on various courses'.[34] These courses included fieldcraft, bomb making and making up demolition sets from four No. 73 grenades ('Thermos' or 'Woolworths' anti-tank grenades) that were attached to a detonator. He was also taught how to make booby traps and the 'skills of dirty fighting, including the use of a knife'. He was given very few weapons and pieces of equipment and so it was up to him to construct his own. He made himself a garrotting wire from cheese wire and two home-made wooden T-piece handles. He also put together various forms of booby traps; these were purposely of his own design to ensure that the Germans were not aware of any standard pattern of trap and so could not learn to disarm them.

He was expected to train and operate alone and keep a low profile within his personal and Home Guard life (indeed if the Germans had come, he had been ordered to destroy any certificates or paperwork that would indicate he was anything other than an 'ordinary' member of the Home Guard). He was told by his X Branch lieutenant to practise moving at night during the black-out in civilian clothing, wearing rubber-soled shoes. Like many of these secret units, in the event of invasion and occupation, they would have access to underground stores of ammunition and food.

He also recalled that he was taught how to manufacture his own explosives using nitric acid and sulphuric acid in equal parts and cotton waste or the use of mixtures of saltpetre, fertiliser, weed killer and sugar. In the 'industrial Midlands, the acids were widely used in the manufacture of car batteries and for cleaning metal castings. They were therefore not a problem to procure.'[35]

Like the Auxiliary Units, it seems these industrial saboteurs used the Home Guard as a cover for their secret activities. Had the Germans broken through the coastal crust and hit the Midlands, they would have found a very different situation to what they had experienced in France and the Low Countries. For example, with petrol stations put out of action, fuel would not be easy to get hold of; instead, they would have had to rely on their own supplies, which itself would first have to make it across the Channel, potentially under attack from the

Royal Navy. Once on land, the supplies would have been suspectable to attack from the actions of the Auxiliary Units and the other layers of secret defence. The potential of this one action, to deny the invading army easy access to petrol, could have been huge. Multiply this across the country and the impact of this particular secret group soon becomes apparent.

The industrial saboteur units were highly secret. As such, we still know very little about the men (and potentially women) involved in these groups but it is clear that, if caught in the act, they, like all the other units discussed in this book, would have been tortured and killed. However, their actions could have been hugely influential and one has to presume, they, like their counter-parts in the Auxiliary Units, Special Duties Branch and Home Guard shock squads/guerrilla sections, fully understood this and the bigger picture of their individual acts.

Part II

Anti-Invasion Civilian Forces:
Spies, Wireless Operators and ATS

CHAPTER 6

Civilian Recruitment, Training and Role

As the Germans attacked France in the summer of 1940, civilians took to the roads to try to escape the carnage, resulting in the roads becoming packed with men, women and children, mainly on foot carrying their most valuable possessions. This meant that any attempted Allied counter-attacks were held-up, while also making all on the road vulnerable targets to the Junkers Ju 87 (Stuka) dive-bomber with its terrifying 'scream'.

Another consequence of the mass movement of French civilians was that as the Germans passed through French villages and towns, no one remained to observe and pass on information about which direction the Wehrmacht was travelling in, what vehicles it had and what numbers and regiments were involved. This lack of information added to the confusion and panic that was already manifesting, particularly within the French Army Headquarters. The idea seems to have been suggested at least. In May 1940, Edward Spears, Churchill's special emissary and liaison officer to the French prime minister, Paul Reynaud, asked during a meeting of the French Comité de Guerre about the onslaught of the German advance, 'Why had roadblocks not been organised, with 75mm guns placed on lorries? A simple order to civilians to telephone ahead the direction these columns were heading would have made such preparations possible.'[1]

As such preparations were not implemented, the German forces were flooding through at will and without anyone knowing where they would be heading next. The apparent ability for the Wehrmacht to 'ghost' through defences caused real concern in Britain in the summer of 1940 with a real fear that any intelligence of a German invasion would be severely limited. Fears arose that small parties of assault troops making quick progress in the early part of an invasion, taking strategic points and cutting lines of communication, were going to be almost impossible to defend against. Added to this was the growing fear of parachute troops hitting targets inland and the activity of a 'Fifth Column'. The shock of the defeat in France was, of course, still fresh in the minds of everyone at GHQ (including mainly false reports on the 'successes' of the Fifth Column in mainland Europe). This meant that there was a real keenness to implement a strategy to counter the effectiveness of the Blitzkrieg. Therefore, having intelligence coming in from towns and villages that were being attacked by the enemy would give GHQ a clear and, importantly, up-to-date picture of enemy activity that they could then respond to.

Civilians staying behind, monitoring the invading army and passing the information quickly to high command could prove a real asset. As previously mentioned, Laurence Grand of SIS had set up the HDS. The sabotage wing of the organisation was passed to GHQ Home Forces and combined with the activities of MI(R) to form the Auxiliary Units.

However, the sabotage wing was just one aspect of the HDS. The fact that there was even a sabotage wing connected with SIS seems to be a bit of an anomaly. For an organisation designed specifically for secretive, undercover work, handing weapons and explosives to civilians to quite literally blow things up seems outside of their original remit. It is less surprising, therefore, that there was a second element too – one dedicated to intelligence gathering, keeping track of enemy movements and sending that information on in a timely manner.

Alongside Grand, one of the original coordinators of the HDS was Viscount Bearsted. He had worked with SIS and Section D, particularly in Scandinavia where he helped create early resistance networks in advance of the German invasion. Bearsted would remain in charge of the group until it was fully handed over to GHQ. The role of the intelligence-gathering section of the HDS was designed, initially at least, to act over a longer period of time and not get involved in the invasion. Much like the Auxiliary Units, 'key men' were identified in vulnerable areas and told to pull together their own cells of observers and messengers. At this point, there were no wireless sets, but dead-letter drops were created along a line, with runners collecting each message and passing it on to the next drop.

The ease with which SIS was apparently willing to let go of what was to become the Special Duties Branch, even though it was very much more in line with its natural role, perhaps points to the fact it had other, more secret, irons in the fire such as the post-occupation highly secret civilian organisation Section VII (to be discussed later). The move towards the military also meant that the Special Duties Branch would now be operating during the invasion period rather than for any elongated period of time (more akin to the role of the operational Auxiliary Units). As the Special Duties Branch was more naturally aligned to SIS than to GHQ, it was decided to delay the complete hand-over, and effectively SIS continued to run this branch alongside the military until a more military 'friendly' version could be created from it. In July 1940, it was agreed that:

> While obstructive activities of the 'D' organisation are being gradually transferred to GHQ Auxiliary Units, it is considered necessary and desirable by GHQ and CSS [Chiefs of SIS] that the Intelligence side of the activities should be maintained and developed.[2]

Part of the reason there was a delay in the complete move over to GHQ was the lack of wireless sets. Although the information being gathered by the spies and observers would undoubtedly be useful, by the time it had reached someone who could make a decision and a difference, the situation on the ground may well have changed considerably. GHQ could obviously see the potential value in such a group, but until wireless sets were introduced, the unit was not that much use to them. By the time GHQ inherited the group it was made up of around 1,000 civilian volunteers, most of whom were in counties that would later have Auxiliary Units operational patrols. The transfer of the HDS-recruited civilians was incredibly smooth; so smooth in fact that many of them may not have realised that there had been any kind of transition. Not a single veteran has ever directly mentioned prior service with the HDS or SIS, even though there may have been around 1,000 of them.[3]

In autumn 1940 Viscount Bearsted was moved to SOE, and Major Maurice Petherick joined from SIS to essentially turn the Special Duties Branch into a force that was more suitable for the military to directly control. At the time of his appointment, Petherick was MP for Penryn and Falmouth, and had at the start of the war been a liaison officer attached to the Paris Embassy.

Petherick designed the complex network of SUB-OUT-Stations, OUT-Stations, IN-Stations, spies and runners and by the time of stand-down in 1944 there were around 3,250 members – civilians, Auxiliary Territorial Service (ATS) and regular forces – all with very defined roles. Their role also morphed into an anti-invasion one, moving away from the post-occupation role it had been designed for by the HDS. There were two reasons for this change. Petherick was likely to have knowledge of other SIS-led post-occupation groups and so there was a need to avoid duplication. Also, as a now military led rather than an intelligence service unit, its key role was to provide critical information during the period in which the military were active against the invader. Once occupied and militarily defeated, the military would have a limited impact, whilst, as we will see later, the intelligence service would come into their own.

Major Rupert Mackworth Arthur Jones joined the Special Duties Branch section of the Auxiliary Units in early 1942. As Officer Commanding, he wrote a document in June 1944 explaining what the role of the unit would have been had the Germans invaded:

> The Special Duties Branch of the Auxiliary Units is organised to provide information for military formations in the event of enemy invasion or raids in Great Britain, from areas temporarily or permanently in enemy control. All this information would be collected as a result of direct observation by specially recruited and trained civilians who would remain in an enemy occupied area. Auxiliary Units Signals are responsible for providing the communications to enable the civilian observers to pass their information to a military HQ. All traffic is by wireless (R/T), using very high frequency sets. Information is collected at IN stations (manned by Royal Signals or ATS Officers) and is passed from there to military formation. IN stations have concealed dugouts in which station crew

can, if necessary, live without coming above ground at all for three weeks at a time. This includes provision for battery charging, feeding etc.[4]

This gives a fantastic overview of the role but, in 1940, just how was such a group recruited, trained and maintained with such high levels of secrecy? Using many of those civilians that came over with the HDS, Petherick was soon extending the Special Duties Branch the length of the country, as had been done with the Auxiliary Units (operational patrols). As with the operational side of the Auxiliary Units, Petherick recruited IOs to travel to key counties. The HQ staff for the Special Duties Branch was relatively small at this early stage and comprised one general staff officer, 2nd grade; one general staff officer, 3rd grade; 11 intelligence officers (all made up to captains), each of whom had a four-seater car and a Royal Army Service Corps driver; and two clerks.[5] Again, at this stage of 1940, with the regular forces and particularly the Home Guard desperate for weapons and ammunition, even this non-operational side of the Auxiliary Units was equipped with .38 pistols and .303 rifles.

IOs (intelligence officers) were a mix of ex-HDS officers (who remained with the civilians they had recruited during the initial stages of the intelligence-gathering group set up by Grand and SIS), regular officers and even civilians.

One of the more remarkable IOs for the Special Duties Branch, who had previously worked for certainly Section D and potentially HDS too, was Major Douglas Mill Saunders, who in July 1940 was IO for Hampshire including areas around Southampton, Portsmouth and the Isle of Wight. Saunders, however, was not your run-of-the-mill officer. Educated at Clare College, Cambridge, Saunders had fought in the First World War in the Bedfordshire Regiment. Pre-Second World War he was the chief executive of the advertising firm J. Walter Thompson. He put the whole company at the disposal of Section D including other senior executives. Saunders would be given the responsibility for 'Press, Propaganda and Rumours'.[6]

By July 1940, however, Saunders was dismissed from Section D, as SOE began to form and take precedence. It was from this date that Saunders seems to have taken his position as IO for special duties in

Hampshire. After a year on the south coast, he was transferred to the King's Royal Rifle Corps, Department of the Adjutant General at the War Office and by June 1945 he was Colonel Directorate of Public Relations.[7]

Another interesting IO within the Special Duties Branch was Arthur Douglas Ingrams. He joined the Territorial Army in the 1920s where he held a commission in the Royal Artillery. However, by the time the Special Duties Branch was extended to the South West, specifically into Devon and Somerset, Ingrams was a farmer (poultry, pig and sheep) living near Axminster on the Devon–Dorset border. It was here that he was recruited as a Special Duties OUT-Station operator (more on his unique bunker later on) by the county IO, Cecil Coxwell-Rogers. By 1942 he was a group leader (what earlier in the war would have been a key man) in the area, which meant he was responsible for other Special Duties personnel in his network.

He must have been an exceptional group leader, as by 1943 he had been promoted to acting IO for the area. This temporary situation was made permanent when Ingrams returned to military service to take on the role. His talent meant that later in the war he was transferred away from his home to the other side of the country to become IO for East Anglia. He would remain in the military after the war, serving in the Middle East.[8]

For a civilian to make such strides in any organisation is a real indication of his talent in this area.

Recruitment, training and role

With the IOs heading out to vulnerable counties, they were soon approaching civilians. These recruits were very different to those being approached by the IOs looking for operational Auxiliary Units members. These were not fit farmer-type civilians. The nature of the work of the Special Duties Branch meant that civilians had to be those that would not catch the attention of the invading German Army. Therefore, pensioners, doctors, vicars, publicans, vets, housewives and even teenagers were identified and recruited. Like the recruitment of the patrol leaders in the operational Auxiliary Units, the IOs went to key areas to find 'key men'. These civilians were to form their own 'intelligence-gathering cells' formed of spies/observers, runners and messengers and civilian wireless operators (often the key men themselves).

Some civilians were approached by the IO to join a cell. Mrs Ursula M. Pennell, near the village of Cley on the north Norfolk coast, remembers being approached by a 'charming young officer' who explained about a network of people 'three miles apart and about three miles from the coast, who would stay put if the Germans came and whether she would be interested.'

Once she had accepted, the officer went on to explain:

> … what I had to do and he told me the names of my contacts. It was a schoolmaster, at the village school in Weybourne, to the east (his name was Edgar Coe and he was the school's headmaster). He was my contact there. The other was a retired schoolmistress at Blackeney that I vaguely knew. If the Germans came I had to gather every information I possibly could. I was given leaflets with the badges and uniforms and those things I had to learn and was told I must never lose them. I kept them in my purses or stuck them in my bra wherever I went. I had instructions to destroy them when the Germans came.[9]

Jill Holman, daughter of Dr Alex Holman, a Special Duties Branch key man who was already running a wireless set from his home in Aylsham, Norfolk, was also approached:

> Colonel Collings, the local commanding officer, asked my father if he thought I'd fold at the sight of a German. My father told him I didn't fold at anything – horses, bulls and schoolmistresses – so the Colonel recruited me. He thought a brat on a horse was unlikely to be suspected of anything. So, I was to ride out and spot choice targets in terms of troops and supply dumps.[10]

Another recruit was Joyce Harrison in Hockley, Essex. In 1940 she was working at County Hall in Chelmsford, Essex. Her husband, who was in the RAF, did not want her to join the Women's Auxiliary Air Force (WAAFs), but she felt she should be doing her bit. At the time of writing, Joyce is 104 and now living in Canada with her family, but she remembers the Special Duties Branch being set up quickly.

This was something very hurriedly done locally, but unfortunately, I can only remember being asked if I was interested, but cannot recall when or where it actually happened. The first thing I do remember was being taken up Gusted Hall Lane to an underground shelter in the woods to receive instructions and introduced to the girl I was to pair up with.[11]

With civilians being recruited in the key, vulnerable counties, training had started with spies/observers being provided with the leaflets printed with details of German regiments, weapons, insignia and vehicles. They were also trained to recognise direction of travel, locations of supply dumps and possible convoy stop points. Once they had witnessed the Germans passing through, they would write their observations down on a piece of paper, in code, which they then deposited at a dead-letter drop.

These dead-letter drops ranged in size and design – anything from a simple rock to a tree stump with a revolving top to an Oxo gravy

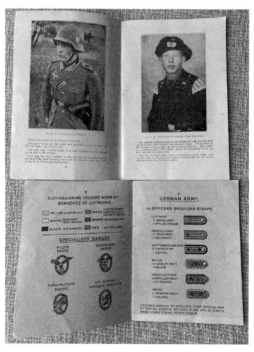

One of the uniform identification pamphlets handed to the Auxiliary Units and Special Duties Branch. Committing the various formations and insignia to memory, the invading army would have been spied on every step of the way. (Ken Welch)

tin. Other examples of dead-letter drops include a farm gate with a horseshoe attached to it. If the horseshoe was facing down, there was no message; if it was facing up, there was one waiting. The runner/ messenger would find the message in a disguised gate bolt on the side of the gate. The bolt was hollow and the message could be concealed within it. Similarly, hollow keys with messages inserted in them were left in doors. All of these were designed to be left in plain sight, meaning the runners could easily leave and pick up messages without attracting attention, and it could be done during the day.

After the message had been left in the allocated spot, a series of runners would take the message and move it to the next dead-letter drop. The number of messengers per cell could be as many as 20–30 people.

The levels of secrecy surrounding the messengers and runners means we know very little about these civilians. A huge majority seem to have passed away without telling anyone, with only a few snippets coming out over the years. However, some, like those above, have talked about their experiences.

George Vater lived in Monmouthshire, South Wales. He went to Newport to join the army in 1940 where, after a medical and IQ test, he was interviewed by a Colonel Hughes who told him he had a special job he wanted him to do. George was asked to swear an oath of allegiance and then sign the Official Secrets Act and was told that from that moment his name was not going to be written down and he was to write down nothing of his training or activities. He was given a large number of documents, marked 'Top Secret' and was given a week to learn everything on them. These documents included the insignia and colours of the German armed forces. He was told he had to learn them off by heart and was tested the following week.

He was given a piece of edible paper on which messages were to be written and by all accounts he did try some. He tried to eat it but found it a bit like chewing gum – a pretty poor standard, gooey and not a very nice flavour.[12]

Like Ursula Pennell, George was then introduced to the rest of his cell.

> One was the vicar of Llanddewi, the Reverend Vincent Evens, Gower Rees the vicar of Llanarth, John Evans, a farm worker, somebody (forgotten his first name) Steele who was a gardener... there were about eight of us. We had the first meeting in the vicarage in Llanddewi and the last word that Tommy Atkins (IO) told us was 'Gentlemen if necessary you all die. You do not break a secret, you die.'[13]

Training was intense but, unlike the operational Auxiliary Units, it seemed to take place exclusively in and around their local area. Joyce Harrison remembers her first training mission:

> We were instructed on the kind of manoeuvre we would be doing and had our first one in the fields off Mt. Bovers Lane in Hawkwell. They chose the first moonlight night; we had to black our faces so they didn't give us away, handed a sealed envelope which we had no idea what it contained and had to cross numerous fields to a hollow tree, leave it there, and get back without being discovered.[14]

She was also trained in how to observe without being seen and her dead-letter drop was a false tree stump with a revolving top, allowing messages to be deposited within it.

Jill Holman also gave some information about the type of training she was involved in:

> We collected information by observations made on the ground such as bombing squad movements, troop assemblages, movements and numbers, vehicle movements, identifications of battalions and regiments and anything else unusual. The information was coded and passed on[15]

With her father operating the wireless set, Jill's role seems to have been mainly as a courier:

> I was mainly a courier and it was my task to take messages concealed in tennis balls, to certain drop-off points. I do not know where these would have been on a map but I knew exactly where they were and also the quickest way to them, even in the dark, because I was very familiar with the area[16]

It seems, from the training at least, that the messengers/runners were expected to act predominantly at night. To know their surroundings intimately and to get from dead-letter drop to dead-letter drop quickly, without being seen. Capture, even without a coded message, was likely to end in torture and death. Perhaps, counting on the confusion that comes as a result of any invasion, the runners of the Special Duties Branch were to move quickly, between rapidly changing 'front lines' to get the information needed to those remaining in command, allowing them to make informed decisions about the next moves the defending British forces should make.

One runner, George Hammand from the village of Aldborough in Norfolk, took researchers to two of his dead-letter drops at the age of 86. He was able to take them to the locations easily, but no trace of either remained. They were both 'small squares in the ground with a wooden or fibrous (non-metal) cover concealed under grass or leaf mould, perfectly blending in with the surrounding ground'.[17] He recalled that he would lift the cover and drop a split tennis ball, with the message inside, into an opening of what looked like an ordinary drainpipe. Both of the locations were on slopes and George believed that he could hear the ball bouncing down the pipe and down the slope to a mystery location at the bottom. He never knew where it would end up, nor did he ever meet anyone else in his cell. He recalled delivering only about four or five messages to each of the locations and was never asked to collect a message.

Incredibly, it seems it was not just human runners ensuring that messages were quickly delivered along the line. The Lincolnshire town of Woodhall Spa had a Special Duties Branch cell operating in it. Two doctors, George Armour and Leonard Herbert Henry Boys, operated from the house of the former. They had recruited a George Bee to be one of the runners within the cell. Bee bred and sold Golden Retrievers and Red Setters and seems to have provided Dr Armour with two Red Setters. At some point, one of these Red Setters, called Sally, was returned to Bee who took advantage of Sally's training as a gun dog to further teach her to swim the River Witham and deliver messages either to or from an observer at nearby Metheringham Fen or Martin.[18]

Initially, and certainly under the HDS, the aim was for messages to be sent by runners the whole length of the line until it arrived in the hands of someone in authority. Although this information was better than nothing at all, the time it would have taken meant that much of the message would be out of date by the time it had reached its final destination.

The obvious answer for speeding up the process was to add wireless sets into the equation, meaning that pertinent and time-sensitive messages could reach GHQ quickly, allowing them to make informed decisions about their next move. Petherick then set about the task of delivering wireless sets to those cells already in existence and to the ones currently being recruited by IOs. Petherick was able to design and implement a complex, but hugely effective, network of wireless operators who played an important role at certain points in the line of communication. As mentioned previously, he allocated them different names: SUB-OUT-Stations, OUT-Stations, and IN-Stations.

By 1941 Petherick had set up Special Duties HQ at Hannington Hall, in the village of Hannington, Wiltshire. The Grade II listed country house had 20 rooms and still stands in 340 acres of pasture of woodland. Just 2.5 miles away from the Auxiliary Units HQ at Coleshill House, Hannington was well positioned. Built by the Freke family in 1653, by the 1920s the Fry family had bought the estate and were still there in the 1940s (although later sold the house back to the Freke family in the 1950s).

A diary entry in Special Duties Branch Senior Commander Beatrice Temple's diary from 24 November 1941 describes her arrival at Hannington.

> Arrived Highworth. DR led to HQ Coleshill House – met by charming Colonel Beyts. Tea with Colonel Major who then led the way to Hannington Hall which turns out to belong to friends of a fellow officer. Butler opened door and maid asked if she could unpack any cases. The Fry family still had 14 servants.[19]

By March 1942 networks were set up in Kent (the trial county), Dorset, Hampshire (including the Isle of Wight), Sussex, Essex, north Somerset, Suffolk, Norfolk, Lincolnshire, Yorkshire, Durham and Northumberland, the Scottish Borders and South Wales. Eventually the Scottish Highlands were also included.

Runners would deliver the coded message written down by the observer that would end up at a SUB-OUT-Station or OUT-Station. SUB-OUT-Stations were introduced slightly later in the war (around

1943) and tended to be positioned nearer the coast. This could be seen as righting an overlooked issue, or as a result of a slightly new role for the Special Duties Branch as an anti-raiding force (in line with the changing role of the operational Auxiliary Units patrols).

One of the more 'famous' members of the civilian side of the Special Duties Branch was Mollie Phillips. She and her father operated the SUB-OUT-Station at Pencarreg in Carmarthenshire. However, it was Mollie's pre-war career that really made her stand out. She had risen to fame as an ice skater, competing from childhood to become a British champion in pairs in 1933 and competing in the 1932 and 1936 Olympic Games. She was one of only four Britons to take part in the 1932 Winter Olympics and was appointed standard bearer, as the other three girls were all under 18. By the late 1930s she was standing for election to the all-male Council of the National Skating Association, taking advantage of the fact that no rule prevented her (the men had never even considered the possibility of a woman standing for election). She was nominated as an Olympic judge, becoming the first British woman in this role and performing it at four Games. She was also the first woman to be assistant referee and then referee at international competitions. In 1941, she was admitted to Lincoln's Inn and studied to be a barrister, completing the course but never practising at the bar.

She operated at Pencarreg between 1941 and stand-down in 1944 after her father was recruited to be a Special Duties group leader in September 1941. A letter, written later by her father, refers to her becoming an operator and transmitting from a separate station to him, suggesting there may have been a second SUB-OUT-Station in the area. After stand-down her father also wrote to Churchill asking for an award of some sort — a medal or similar — be given to members of the Special Duties Branch to remove the stigma from the rest of the population who perceived they hadn't contributed to the war effort. His pleas, it seems, fell on deaf ears, presumably because of the Official Secrets Act. After the war, Mollie was appointed to lead the Girl Guides in Cardiganshire, was a Justice of the Peace and spent 15 years as a member of the Police Authority, being awarded an OBE in 1978.

SUB-OUT-Stations and OUT-Stations were often placed in locations that reflected the occupation of the operator. For example, the SUB-OUT-Station where George Vater's messages would end up was at Llantilio Crossenny Church, where there were a number of wireless operators (presumably to share the burden, but also to shift suspicion away from one individual). This included the Reverend H. Vincent Evans, Richard Albert Sluman (clerk in Holy Orders, vicar and rector) and John Owen, a farm worker.

The wireless set was in the altar in the church, with a lightning conductor that reached the length of the spire used for supporting the aerial. Vater also spoke of a loose stone in the churchyard wall at St David's Church, Llanddewi Rhydderch, where he was to leave the message he had collected from the previous dead-letter drop. The Reverend Evans was the vicar at St David's, just four miles away from the wireless set at St Telio's church.

Vicars made the perfect cover for the Special Duties Branch, as they were likely to be treated with little suspicion by the invading army and could wander around their local area without attracting unwanted attention. Indeed, one of the more mysterious runners was the Reverend James Tindall Soutter. He was a Church of Scotland minister and a runner for the Smeaton House Estate wireless set. He was born in 1885 and was a member of the Great Britain Olympic team in 1912 where he won a bronze medal as part of the 4 x 400m relay in Stockholm and also competed in the 800m and the 400m. He saw service during the First World War as a chaplain in East Africa and France before returning to Scotland in 1917 as the minister at Whitekirk. However, in October 1959 he simply disappeared; he went out for a walk, reportedly with his passport, and never came back. He was declared dead in 1966 but his body was never found.

Another good example of the type of civilians recruited belonged to the Longhorsley OUT-Station in Northumberland. The wireless set was in a hidden room at Longhorsley Tower. A rectangular structure, four stories high and thought to date from the 16th century, it is now a Grade II listed building. Having fallen into some disrepair, it was renovated in the 1930s and was home to a Charles Webb. Born in 1886,

Charles was a solicitor and a member of the Observer Corps (Master Observer). A man therefore not likely to attract the attention of an invading force but more than capable of working effectively in passing information on about them. The other operative was the Reverend Frank Wright. He was also an air raid warden and as a 67-year-old vicar was less likely to attract the attention of the Germans. Likewise, both of the men's volunteer roles meant that they could train easily enough, as they were expected to be walking around the village at times when others were indoors, so no questions were asked.

The room that held the wireless set was not discovered until after the war when Charles Webb's son and his friend found the concealed entrance. In order to gain access to the room, all the tools and bottles had to be removed from the shelves in the corner of the garage. A shelf was then folded down exposing a bolt which needed to be undone, removing the panel and allowing access to the door behind. This opened into a small, soundproofed room that, when discovered, was said to contain a wireless and accessories and also a bench and two chairs.

The Great Glenham OUT-Station in Suffolk highlighted the levels of ingenuity involved in the disguise of wireless-set locations. Operated by Charles Kindred, the wireless set was hidden in a mobile chicken hut with a concealed area at the far end. A catch was opened by poking a finger through a knot hole and entry was gained to a small chamber housing the set. The aerial was run up a nearby oak tree, with messages left under an old ploughshare, which could be collected from inside the hut by removing a floorboard.[20]

Another great example of a genius OUT-Station was Smeaton in East Lothian. Located on the Smeaton House Estate. It was a hidden underground construction made up of two concrete rooms, one for equipment and furniture, the other for holding radio equipment. Pigeon-holes contained booklets of German units and equipment. In one pigeon-hole was a concealed switch which would open a wall section to reveal a small annex containing the wireless equipment.[21]

The bunker of Arthur Ingrams on the Devon–Dorset border was nothing short of spectacular. David, Arthur's son, remembers that during the Easter holidays in 1941 a group of 7–8 soldiers came to work on the site. They excavated a large hole (around 3m below ground level) alongside some back-to-back privies, situated in the garden of the Ingrams's house. All of this work, David remembers, was done by hand, without the use of any mechanical diggers, as they would have been far too noisy and conspicuous.[22] To conceal such a large project from prying eyes and reconnaissance aircraft, the spoil from the hole was spread on a nearby vegetable patch and covered with topsoil or thrown down a slope which dropped down next to the hole.

Much like the OBs of the Auxiliary Units patrols, an Anderson-like shelter was dropped into the hole, with vent pipes for taking out stale air and bringing in fresh air. At this early stage it was one chamber, but the most remarkable aspect about the bunker was its concealment. We have already seen some of the extraordinary lengths and levels of ingenuity involved in such bunkers, but Ingrams's example takes it to a new level. Utilising the privy, the entrance to the radio bunker was situated under the wooden box seat. Opening the door of the privy, you were confronted by the box seat, which was, as you might expect, firmly fixed in place.

However, by going back outside to the base of a concrete rose arbour post, one could open a disguised box, which contained a latch-rod. Turning the latch-rod 90 degrees released the entire box seat, allowing the civilian wireless operator to then return to the privy and lift the whole system up, revealing a ladder making its way down into the bunker. A similar system from inside the bunker allowed the occupant to bring the box seat back down, re-securing it to the ground.

Once down the ladder and inside the bunker you could walk (hunched due to height restriction) along a short corridor to enter the main chamber itself. Later on, there were some quite considerable amendments to the bunker, which meant splitting the chamber in two.

The two chambers were designed to become a map room and a radio room, separated by a partition of old railway sleepers. These sleepers made a false wall, meaning anyone who somehow gained access to the bunker would not immediately be able to put the wireless (and its operator) out of action. The release mechanism for the 'wall' was ingeniously disguised on a shelf at the other end of the chamber. Along the side-end of the shelf were three cup hooks, one of which was a release mechanism – if pulled, it would then allow you to raise the railway-sleeper wall (once the table and bench had been folded away). You could then enter the radio room, in which Ingrams would be transmitting the information he had received from the last runner in the line. The false wall meant that he had time to continue transmitting until the last possible moment if a German patrol had found its way in.

The last messenger in the line in this case was a Mrs Medora Byron Eames, a farmer's wife from the nearby Woonton Farm, who was in her fifties during the war. Her job as a runner was to take the messages from a dead-letter drop and deposit them at the wireless location where Ingrams would send the information on via his wireless set. She was to take the coded message to the hedgerow on the boundary of Ingrams's house. In the middle of the hedge was a tree stump. This was no ordinary stump though: the top of the stump swivelled round to reveal a pipe heading down the stump and into the ground. The message, now in a split tennis ball, would be dropped down the stump where it would roll its way down into the bunker under the outside privy, arriving next to where Ingrams would be operating the wireless.

Medora is thought to have taken over operating the wireless set once Ingrams had been promoted and taken his place as IO in Suffolk. She, like so many, said very little about her role and died without saying much, if anything, about her experiences.

Once the message had reached Ingrams, he could send the information on. With the wireless set in a bunker, sending messages was going to be difficult. Like other OUT- and SUB-OUT-Station sites, aerials were sent up trees. Three tall conifers in the garden surrounding the outside privy were utilised to attach aerial feeder cables upwards, allowing for signal to be maintained. Even the aerial feeder cables going up the trees were disguised.

One member of the Auxiliary Units Signals support, Stan Judson (more on Stan and his colleagues in the next chapter), explains how:

> The aerial would be up a tree, a selected tree which often was most difficult to climb, so what we had, we usually got a hammer, tied a string to it and threw it. Pick a tree with fairly few branches lower down, and if you study trees you'll

find that they have a black line coming down, because they get dust on them and the rain, the water finds its path and it doesn't make a channel but usually a black line which is ideal for concealing the black cable up to the aerial.[23]

The wireless location of the cell in Woodhall Spa (the cell that had Sally the gun dog delivering messages across the River Witham) was slightly less sophisticated but nevertheless effective. The wireless station was an early box type, where the set was buried in a metal-lined wooden box with a concealed cover. The set was located in an outhouse used to house George Armour's other red setter. The dog had his bed on top of the cover which provided a good way to avoid accidental discovery.

There is no evidence that any of these bunkers were 'accidently' discovered by civilians as some of the OBs of the Auxiliary Units were. There do seem to have been some close shaves though. One incident just outside Charing in Kent involved chicken farmer Adrian Monck-Mason. The son of a high-ranking Royal Artillery colonel (George Monck-Mason), Adrian was a lieutenant with the Royal Field Artillery Special Reserve during the First World War, and during the inter-war years he appears to have briefly been British vice-consul in Skopje, Macedonia between 1924 and 1925.[24]

However, in the 1930s he had bought a 32-acre farm at Stonestile in Charing on top of the North Downs. Such an elevated location lent itself well to wireless transmission. Before the war, the farm had been a commercial egg farm, which proved impossible to maintain under war conditions. However, Monck-Mason continued to raise chickens with much of the rest of the farm converted to arable growing.

The wireless set was located under one of the chicken sheds. One day, on his way to the hideout, Monck-Mason saw a Royal Corps of Signals soldier wandering around nearby with a tall fish-pole aerial extending from a knapsack radio on his back. He approached the soldier to ask what he was doing, to which the soldier replied that they had picked up signals from a strange source in the area. They did not recognise the code and had come to the understandable conclusion that a German spy was active in the area. Monck-Mason said that he would certainly keep an eye out for suspicious characters and, reassured, the soldier went on his way.[25] Monck-Mason continued to train and broadcast messages undetected throughout the rest of the war. It is said that both Montgomery and Alan Brooke both visited the site later in the war.

Monck-Mason's wireless set location was not the only one to be located by the army. The OUT-Station at Donnington-on-Bain in Lincolnshire was run by local coal merchant Harold Gray.[i] The set was another early version in a metal-lined box buried in a wood. One evening Gray and his assistant were using the set when they were overheard by an RAF officer and his WAAF girlfriend who were 'courting' in the woods. The couple crept away and called in the army who quickly encircled the wood. Gray realised that they had been discovered and managed to conceal the radio set before they were arrested. They spent the night in jail before being released in the morning, after their identities had been confirmed.

With so many of these civilians not telling anyone of their role during the wartime years, researchers often have to go on very little evidence to try and tie together clues of activity around the country. One good example of this is in East Devon. An Auxiliary Units Signals soldier who left behind a map and some descriptions of OUT- and SUB OUT-Stations (more on this later) included evidence of a SUB OUT-Station in the village of Clyst St Mary, just outside Exeter. Now near the M5, it once stood on the main road running from Exeter to Southampton and would have proved to be a useful link for an invading army either coming from the South West eastwards or moving into Devon and Cornwall.

With nothing else other than a vague map and the testimony of an individual to go on, like so many other areas where researchers know that there was a SUB-OUT-Station or OUT-Station but very little other information, it was looking like a dead-end. However, after a talk on Auxiliary Units in the local area, the author was approached at the end by an audience member who talked about rumours that

---

i   Harold's brother, Bernard, was a noted war correspondent being the first to report from a bombing raid over Germany. He was last seen boarding submarine HMS *Urge*, never to be seen again. The wreck of HMS *Urge* was only confirmed as being discovered off the coast of Malta in 2021.

spread around Clyst St Mary during the war. These local rumours consisted of wartime 'spies' operating out of The Malster's Arms, one of the pubs in the village. The licensee in 1939 and during the war was Mrs Elizabeth Westaway. Born in 1869, Elizabeth was a widow and a publican, a combination that seems to have been perfect for a Special Duties Branch civilian recruit. Research continues.

All of these civilians fully understood the dangers of volunteering for the Special Duties Branch, and that, in all likelihood, if the Germans invaded, their life expectancy would be very short. It was also probable that, out of the two branches of the Auxiliary Units, it would be the group that would fall first. With so many civilians involved (possibly up to 20–30 within each cell, including spies/observers, messengers/runners and operators) it is likely the Germans would have caught one of them before long. Although as much effort as possible had been put into avoiding too much connectivity between individual members of a cell (so that one messenger/runner did not know who the next along the line was), just one person being taken out of the line could have had the potential to bring the whole cell down.

Wireless operators were especially at risk. Transmitting often from a set location meant that within a relatively short period the German Army would have tracked them down, and no matter the level of sophistication of your wireless base, they would eventually have been found – the Germans hunted SOE wireless operators tenaciously in occupied Europe and usually found what they were looking for.

Likewise, and something the operational patrols of the Auxiliary Units also had to contend with, if the invading army got wind of a spy network passing information on, there were likely to be ramifications for the rest of the population. Whether a network could continue operating in the face of individuals being taken as hostages, or swathes of the population being wiped out, is something, thankfully, they never had to find out.

CHAPTER 7

Signals and ATS

To make the most of the network of civilian spies, runners and messengers established under SIS, and the continuing recruitment of increasing numbers of them, a more military 'friendly' version (where information would reach key military decision makers quickly), of the organisation was top priority. The introduction of the wireless sets and the system of OUT- and SUB-OUT-Stations meant that this was now possible. However, wireless sets capable of being operated by civilians needed to be designed, manufactured, distributed and maintained in large numbers.

Ensuring that wireless sets were successfully distributed and running optimally meant that specific expertise had to be brought onboard quickly. The source of such expertise was found in a number of places, from groups of regular officers and signals men to civilian 'radio hams' that came together to form the Auxiliary Units Signals.

Auxiliary Units Signals

In September 1940, Gubbins recruited Captain John Hills. Hills's previous role had been Technical Maintenance Officer at No.1 Special Wireless Group (Y-Service). Gubbins wanted Hills to produce a new wireless system for the Special Duties Branch to help accelerate its move to military command and away from SIS.

By the time Gubbins left the Auxiliary Units to join SOE in November 1940, planning for the new set had barely left the drawing board. However, the new head of Auxiliary Units, Colonel Major, and Petherwick at the Special Duties Branch worked out how to move the transition more quickly and bring on board the necessary people and technology. Hills's part in this seems to have been pivotal.

In late 1940–early 1941 Hills, now with the title, Officer Commanding Auxiliary Units Signals, started to recruit 'radio hams' – some of whom were civilians who had a pre-war passion and expertise for radio sets. This new team began the process of designing and manufacturing a new radio set.

One of the first men to be recruited was Captain Ken Ward. Ward was to be Captain, Adjutant and Workshop Officer. Ward had, like Hills, been a part of the Special Wireless Group. In January 1941 Ward made his way to The Bull at Long Melford, Suffolk, where Hill was based. Also based there was Captain Freddie Childe, the newly appointed Special Duties Branch IO for Suffolk. Childe took Ward to a room in the pub that had been converted into an office, where Ward signed the Official Secrets Act and had his role explained to him.

A pub and a baker's shop (where Ward was to be billeted) were obviously not ideal places for a highly secret organisation to be based, and so a search began to find a more suitable HQ. The manorial house, Bachelor's Hall, just outside the village of Hundon in Suffolk, was identified. It had recently been vacated by a Manchester regiment as Ken Ward describes:

> Our first problem was to find a convenient, out-of-the-way base, preferably in East Anglia – the first area to be developed – where we could establish our activities. This resulted in us taking over Bachelors Hall, Hundon, (Suffolk) between Haverhill and Stratishall. It had recently been vacated by a Manchester Regiment and was pretty shoddy, but isolated, with plenty of accommodation and sufficient outbuildings for workshops and stores, and standing in several acres of ground, far from any other dwellings. It had a large kitchen with an Aga cooker, plumbing and hot water, etc. The main disadvantage was lack of electricity; so lighting was with pressure lanterns and in workshops soldering irons were heated with blow lamps.[1]

So, the task of designing a suitable wireless set was now very much underway. Finding funding for such a task was not too difficult either. Although SIS had given up direct control of the Special Duties Branch, by placing an SIS man, Petherwick, in charge. It also retained some control of the Special Duties Branch budget.

Hills's first radio set was the Savage set (manufactured by Savage and Parsons Ltd of Kingsbury). These were around the size of a shoebox and about 50 were produced in late 1940–early 1941. Indeed, it was Savage sets that provided the first radios for a trial taking place in Kent. The trial was designed to see how well a network of civilian wireless operators could work within a military set-up. It seems in Kent, at least initially, the Special Duties Branch IO was the same as the Auxiliary Units, with Peter Fleming working out the details.

> In Kent, a pilot scheme with a few civilian-operated coast stations (OUT-Stations) working to a Base Station (IN-Stations) at the static division, working with the county IO Peter Fleming, was already in place. Our brief was to establish similar networks along the coast from Berwick on Tweed to the Devon border. Close liaison with the county IOs was necessary to ensure that locations were suitable for siting concealed sets and aerials.[2]

While the trial itself was successful, the radio sets were proving to be increasingly troublesome. They were, according to Ken Ward, 'difficult to open, difficult to repair and not very well built'.[3] As a result, Ward and his team decided to come up with their own set. With a number of radio hams now on board, including Sergeant Ron Dabbs, remarkably a replacement was built within two weeks. It was called the TRD (Transmitter Ron Dabbs). It was housed in a metal case about 15 inches long, 9.8 inches wide and 9.25 inches high. It was deliberately designed for simple operation, with minimal controls and the transmitter set at a fixed frequency. The frequency was very high (60 or 65 MHz) and at the time it was not thought that the Germans would be able to trace such signals. The TRD used voice in plain language to transmit the information or very basic word codes. The frequency system meant that anyone using a 'normal' receiver would only hear a noise rather than a clear message and was the reason why only basic word codes were used, as there was a (misplaced as it turns out) belief that they wouldn't be heard in any case.

It had a range of 30–60 miles (and could occasionally reach much greater distances depending on the atmospheric conditions). At first the team were creating the sets themselves and gradually replacing the Savage sets that had already been sent out. The workshop was managing to produce seven or eight sets a week, a remarkable effort for a relatively small team. However, as the network of civilian wireless operators continued to expand, a commercial-like arrangement was needed to increase production while maintaining quality. By 1942 a contract had been given to Peto Scott Ltd, with Arthur Ward as contract manager. Throughout the war, the TRD was adapted and improved, but the level of secrecy remained so high that little is known about what these changes were. By the summer of 1944, 250 original TRD sets and 64 adapted sets were distributed across 30 IN-Stations, 125 OUT-Stations and 78 SUB-OUT-Stations, plus the headquarters for IOs[4], from Scotland to South Wales.

It was not just the various versions of the TRD sets that made up these numbers though. The WS17 set operated at a similar frequency and may have been introduced to allow for more effective communication between SUB-OUT- and OUT-Stations.

So, with a number of different bits of technology across the country, the signals team were required to go out to maintain the sets, check, change and recharge batteries, establish new sites, disguise aerial settings and more.

Therefore, groups of Auxiliary Units Signals men were dispersed throughout the country to service SUB-OUT-, OUT- and IN-Stations. Arthur Gabbitas, a member of the Auxiliary Units Signals, left some information, particularly about his recruitment (in November 1940) and his role as one member of a three-man team maintaining the wireless network:

> I was called up in 1940 to Catterick and trained as a wireless operator. At the end of our training, we were chosen for varying theatres five of us were designated to go to Auxiliary Units, although we weren't aware of what it was all about. We went down to Coleshill, where we spent several weeks whilst they were assembling the Signals HQ where they were building sets and trained in the use of these sets. I was then sent to Winchester where I spent some time and was then moved on to Buckland St Mary near Taunton, and then later on up to Lincoln where I continued until we were disbanded in 1944.
>
> We were in civilian billets and had to start work at eight o'clock in the morning. There were three of us: two wireless operators and an instrument mechanic. While one operator was at the Base station the other operator and the mechanic went to the OUT-Stations to take their batteries and charge them

so they always had fully charged batteries; if necessary, to check hidden aerials in the trees that they were still firm after the winds and that the down leads were still hidden under the bark. Of course, if there had been any operational requirements, we would have left our civilian billets and gone to our stations.[5]

Another member of the Signals support team was Bert Davies. After a period at Coleshill he was posted to the support team in Carmarthen and spent time servicing a number of OUT-Stations, including one in a church altar.

He also remembered, when his team were fitting or maintaining radios or batteries, they would not stop for more than a week at any time in any locality, presumably for security reasons in case of German invasion, but equally to avoid drawing too much attention to themselves with the local population. He was also able to confirm other information that we have a limited amount of detail on, particularly how radio messages were sent. He believed that messages should have been sent by the civilian operator using an encrypted standard army code sheet, but most were in fact sent in 'plain language'.

Stan Judson also confirmed that all messages were voice and not Morse code. He also remembered some of the difficulties in servicing and maintaining OUT-Stations without drawing attention to what they were doing. This became particularly tricky when other army units moved into areas where wireless sets were hidden.

Stan remembers servicing the wireless set at Woodhall Spa (the wireless unit that was run by Dr Armour and his red setters). At one point during the war an Ack-Ack unit was brought into the area, using the doctor's large garage as a store.

> The aerial was not in the garden, it was on a tree in the back of this empty garage. Well, what happened, later on the Army decided to put an Ack-Ack unit and all their guns in this garage, and their cook decided that the tree was just right for chopping his wood, and he severed the cable which was on this tree. So, we decided we would put a cable in another tree in the garden, which we did, but in case he discovered the old aerial – they had a sentry marching up and down and while he was marching I got over the fence and up the tree and recovered this aerial.[6]

Unfortunately, this wasn't the end of their trouble at the site:

> The guttering on this garage was very old, it began to leak, and if there was a rainstorm the water poured down on this shed and into our set in a box. So we then decided we'd have to move the set into the house, which we did. And everything worked alright until Jerry came over and dropped a bomb on the house.[7]

The incident Stan described took place on 17 August 1943 and the bomb was a huge parachute mine which caused substantial devastation. Dr Armour's wife was seriously injured and his children trapped. Dr Armour was away in Scotland at the time, but his son remembered how his father had been very anxious that the police might discover the set in the ruins before he had a chance to retrieve it.

Another member of the Auxiliary Units Signals team, Roy Russell, talked about his role travelling around the country, servicing and fixing wireless sets. The main faults, as he remembered, were usually with the aerials though:

> Communication at the high frequency we used required accurate direction for reliable reception. High winds or even branch growth could alter the delineation and lose radio contact. It would then be necessary for one of our several volunteers to go up the tree.
>
> He would be hauled up, standing in a noose of rope thrown over a high branch. The other end was attached to my Humber car, and by slowly backing, he would be drawn up the tree. Sometimes he had to climb the last few feet, carrying a bag of tools on his back. This was a job we shared in view of the risks involved.[8]

Russell, Gabbitas, Davies and Judson are just four examples of the men of the Auxiliary Units Signals who were constantly going around the country ensuring the radio sets, aerials and other equipment were in good working order. The work undertaken by the Signals men changed the dynamic of the Special Duties Branch from an effective but relatively slow-moving organisation under SIS to one that was able to pass on information quickly.

We have a picture then of the British public spying on the invading army, passing messages through dead-letter drops and messengers, ending with civilian wireless operators, whose sets were maintained by small groups of highly trained Signals men.

But where were the messages ending up? How could the network ensure that they reached the decision makers in a timely manner? Most of the civilian wireless operators had no idea who was receiving the messages, often only getting a 'Received' reply to confirm receipt of the information.

They may have been surprised to learn then that many were literally speaking to women of the Auxiliary Territorial Service (ATS), sitting in secret disguised bunkers, rather like those used by the operational Auxiliary Units.

ATS

The network comprised SUB-OUT-Stations and OUT-Stations which would send their messages to an IN-Station. These were staffed by military personnel who would be able to pass the information on directly to GHQ Home Forces and local units (although not the Auxiliary Units – more on this later).

Initially, IN-Stations were manned by the men of the Auxiliary Units Signals but soon, with the network expanding, the need for extra bodies (and to free up military manpower), it was decided that new wireless operators should be recruited from the ATS (the women's branch of the British Army).

The term 'Secret Sweeties' was first coined by David Lampe in his 1968 book *The Last Ditch*. The origins of this term are still unknown, and it is not something that has come up in any paperwork seen by the author or other researchers and, rather unfortunately, like many aspects of the Auxiliary Units, it has stuck. The term, apart from being unacceptable in the modern day, does a huge disservice to their role and the sacrifice they were willing to make had the Germans invaded.

Their role would have been to head to their secret underground bunkers as the Germans entered their area, and they would have been expected to stay underground for up to three weeks. Such a period of time in dark, dank conditions, while receiving potentially hugely important information and then passing that information on clearly and concisely in a timely manner, meant that finding the right type of person was crucial.

The first ATS operators were recruited by the chief controller of the ATS, Lady Bridget Helen 'Biddy' Monckton, the Countess of Carlisle. These first recruits were critical in setting up the trial cells in Kent at an IN-Station in Hollingbourne. The wives of some of the first Auxiliary Units Signals men were also brought into the fold, with Kitty Hills, the wife of Major John Hills, and Thea Ward, wife of Ken Ward, being two of the first Special Duties Branch operators in East Anglia. Forty-three ATS women were recruited during this initial stage.

However, as 1941 drew on, the recruitment of ATS was stepped up and Beatrice Temple was brought on board to head up the Special Duties Branch ATS. Temple was the niece of William Temple, the then Archbishop of Canterbury, and had already served for several years in the ATS. Her role as Senior Commander of Auxiliary Units ATS included the organisation and recruitment of ATS women who would be stationed at IN-Stations across the country. She was also responsible for their welfare.

These recruits were found in a number of places. Some were existing ATS officers, ATS other ranks, members of the Voluntary Aid Detachment (VAD) or the First Aid Nursing Yeomanry (FANY) or even, in a few cases, civilian women not engaged in war work. The first interview, rather bizarrely, took place in the public lounge on the fourth floor of Harrods in Knightsbridge.

Prior to and during the interview, the women were not told what they had 'volunteered' for or what qualities they were expected to display. Unknown to them, Beatrice Temple was not so much interested in what they were saying, but rather how they were saying it. It was critical that they had clear voices as all communication was via voice rather than code. Some women never heard anything more from their chat with Beatrice; others though were invited to the next stage.

They were told to go by train and get off at Haverhill station in Suffolk and head to the Rose and Crown pub. There, an army car with the number '490' would meet them and take them to a large farmhouse effectively in the middle of nowhere. In the farmhouse the women were given a slip of paper by an officer of the Royal Corps of Signals and were asked to read the contents into a microphone.

After a cup of tea, they were sent on their way, none the wiser as to their potential role, and put back on the train. Those whose voices were considered clear enough were then invited, much like the men of the Auxiliary Units, to visit the post office at Highworth and were picked up from there and taken to Hannington Hall. Only after they had arrived and signed the Official Secrets Act were they told that they were now part of the Special Duties Branch of the Auxiliary Units.

After training at Hannington, and in already established IN-Stations across the country, the ATS women were sent to their own stations. Many IN-Stations had an above-ground 'hut' which was to be used for training and practice, as well as giving a reason as to why ATS women were making their way to and from the location. However, had the Germans invaded, the ATS women would have made their way into their bunkers and begun their period underground, transmitting crucial messages (although in some cases bunkers were not built until later in the war and so ATS teams would have found themselves even more exposed working on the surface).

Again, like the operational patrols, training and exercises took place regularly. Every month, the ATS women were expected to enter their bunkers and live and work in them for the duration of the exercise.

In notes issued to all Special Duties Branch IOs in 1943 it was clearly stated how important the continuation of training was, even though the threat of invasion had greatly diminished.

> We consider that any group which practices fifteen times in the two month period is good
>
> It will, we think, be a stimulus to the maintenance of enthusiasm if members realise that by being a trained body in the defence of the country, they are actively assisting in providing reinforcements for theatres of war. A greater than ever responsibility will be laid on us as new offensives become developed.[9]

By stand-down it is estimated (based on a memorandum from Major Jones) that there were 30 IN-Stations, 125 OUT-Stations and 78 SUB-OUT-Stations. The nature of the OUT- and SUB-OUT-Stations mean that most have disappeared without a trace, with researchers relying on written and verbal testimonies from veterans. They were often within the house of the operator, an outbuilding or, if away from a residence, quite often simple shallow holes in the ground where the radio sets were kept.

However, the IN-Stations, or 'base stations' were very different. As has been described, many IN-Stations had huts or 'met huts' associated with them. Named met huts because they were furnished as though they were a meteorological hut, including barometric charts and other meteorological paraphernalia they were constructed in a number of ways: some were wooden huts, others Nissen-type buildings and some seem to have taken advantage of existing structures. Most of the IN-Stations were near or actually within the grounds of the local army HQ. This meant that incoming messages could be immediately passed on. For those IN-Stations a little further away, field telephones and GPO land lines were used to convey information. However, once the Germans had entered their area the ATS women would disappear to their nearby underground bunkers. Like the OBs used by the patrols of the Auxiliary Units, the underground bunkers of the IN-Stations have tended to survive or at least give us an impression of what working in such conditions might have been like.

It seems the first IN-Station bunkers were built in 1942. The Royal Engineers were brought in to dig and build the bunkers (all unaware of their intended purpose). Very much like an Operational Base, an IN-Station had a disguised entrance hatch that could be opened in a variety of ways. Unlike OBs though, the ladder leading into the bunker was one that could be removed. The permanent ladder of an OB allowed the patrol to go to and from operations. With the ATS women not expected to leave the bunker once ensconced inside, removing the ladder once in meant that it was another obstacle for any enemy soldiers who found the entrance.

Indeed, specific instructions were given to IN-Station operators in the event of the bunker being discovered.

No action whatever will be taken by the crew until it is definitely ascertained that the enemy have discovered and are about to open one of the hatches. When there is no doubt upon this point, the code word 'Scramble' will be transmitted three times.

When the enemy have discovered the secret entrance to the op room all sets, valves etc, will be carried into the chamber farthest from the hatch which the enemy appear to have discovered, all papers destroyed by fire and the sets rendered unworkable.

When this action has been taken, the crew Detachment Commander will lead the party and will get out as quietly as possible, followed by the two other operators.

The OC Det (Officer Commanding Detachment) will make every effort to kill the enemy. If, however, the party is too large for him to tackle, he will endeavour to escape capture and to make his way to join up with the nearest British troops.[10]

Edwina Burton, one of the ATS subalterns operating in Kent, remembers being trained to use weapons in case they were overrun. She was trained in using rifles, revolvers and sub-machine guns. Although the rifle and revolver practise did, by all accounts, not go so well, she enjoyed using the automatic weapon, spraying the target with bullets rather more successfully.[11]

One would imagine they would leave one bullet for themselves and, indeed, ATS subaltern Barbara Culleton remembered that she was issued with a cyanide tablet, to be used if the worst happened and she was about to be captured by the enemy.

It was in a tin and if it had ever been opened, they would have wanted to know why. All strictly secured but it was there, just in case. We were told the most horrific stories of what would happen if the Germans did invade. It didn't sound very pleasant, so maybe it was the best thing to do.[12]

Unlike the OBs of the Auxiliary Units, IN-Stations were made up of three chambers. The first chamber acted as a storeroom for spare equipment for the radio sets as well as anything the ATS women would need during the weeks they were expected to remain in the bunker. The second chamber was the wireless room, where the wireless sets would be operated. This chamber also housed the living quarters where bunks would allow one of the two ATS women in the bunker a place to grab some rest. A doorway would lead to the next chamber in which spare batteries and a generator were located. During training, the Auxiliary Units Signals teams would visit each bunker, check the sets and replace batteries. However, in the event of an invasion it would be impossible for the Signals teams to be wandering around the country replacing batteries. It would then fall to the ATS women to recharge the batteries themselves. Pipes took the poisonous exhaust fumes out of the bunker, but the danger of having petrol, oil, kerosene and batteries in a restricted underground space goes without saying. A bucket of sand was in place to sprinkle on any spilt fuel, as any fire would have been immediately disastrous.

The doorway between the wireless room/living quarters was sealed to ensure none of the invisible, but potentially deadly, fumes from the generator made their way into the part of the bunker where the operatives would be spending most of their time. The danger of spending extensive time underground with the generator, which the ATS women staffing the bunker would have done in the event of an invasion, is perfectly demonstrated by an incident remembered by Arthur Gabbitas. During an exercise, Arthur and his colleague, Alf Ellis, spent a large amount of time in a bunker.

> Early in the evening Alf's eyes glazed over and he collapsed. Fortunately, two officers were present to supervise the exercise but it still proved difficult for the three of us to lift the dead-weight person up the vertical ladder. We managed to drag him across the field to the staff car and rushed to the General Hospital where we received oxygen, though experiencing dreadful headaches. The next morning Alf and I were most annoyed because the attractive auburn-haired night sister had spent most of the night chatting to the officers and ignored us.[13]

Ellis's headache was not helped by the fact that during the effort to take his collapsed body out of the bunker, Gabbitas and the two officers inadvertently broke his nose!

The dark, dank and potentially dangerous conditions in which the women of the ATS would have entombed themselves if the enemy had come is very clear. As has been described, a key part of their training was spending large amounts of time in the bunkers, receiving and passing on practice messages. The conditions, as well as the relative loneliness of spending such prolonged periods of time underground, with maybe just one or two others and sometimes on their own, took its toll. There is at least one example of an ATS girl committing suicide while in the bunker, tampering with the exhaust on the generator.

Lord Bridgeman, Director General of the Home Guard, was an advocate for expanding their role to incorporate guerrilla warfare. (Author's collection)

Irene and Frederick Lockley – October 15th 1940
18years 22years.

Irene Lockley on her wedding day in 1940. Post-war, Irene, would reveal some of her Section VII training when 'dealing' with a persistent door-to-door salesman. (Jennifer Lockley)

Barbara Culleton, a member of the ATS team who were to receive information from civilian Special Duties Branch cells in their secret bunkers. She was given a cyanide pill in case of capture. (British Resistance Archive)

Elsie Rees told no one of her involvement in the Special Duties Branch. Only when relatives found specific paperwork in her belongings after her death did the story emerge. (Philip Smith)

Airlie Campbell joined the Auxiliary Units ATS in 1942, she was stationed in a number of IN-Stations throughout the rest of the war until stand-down. It was whilst at one of these IN-Stations that she met her future husband Clive Gascoyne, an Auxilier who accidently found her bunker. (Jim Gascoyne)

Joyce Harrison worked at County Hall in Chelmsford, Essex. Only later in life did she reveal her role as a runner/observer in the Special Duties Branch. Her first training session involved a moonlit night, blacking her face and delivering a sealed envelope to a hollow tree without being discovered. At the time of writing, Joyce is 104 and living in Canada. (Joyce Harrison)

The cup hooks in Chirnside 1 Special Duties Branch civilian wireless-set bunker. Turning one of these released a false wall revealing the radio room. (British Resistance Archive)

If a German patrol opened the door to the Chirnside 1 bunker, all they would have been confronted with was a run-of-the-mill outside toilet. (British Resistance Archive)

The fake tree stump that was in the middle of a hedge row on the border of the garden. Here, the message in a tennis ball would be placed. (British Resistance Archive)

By turning a disguised latch-rod, one is able to then return to the toilet and lift the whole system, revealing a ladder leading into the bunker. (British Resistance Archive)

The different kinds of dead-letter drops used by the Special Duties Branch. A split tennis ball with a message, a hollow key and a false gate bolt. (Martyn Allen)

A close-up of the false gate post where a message could be placed. Runners would know whether a message was secreted by the direction of a horseshoe on the gate itself. (Martyn Allen)

Two hollow keys that could easily be placed in doors. Picking up and delivering information in 'plain sight' would have been crucial in order to get it to authorities in a timely manner. (Martyn Allen)

Ron Dabbs was one of the 'radio-hams' recruited into the Auxiliary Units Signals team. He headed a team that created a suitable radio set for civilians in the Special Duties Branch to use. Remarkably the team achieved this in just two weeks (British Resistance Archive)

With no known TRD sets in existence, this example was built by Malcolm Atkin based on descriptions and notes by Auxiliary Units Signals personnel. (Malcolm Atkin)

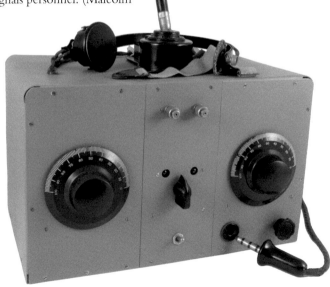

Above: The Thompson sub-machine gun was provided to Auxiliary Units before the Home Guard and, in some cases, the regular army too. (British Resistance Archive)

All members of the Auxiliary Units were issued a pistol, quite often the Smith and Wesson shown here. This is in contrast to Home Guard units, which struggled initially to secure weapons and ammunition. (British Resistance Archive)

A knuckle-duster utilised by the Auxiliary Units and Section VII alike. A silent weapon, perfect for dispatching of sentries. (British Resistance Archive)

Below: The Fairbairn-Sykes fighting knife. Distributed to the Auxiliary Units and a weapon that was held with some pride by patrol members – making them stand out as the elite. (British Resistance Archive)

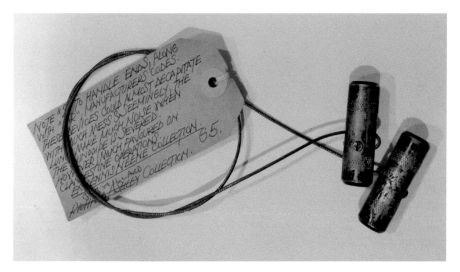

A garrotte used by Auxiliary Units patrols and members of Section VII. A brutal but effective way of dispatching the enemy silently and effectively. It epitomises the brutal nature of the fight these units would bring. (British Resistance Archive)

A collection of the key silent killing weapons the Auxiliary Units would have utilised in the event of an invasion. A brutal, ruthless and suicidal campaign of chaos would have ensued had the Germans come. (British Resistance Archive)

The key for the Auxiliary Units was not to get into a running battle. Even clubs and truncheons would have been used against sentries to gain access to targets. (British Resistance Archive)

Map of the Special Duties Branch radio network. Based on a hand-drawn map left by a member of the Auxiliary Units Signals, many of the civilian wireless-set locations remain unknown. (British Resistance Archive)

Undoubtedly, had the Germans come, the members of the ATS in the Special Duties Branch would have played a crucial but suicidal role in passing on information. Lampe, in *The Last Ditch*, talks about 93 ATS subalterns recruited. However, more recent documents that have come to light since 1968, seem to suggest that there were many more. During the life of the ATS Special Duties Branch, it seems much more likely that there were nearer to 150. Women moved within the organisation to HQ or to stores; others left to get married or have children. But all of them, during their time in the organisation, fully understood the risk they were taking and what was in line for them if the worst happened.

CHAPTER 8

Secrecy and Change of Role

The secrecy surrounding all of those in the Special Duties Branch was incredibly high. This is demonstrated by the likely number of people involved in all its areas and the very low percentage to have come forward and talked about their role.

That remarkable level of secrecy was maintained throughout the war. The fact that there are no recorded accidental discoveries of civilian wireless-set locations (unlike the discoveries of the OBs of the Auxiliary Units) tells its own story. Throughout the entire organisation the emphasis on secrecy was absolute.

Although the operational Auxiliary Units and Special Duties Branch were, for the most part, connected at the highest level of command, further down the chain there was little-to-no knowledge about each other's existence.

A document from the National Archives shows just how seriously this secrecy was being taken, even relatively late in the war when the threat of invasion had diminished. The document, dated 7 November 1943, states that:

1. Knowledge of the existence of the Auxiliary Units should be confined to persons who need it in the course of duty. As however a considerable amount of correspondence of a purely administrative and non-committal nature refers to these Units, it is not necessary for documents containing a bare reference to them to be marked SECRET

2. The functions of Auxiliary Units are MOST SECRET and any documents which refer to, or in any way suggest, their functions, or give any indication of their strength, will be graded MOST SECRET. Correspondence referring to their functions will be addressed personally to one of the officers specified in para 3; at GHQ it will be addressed personally to the M.G.G.S (Major

General General Staff), Colonel, G.S. (General Staff) or G.S.O 1 (General Staff Officer Grade 1)

3. Knowledge of the functions of Auxiliary Units before STAND TO will be confined to the following officers:
   a. At Command HQ
      i. G.O.C-in-C
      ii. B.G.S
      iii. G.S.O.1 or where none exists, the G.S.O.2 (Int) or the G.S.O.2 (Int a)
      iv. G.S.O.2 (Int b)
      v. G.E. (sufficient information for construction work only)
      vi. C.S.O (sufficient information to enable him to be aware of the general duties of Auxiliary Units)
   b. At HQ of Corps in touch with Auxiliary Units
      i. Commander
      ii. B.G.S.
      iii. G.S.O.2 (Int)
      iv. C.E. (sufficient information for construction work only)
      v. C.S.O (sufficient information to enable him to be aware of the general duties of the Auxiliary Units)[1]

The nature of the information being collected by the civilians in the Special Duties Branch, who were largely operating in the same areas as their operational Auxiliary Units patrol cousins, would have been hugely useful to those patrols. Instead of having to rely on one man looking out from his observation post or searching for targets on the way back from a mission at night, information coming into them in a timely manner could have made them more effective.

In some parts of the country, there might have been a link-up, with messengers apparently leaving information at dead-letter drops for Auxiliary Units patrols. The nature of being in such a secret organisation, with little-to-no idea of who else was in their group, means it is likely that some of this apparent link-up may be the result of confusion on behalf of the veterans. Oxenden, in his *Official History and Achievement of the Auxiliary Units*, mentions one example of a meeting between a key man of the Special Duties Branch and a group commander of the Auxiliary Units.

In May 1941, two fire-watchers, talking nearer and nearer to the point, turned out to be a Group Commander and a Key Man, Special Duties. The latter had no near prospect of getting an OB and was invited by the other to share his. The Commander was approached through the IO, with the result that a special conference on the link-up question was held in July. It was decided that this should only take place on a fairly high level – G.C. to Key Man – and in special circumstances; in no case would OBs be shared. Following this, a few exercises were run jointly by the IOs of the two sides, during the ensuing year, but they seemed to lead to nowhere, and with our changing operational policy, the link-up was allowed to die a natural death.[2]

The separation of the two groups is highlighted by the fact that Oxenden was asked to only write about the Auxiliary Units and not the Special Duties Branch in his official history. Indeed, throughout he very clearly separates the two groups whenever he mentions the Special Duties Branch. It might be that an official history of the spies, wireless operators and ATS women exists but, if so, it has yet to be released or found.

Speaking to veterans of both groups, there is a general acceptance that they had no idea about each other at grass-roots level. Auxiliary Units veterans turning up to the first reunion at the British Resistance Organisation Museum, in Parham, Suffolk, in the late 1990s were shocked to find that not only was there a separate group of spies and wireless operators, but their own unit was a national one, and not just confined to their particular area.

There is one remarkable exception to the Auxiliary Units and Special Duties Branch being kept entirely separate on the ground. It involves Private George 'Clive' Gascoyne of the Lynsted Patrol (Lynsted is situated between Sittingbourne and Faversham in Kent) and ATS Second Subaltern Airlie Abinda Campbell.

While on patrol in his local area, Clive Gascoyne happened upon a disguised hatch, very much like his own OB entrance. Recognising that this was likely to be too close to his own bunker to be another patrol, he decided to investigate. Finding a way into the bunker, Clive made his way down the ladder where he was confronted by Airlie who was pointing a revolver at his head.

All Clive knew was that a mystery woman with a gun was in a bunker with wireless sets, and all Airlie knew was that a strange, heavily armed man in denims had just discovered and descended into her IN-Station.

They eventually agreed not to shoot each other and went their separate ways, but not before they had started chatting and presumably swapped contact details, as by January 1944 they were married, and in May of the same year Airlie had left the ATS to give birth to their first child. Because both had signed the Official Secrets Act, they could never tell anyone how they met. This amazing story demonstrates two things: firstly, it highlights just how the two organisations were kept completely separate despite their commonality in terms of senior command. Secondly, it shows just how close units of the Auxiliary Units and Special Duties Branch were geographically located to one another.

Change of role

Like the operational Auxiliary Units patrols, the role of the Special Duties Branch morphed as the war went on. Indeed, while the Auxiliary Units' role faded as the likelihood of invasion decreased, the Special Duties Branch, and particularly the ATS teams in the IN-Stations, became increasingly relevant and useful.

As the operational patrols began to train for German raiding parties, so did the men and women of the Special Duties Branch. This became particularly important in the run-up to D-day, when the fear of Germans coming across the Channel to disrupt training and destroy ships and landing craft was a very real one. The location and nature of the IN-Stations meant they were well positioned in case of an enemy attack on a local HQ, particularly if local lines of communications had been broken by German parachutists.

Indeed, this is emphasised by the IOs 'Monthly Notes' in August 1943, which stated that IN-Stations should be manned 'by night, as well as by day, in all raid areas'.[3] This new anti-raiding role also saw an increase in the distribution of the WS17 wireless sets. These sets, although less secure than others, particularly the TRDs, were quicker and more efficient, which in an anti-raiding role was considered far more important.

It was not just the anti-raiding role during the run-up to D-day where the members of the Special Duties Branch may have played an important role. There is some evidence that the network of spies, wireless operators and ATS teams were asked to spy on their own population.

Harking back to its origins as an SIS-led organisation (and as an organisation still partially funded for a time by SIS), the Special Duties Branch operatives were asked to perform another, potentially critical, role in the run-up to the invasion of Europe. In 1943 and early 1944, there was no real reason to keep the group and its hugely complicated system of spies, runners, civilian wireless operators and ATS women in place. The Germans were not coming and yet the group was not stood down until the summer of 1944.

From a spying perspective, all of the civilians had already demonstrated their ability and commitment to the cause over the past couple of years. Adding to this, most had also signed the Official Secrets Act and so could be trusted to be told snippets of information and listen out for others talking more openly about the forthcoming invasion. Virtually nothing is known of the spies and runners involved in the Special Duties Branch and it might be that their role morphed into listening into the conversation and gossip of locals and, more importantly, members of the armed forces stationed in their area.

The need to keep the location and timing of the invasion under wraps was key. Any decent German spy would have been listening out for the same information and so if a Special Duties Branch spy was able to identify a possible leak or a soldier letting out too much information when at the pub, then it would be possible for the authorities to plug that leak. This would certainly go some way to explain why the complex network was kept up for so long. It could also explain why there appears to have been Special Duties Branch groups in Worcestershire and Herefordshire. Lowry and Wilks have identified a couple of possible sites in their *The Mercian Maquis* book, which of course could not have been playing the same anti-invasion role as those on the coastal crust.

This internal security role has been further enhanced by the stand-down letter sent by General Franklyn, Commander-in-Chief of GHQ Home Forces. One paragraph from the letter, in particular, highlights what role the Special Duties Branch might have played.

> In recent days while our own invasion forces were concentrating, an additional heavy burden was placed on those of you responsible for the maintenance of good security to ensure that the enemy was denied foreknowledge of our plans and preparation. The Security Reports provided by Special Duties have proved of invaluable assistance to our security staffs.[4]

Another possible reason, and again linked to D-day, was the Special Duties Branch role in Operation *Fortitude*. *Fortitude* was the Allies' operation to put Hitler and the Nazi high command off the scent of where the D-day landings were to take place. It came in two parts: *Fortitude South* and *Fortitude North*. *Fortitude South* was to persuade the Germans that the attack was coming across the Straits of Dover to land in the Pay-de-Calais, and *Fortitude North* hinted at an invasion leaving Scotland to land in Norway.

Fortitude was implemented in a number of ways. In the south–eastern corner of Britain, an entirely fictitious army group was created. The First US Army Group (FUSAG) was placed under the 'command' of General Patton (who was currently unemployed, but who the Germans respected and expected to play a major role in an invasion). Created to 'threaten' the shortest route across the Channel, *Fortitude South* included groups of inflatable tanks positioned to catch the eye of any German reconnaissance planes and any German spies that may have avoided detection. Alongside inflatable tanks, dummy aircraft and landing craft were placed at probable embarkation points, with Patton visiting many of them accompanied by a photographer to make sure the Germans saw what they wanted them to see. *Fortitude North* had similar aims and roles with the entirely fake British Fourth Army 'headquartered' in Edinburgh Castle.

One tactic that covered both *Fortitude South* and *North* was the use of fake radio traffic to simulate the normal radio traffic of army groups training and communicating. With a group of civilian and ATS wireless operators already in place, it seems that the Special Duties Branch was ready made to help in this deception campaign.

Warwicker contends that '200 standard War Department No. 17 radio sets'[5] were issued to Special Duties Branch throughout the South East and East Anglia. Operatives were told to work the sets night and day in the same areas, transmitting 'any old rubbish'.[6]

The WS17s were known to be easily intercepted by German radio listeners and it looks like this knowledge was used in an attempt to further persuade the Germans that the likely location of the long-anticipated invasion of occupied Europe would be Calais. Warwicker's claim is backed up Roy Russell who, in his memoirs, also remembered the effort of the Special Duties Branch around D-day.

> Our tiny contribution, although I only guessed at the time, was to step-up our on air-traffic. We made hundreds of meaningless five letter coded group messages and transmitted them to our OUT Stations for their 'dummy traffic' responses; round the clock.[7]

There has been some uncertainty as to just how much Special Duties Branch did take part in *Fortitude*. Apart from Warwicker and Russell's testimony, there is little other evidence pointing to the use of WS17 sets. Indeed, one of their colleagues, Ken Ward, contended that the WS17 sets were used to allow the ATS teams to communicate from the met huts to the army/divisional HQ when it was realised that the HQ might have to move in the event of a German invasion.[8]

A directive sent to the British No.5 Wireless Group and the American 3103rd Signals, the two 'official' wireless groups that were sending misleading radio signals for the Germans to pick up on as part of *Fortitude South*, also casts doubt on the role of the Special Duties Branch's role:

> You must realise that the enemy is probably listening to every message you pass on the air and is well aware that there is a possibility that he is being bluffed. It is therefore vitally important that your security is perfect.[9]

The likelihood, therefore, is that IN-Stations and OUT-Stations sending and receiving meaningless messages would go against the aim of the deception. However, no matter the level of truth behind the stories of involvement in Operation *Fortitude,* it would go some way to explain why Special Duties Branch was kept active so late in the war – although it was stood down earlier than the operational patrols of the Auxiliary Units, the civilians, ATS and Signals teams that carried on until July 1944.

Stand-down

Elsie Rees (née Jones) was a very intelligent and astute woman working as a solicitor's clerk in Monmouthshire. She had, by March 1942, married Glyndwr Rosser 'Glyn' Rees of the Indian Army and while her husband served in Iraq and North Africa, Elsie stayed with Ceiriog and Ethel Smith, her brother-in-law and sister, and lived and worked as any other 'ordinary' civilian during the course of the war. It was only after Elsie's death in 2003 that the true nature of her role in the war came to light through some paperwork found amongst her belongings. Her role as a solicitor's clerk saw her working for Colonel Kenneth Treasure, a local solicitor. Treasure, like his father before him, qualified as a solicitor in 1937 and joined the family firm. For much of the war he was in the Monmouthshire Regiment, serving in the Far East. However, by February 1944 he was back in South Wales and at some stage took over the role as the key man in the area, likely taking the place of his father. This cell had a sophisticated underground bunker and was an allocated SUB-Outstation reporting into the Coed-y-Caerau OUT-Station.

Elsie was anything but an 'ordinary' civilian; she was a highly trained observer/spy, a fundamental part of this Special Duties Branch cell. Like so many others in the organisation, she told no one of her role. The documents found in her belongings were the first clue to her relatives and friends and give a rare insight into the process of shutting down a highly secret and nationwide organisation.

Three documents were found including the stand-down letter from General Franklyn to Colonel Douglas (head of the Special Duties Branch), in which he described the internal security role that the Special Duties Branch played in the run-up to D-day, as discussed above). Like the stand-down letter sent to the operational patrols of the Auxiliary Units, it made it very clear that despite their role coming to an end, secrecy was still of paramount importance.

> As no public recognition can be given for this job so well done, it is my wish that a copy of this letter be sent to all members of the Special Duties organisation as my own acknowledgement of the value and efficiency of their work.[10]

As the letter was found in the possession of Elsie, it seems, in South Wales at least, copies were passed on.

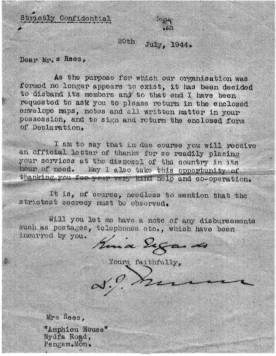

A remarkable document from Elsie Rees. It confirms the stringent approach to the collection of equipment and materiel associated with Special Duties Branch at stand-down. (Philip Smith)

Another document was a letter from Colonel Douglas in which he thanks all members of the Special Duties Branch for their service 'keenness and enthusiasm which has been an inspiration to us one and all'.[11] He summarises the current state of the war and how the Allies were in an advantageous position and on the 'eve of, and fully prepared for the greatest tank battle of the war'.[12]

These letters were delivered in early July 1944 and were both very similar to the letter received by the operational patrols of the Auxiliary Units. However, the third document gives real insight into the logistics around dismantling such an organisation.

Dated 20 July 1944, the letter confirms stand-down but also requests the return of all training materials. The effort to gather all equipment associated with the Special Duties Branch seems to have been comprehensive, certainly in contrast to the Auxiliary Units, where we have seen huge amounts of explosives and arms remaining unclaimed right into the 1960s and 1970s.

The nature of the materiel and equipment used by the Special Duties Branch, although not as immediately 'dangerous' as the weapons of the operational patrols, was highly sensitive.

The letter, which is headed 'Strictly Confidential', states:

> As the purpose for which our organisation was formed no longer appears to exist, it has been decided to disband its members and to that end I have been requested to ask you to please return in the enclosed envelope maps, notes and all written matter in your possession, and to sign and return the enclosed form of Declaration.[13]

It was not just the written material that was so thoroughly collected though. The TRD wireless sets distributed throughout the vulnerable counties were collected without exception. It was not GHQ collecting the wireless sets but SIS, which had kept a subtle but steady hand in the Special Duties Branch throughout its existence.

Every single TRD set was collected and apparently destroyed. There are no remaining original sets in existence. The only example being made in the last few years based on drawings and descriptions.

Inner Control network

Among the many mysteries that continue to surround the Special Duties Branch is a set of Inner Control stations that stretched across the width of the country. Unlike a majority of the IN-, OUT- and SUB-OUT-Stations, which were based around the coastal crust, these Inner Control stations, as the name suggests, were located inland.

Certainly, information from a number of IN-Stations and regional HQs seemed to be ending up at Reigate, Surrey where there was a large underground complex built at the top of Reigate Hill as a divisional command bunker. It is likely the Special Duties Branch moved into an existing underground complex and that the ATS women at Reigate were based in met huts, like those in other locations were, during training. Indeed, when Beatrice Temple visited the site on 15 June 1943, she noted she had visited a 'new hut' which was 'very grand'.

Alongside Reigate, a map left by Major R. M. A Jones, Commanding Officer of the Signals group of the Auxiliary Units suggests another chain of internal stations, reaching from the Signals HQ at Bachelor's Hall in Suffolk, and connecting Ousden, Suffolk; Ware in Hertfordshire; Chesham in Buckinghamshire; and Hickleton Hall (Doncaster, Yorkshire) to Coleshill House HQ.

Some of these IN-Stations may have existed as part of SOE/SIS transmitter stations or Y intercept stations and, like Reigate, Special Duties would have taken their place at an existing site.

As stated, the network stretched east to west, connecting the Suffolk coast to the HQ at Coleshill. The exact purpose of the Inner Control is yet to be determined. The fact that it seems to link Bachelor's Hall with Coleshill House might give some indication that there was some direct communications between the two, across the network.

The exact location of most of the Inner Control stations is also unknown. Most were probably met huts and so very little evidence would remain today.

Limited role

Had the Germans invaded, all members of the Special Duties Branch, from civilian observers, runners and radio operators to the Signals team and the ATS women staffing bunkers would have been active for a minimal amount of time. Each of them fully understood the huge risk they were taking, but their role was limited.

It was simply an information-gathering service, one that, once in the hands of the military, allowed vital information to be passed on quickly to those in a position to make decisions about the positioning of British regular forces. There was no analysis of the information being gathered within the Special Duties Branch; it was simply a tool to get the information quickly. The Blitzkrieg of mainland Europe struck fear and uncertainty into the senior figures of GHQ. Undoubtedly, the Special Duties Branch developed as a result of this, and the introduction of wireless sets meant the information could travel faster than the invading army.

However, this would have likely been for a very short amount of time. The fixed locations of the civilian wireless sets meant they were going to be tracked down quickly by the invading army. Runners potentially criss-crossing front lines, in and out of German-held territory, were unlikely to have lasted very long. The Signals teams, after invasion, could no longer carry on monitoring and maintaining radio sets; and ATS women were only too aware that, once the Germans reached their area, they would be underground until the Germans discovered them or the British liberated them.

Despite this, all were prepared to do their duty and to carry on for as long as possible. Like the operational patrols of the Auxiliary Units, there was no public recognition at all for their commitment. Apart from the few remaining ATS bunkers, there is also very little tangible evidence of their roles and potential sacrifices, with most going to the grave without telling anyone. That in itself is a credit to their ongoing and absolute commitment to the secrecy they were urged to keep.

Part III

Post-Occupation Resistance

CHAPTER 9

SIS Section VII

SIS's role in the early stages of the Auxiliary Units and, in part at least, throughout the life of the Special Duties Branch has been discussed. The fact that SIS was willing to hand over both arms to the military, without much of a fight, makes sense when one considers the role both units were to play.

As both were to act solely during the invasion stage and not for any long post-occupation role, it made sense that the military had control over both, allowing GHQ to integrate them into the overall defensive strategy. However, SIS had already begun to put into place another secret civilian group that was trained only to act after occupation had taken place. The civilians recruited to this organisation, called Section VII, were given only the very basic information needed to undertake their future task. They certainly had no idea they were working for SIS but rather were informed that it was something vaguely to do with British intelligence.

This was due to the high levels of secrecy surrounding the group but also because SIS (later MI6) was not meant to be operating within the UK, with its remit set outside of the country (and MI5 operating within the borders of the UK). As with the HDS, civilians were sought out to volunteer for a highly secret role. However, unlike HDS and the resulting Auxiliary Units and Special Duties Branch, the civilians being approached by SIS for this group were not to be active during the period of invasion. Instead, they were to remain inactive until the occupation had started. At this point, the men and women of Section VII would start their work. Some were messengers and wireless operators; others were saboteurs and resistance fighters, more in line with the French resistance groups. In the years since the end of the war, and certainly since David Lampe's *Last Ditch* was published in 1968, the role of the Auxiliary Units has been described as the 'British Resistance'. However, as we have discovered, the Auxiliary Units were an anti-invasion unit; Section VII is much more representative of what would have been a British Resistance force had the Germans come and stayed for any length of time.

The story of Section VII starts in the spring of 1940, when SIS was beginning to replicate some of the planning work on resistance forces it had been discussing with European countries as part of Section D. Now with Britain under threat, SIS had the experience and the opportunity to set up a post-occupation resistance in advance of any invasion.

In a counter-factual scenario where the British had been defeated militarily, the royal family whisked away out of the country (probably to Canada), with Churchill lying dead in the smoking ruins of Whitehall, the Germans would in all likelihood be setting up an administration much like they had in other parts of occupied Europe.

Using a British figurehead (possibly one or a combination of Lord Halifax and Lloyd George), the Germans would have begun the rapid occupation of the country, potentially dividing Britain, as it had done to France, into occupied and unoccupied zones (and thus reducing its need to allocate much-needed resources across the whole country). In this scenario, SIS had begun to work out how an underground resistance force might work, how it could pass messages on from occupied territories to unoccupied areas, how acts of resistance against the occupying forces could be coordinated by those British leaders carrying on the fight from elsewhere and even how information about the occupying force could be transmitted to an exiled British government.

All of this was being considered very quietly, ensuring the military did not get to hear about it. Indeed, the level of secrecy (and age of those recruited) meant that information has only come to light very recently indeed. In the 2010 official history of MI6, Keith Jeffery gives the first indication of Section VII and its role (Section VII was officially the accountancy arm of SIS and so acted as the perfect cover for this group – not arousing suspicion from anyone who overheard conversations about the cells). It is very brief but does give a little and the only 'official' insight into how this group began and how it expanded. Jeffery states that by July 1940, there was active recruitment of civilian 'agents'. The section was led by Valentine Vivien, head of Section V (SIS counter-espionage); Richard Gambier-Parry, head of Section VIII (communications section focusing on improving the communications systems of SIS); and SIS agent, David Boyle (a close friend of SIS chief Stewart Menzies and head of Section N which focused on the interception of diplomatic mail). They initially recruited six agents across the country and provided them with and trained them on wireless sets. They then ran a war game to check the effectiveness of the group.

> They trained and equipped six agents with wireless sets in Norfolk, Suffolk, Sussex, Somerset, Cornwall and Devon, deployed mobile signals units across home commands and successfully ran a war game code-named 'Plan 333'. This had produced good signalling and 76% deciphered messages.[1]

After this successful trial, SIS extended its recruitment, which Jeffery claims to have included 24 'head agents' with wireless sets.[2] Like the recruitment of civilians to the Special Duties Branch (which after all was very much an SIS enterprise before being handed over), recruitment was restricted to those who 'by the nature of their occupation could remain in enemy controlled territory and continue their occupations without arousing suspicion'.[3] So doctors, dentists, chemists, bakers and small shopkeepers were all targeted. Not only did these professions allow the agents to continue their work post-occupation and move around easily, but it also allowed them to receive visits from many people, without drawing attention to themselves.

All of these recruits will have signed the Official Secrets Act and we know almost nothing about these early agents. Another factor of recruiting such agents is that most would be beyond the age of call-up. This meant there wasn't a constant need to find new recruits, nor would the cell network be put at risk if they were called into the regular forces. The negative side for historians is that, as a result of their age, most had died long before anything about Section VII had come to the surface.

However, there appears to be one exception to this rule. In the Derbyshire town of Matlock one Section VII agent was able to tell his story. Peter Attwater was a 14-year-old ARP messenger when, in late May–early June 1940, he was approached by a local journalist and ARP organiser for the area, Frank Ford. Ford had got to know Attwater in his duties with the ARP and recognised him as a teenager with a good memory and artistic skills. Attwater was also a member of the Air Training Corps and as an air cadet had received some military training, including weapons handling and how to operate a wireless set.

He was introduced to a Captain William Lawrence who was attached to a 'mysterious military intelligence establishment at Matlock Hydro with the seemingly innocuous role of billeting officer and quartermaster'.[4] It seems likely that Lawrence had been seconded to SIS to manage the network and used his role at the Hydro as his cover.

Attwood described being taken to a 'Zero Station' which is the same term used by Special Duties Branch later in the war and one that perhaps points to similar beginnings with SIS organisations. He knew of the existence of three wireless stations in the local area, but the one he was connected to was at 135 Smedley Street, Matlock.

> At the time the building was the premises for a working tailor's shop belonging to Mr H Toplis. Although the wireless station remained there throughout its operational life, under active service conditions the equipment was portable and would have been moved around to avoid detection.[5]

This is an interesting contrast with the wireless sets of the Special Duties Branch, which were static, either associated with the job of the operator or in a bunker. It highlights the difference of the two roles the groups were to play. Special Duties Branch were not expected to last for any length of time. Its role was to collect information on the invading army and as individual cells they were, frankly, not expected to survive any longer than two to three weeks. The civilians of Section VII, however, in their roles of post-occupation resistance, were expected to last for a much longer period – passing information for weeks at a time and carrying out acts of sabotage for, if possible, the duration of the occupation.

Attwater signed the Official Secrets Act and was introduced to two female recruits, a Mrs Key and Miss Swans. Key and Swans were wireless operators working under the 'keeper' Mr Toplis in his tailor shop. The wireless set was hidden in an alcove behind a rack of uniforms in the back of the shop. A revolver and a grenade (with its pin stapled to the table to allow for a quick one-handed withdrawal) were always kept beside the wireless set. A window in the room provided the only escape for the wireless operator (and the wireless itself).

Like the Special Duties Branch operators, the wireless operators of Section VII units did not know who they were sending information to (and only received the message 'Received, Control Out' during training).[6] Attwater's role was one of a courier and observer (again very close to the roles to be played by civilians during the invasion period under Special Duties Branch). He learnt how to move through the town at night without being discovered (using his work as an ARP messenger as cover). He also had a specific task to identify an abandoned building (he found a stable) where any fugitives of the occupation could be hidden before moving along an escape line.

Attwater also described other training he took part in:

> The Winter Gardens at the Hydro were transformed into a display of German (and later Italian) uniforms displayed on dummies, badges, equipment, army signs with many photographs of German vehicles and markings, and senior German officers' individual uniforms and decorations and accompanying security staff so that they could be studied and memorised for later reporting if they were seen in the area.[7]

The role of Section VII seems to have been a combination of Auxiliary Units and Special Duties Branch, something that is highlighted by Attwater's memory of various caches and dumps spread around the town.

> An ammunition cache was kept at the Masson Cavern. There were also locations for rendezvous and hiding, such as Jugholes and a tree-filled ravine on Masson hillside known as Northwood (after the war it was incorporated into a quarry). There were extensive quarry workings in Matlock at the time where magazines

of explosives were hidden. If the invasion signal had been given there were unit members who would have emptied these magazines to store the contents in other secret locations.[8]

There were also fuel dumps around town (including a store full of 2-gallon petrol cans secreted amongst logs, to be used in the making of Molotov cocktails, with a spigot mortar and a number of mortar bombs hidden in a scrap iron dump behind Matlock Town Hall). Later in the war, in early 1941, Attwater was invited to a meeting in Birmingham attended by six other young men (likely to all be couriers as Attwater was). The others came from Birmingham, Manchester and Nottingham and would be his contacts had the invasion occurred. Each was given a codename and the meeting was run by a strict, ex-NCO-type disciplinarian and, according to Attwater, 'the most frightening man I have ever seen'.[9] There were other 'smartly dressed civilian instructors' at the meeting who focused on the safety phrases to prove the recruits' identity to each other. These were very likely to have been SIS agents. Indeed, the codes they were given points markedly towards a secret service approach.

> On meeting they were to follow the traditional British habit of discussing the weather: each of the seven men had a key word they would use, which together spelt out the word BRITISH, thus **B**lizzard, **R**ain, **I**ce, **T**hunder, [more] **I**ce, **S**now, **H**ail. Attwater had to work the word 'Ice' into a conversation with a contact.

Peter Attwater has given us one of the only first-hand accounts of an individual in Section VII. However, there is a large amount of second-hand information that has come to the attention of historians over the past few years. Much of this has come through relatives recounting stories told by family members.

Nottinghamshire provides another example of a possible Section VII. Ex-mine worker Eric Deverill told his son, Ian, just before he died in 2004, that he had a secret role during the war. In 1940, aged 18, Eric was approached by a Colonel John Chaworth-Musters DSO of Annesley Hall to lead a cell of five men comprising three colliery workers, Jack Attwood, Jack Kirk and Charlie Bramley; a poacher called Kelly Cooper; and Frank Saint, the gamekeeper at Annesley Hall.

Chaworth-Musters had served during the First World War: he'd commissioned in the South Notts Hussars, serving in Egypt and taking part in the Gallipoli campaign at Suvla Bay in 1915 before returning to Egypt and Palestine. By the end of the war, he was with the Warwick and South Notts Hussars Machine Gun Battalion in France. He had inherited the Chaworth-Musters estates in 1921, which included Annesley Hall and the associated park.

This is important, as it seems a bunker of some sort was built in the dense pine forest on the Annesley estate. With the hall itself a likely option as a German HQ after any occupation, it was a key target, and so the bunker will have been well positioned. The cell had also placed explosives in two nearby main railway tunnels, the local electricity sub-station and the telephone exchange.

Post-war, Ian had written down the stories his father had told him and had soon begun to collate quite an incredible story. His father, by all accounts, had become slightly concerned by Ian starting to dig for further evidence and took steps to keep the secret, as Ian describes:

> Eventually I aroused my father's suspicions and he became so horrified with the amount of information I'd accumulated, he contacted the intelligence services who talked him through destroying any documentation that might verify his activities. On his death, the lack of paper and photographic evidence of his life was shocking to our family – the house appeared to have been professionally cleaned.[10]

The fact that Ian believes his father contacted the 'intelligence services' for advice on how to clean up is interesting. An ex-colleague of Eric's has also contacted the author. He worked with Eric at Annesley Colliery, and they knew each other well. He remembers in the mid-1980s Eric confiding in him that he and his wife, Joan, had received a 'reminder' that they were still bound by the Official Secrets Act. The fact that his wife was included in this reminder makes it all the more mysterious. Was Joan the wireless operator with the group of colliery workers acting as the sabotage wing of the cell?

Another interesting piece of evidence is a piece of documentation that Eric's son Ian saw before his father destroyed everything. He remembers clearly that he saw two different identity cards identifying him as 'Captain Eric Deverill, Military Intelligence MI7'.

MI7 was the press and propaganda section of the War Office in the early months of war, before being transferred to the Ministry of Information around June 1940. It seems a strange fit then for an 18-year-old mine worker to be connected to this group. Might the answer actually be connected, not to MI7 but Section VII? It certainly makes sense, matches to the type of cell and the type of activity Eric and his comrades were looking to undertake.

Another possible Section VII is located in Yorkshire. A letter from Jennifer Lockley reached the author telling of how her mother had suddenly revealed her wartime role over an 'aperitif' during her final years. Her mother, Irene, lived in the village of South Milford in the West Riding of Yorkshire, near to Leeds. She told her daughter that Churchill had ordered groups of people across the country to become 'urban fighters if the invasion had happened'.[11] Irene described her particular unit as a 'special group, usually related by blood or marriage, who met underground and trained to kill, maim and cause as much damage to the enemy as possible'.[12]

It seems that Irene's father, already a member of the Home Guard, was also in the group, alongside herself and a cousin who was a butcher and two more male relatives. They 'were taught how to derail trains, how to make Molotov cocktails to throw into enemy tanks and other vehicles, how to garotte, unarmed combat, recognise aircraft and may other skills related to warfare.'[13]

Her group met in an old quarry near their village, going under a trap door that led into a secret underground room, where there was a radio and where she learnt Morse code. Again, much of this sounds very similar to the Auxiliary Units. However, with none operating in the area, with women very much part of the units and radio sets belonging to each cell, it is likely to be associated with Section VII. Irene only told her daughter this information the day after the 50-year rule had passed on the Official Secrets Act that she and her relatives signed when joining the group. Her revelation, however, did start to make sense of memories from Jennifer's childhood. One particular story highlights the skills these civilians were armed with. In the early 1950s, Jennifer remembers a pots and pans door-to-door salesman coming around to their house. His sales technique was somewhat aggressive, and he would not take no for an answer from what he perceived to be a 'normal' housewife. When the salesman put his foot in the door to continue with his patter, Irene's wartime training seems to have kicked in. Jennifer remembers the man suddenly summersaulting through the air, pots and pans flying, landing with a bang. Presumably somewhat shocked, he grabbed his wares and fled. This story not only highlights the impressive nature of the skills and training these civilians received but also why women were eagerly recruited. The presumption made by the salesman would have been the same as that made by any soldier in an occupying force.

Another woman involved in a very similar group was Priscilla Ross (known as Joyce or Judy) in Hornchurch, East London. Her daughter, Susan, describes her mother as skilled in archery and fencing and an accomplished horsewoman.

In 1940 Priscilla was 18 years old, living in Hornchurch with her mother (her father had been gassed in the First World War and had died of septicaemia by the time Priscilla was 11). The cell Priscilla was a member of had its base under the local church. The entrance could be accessed by sliding the top of one of the tombs in the cemetery to the side and climbing down.[14]

She too was taught unarmed combat and how to make Molotov cocktails. Just in the brief details we have of Priscilla's units, the connections with those of Irene are clear. Women and men were being recruited in inland towns and cities across the country. They were being trained in unarmed combat, in the production and use of Molotov cocktails and how to use communication equipment.

The fact that women were involved pushes these groups away from the military and much more in line with the activities of SIS. SIS seems to have had no problem with the recruitment of women or teenagers. In other parts of the country, there is evidence of recruitment of teams of teenagers trained as assassins had the Germans invaded and occupied Britain. Four teenage 'sharpshooters' were picked out from a school cadet corps. They were, according to John Warwicker, put through 'sophisticated training in marksmanship, disguise and deception'.[15] These four boys had a cover story that they were training as Home Guard messengers. They were provided with a range of weapons including a .22 rifle with telescopic sights (like those provided to the Auxiliary Units), explosives and an underground base. Interestingly the training was undertaken by 'two hard, mature men dressed as Army NCOs in battledress without insignia'.[16] This is a very similar description to the NCO-type of 'scary' men brought in to teach Peter Attwood and his fellow teenagers in Matlock. It seems very likely that SIS was bringing ex-regular army NCOs into the intelligence service to train young teenagers in a whole range of anti-occupation tactics.

The training of civilian snipers under SIS also appears to have taken place in Liverpool. William Hughes had served with the King's Liverpool Regiment in the First World War, where he specialised as a 'sharpshooter'. He served as a teenager in 1914 until he was captured during the German Operation *Michael* offensive in March 1918, by which time he was a lance corporal. By the beginning of the Second World War, he was 42, with a family of nine to look after. He did, however, like many of his age, volunteer for the Home Guard, but his story is not quite as simple as that. Unbeknownst to his wife and children, William had joined what he later described as a 'special auxiliary unit' that was set up when the fear of invasion was at its height.[17]

His group were billeted in secret tunnels under St George's Hall and in the disused feeder tunnels that were created when the first Mersey Tunnel was built. It was here they stored all kinds of weapons and explosives. William believed there were special 'hit squads' set up along the south Lancashire coast to target paratroopers, as it was felt this is where they would land to then move immediately south to seize the docks in Liverpool.

However, William's role was not as a combatant but as an instructor, teaching those who came to the tunnels how to become an effective sniper. With his experience during the First World War and as an ex-NCO, this seems to fit very well with the other evidence from Matlock and the other teenagers Warwicker spoke to.

Indeed, stories of tunnels being used as HQs and also explosives and weapons stores bear a remarkable similarity to the Hydro at Matlock as well as the other dumps described by Peter Attwater.

These teenagers were, from an SIS perspective, perfect recruits. Motivated to take on the invader, and with the naivety of youth, they also had the fitness and natural athleticism to complete a hugely physical task. Undoubtedly, had the occupation come and these boys were called into action, they were unlikely to last very long. The author's own grandfather, Anthony Butcher, was a teenager based in Surrey during the war. 'Tony' did not reveal his own role but hinted of something highly secret, telling his new wife in the early 1950s that he was involved in something he could not tell her about but mentioned special training and dum-dum bullets. Like Peter Attwater, Tony was also an ARP messenger and a member of the ATC and had specific training in wireless operation. No hard evidence has been found to confirm Tony's role. Like Ian Deverill found with his father, there is very little evidence of any official paperwork from the period, and his wife (the author's grandmother), although convinced that Tony was 'up to something' in the war, knew, or at least said, nothing to her family.

Just how many teenagers were recruited during the early part of the war is unknown. Almost all of them died without telling anyone, belonging to the generation that took the signing of the Official Secrets Act as a lifelong commitment.

These groups, waiting for the German Army to push inland and begin occupation, represent the 'true' British Resistance. It was they, who had been told to keep on with their daily work until the Germans had taken control, that would have represented Britain's ongoing struggle against the enemy, even in the face of a military defeat.

Conclusion

On 4 June 1940, Churchill delivered one of his most famous speeches. In the face of the now inevitable military defeat in France and in an effort to both check the mood of the public, which was jubilant at the number of troops returning from Dunkirk, as well as preparing them for a possible invasion. He spoke about the reality of the situation, and in his concluding remarks he uttered some of the best-known sentences in Britain's history.

> We shall go on to the end, we shall fight in France, we shall fight on the seas and oceans, we shall fight with growing confidence and growing strength air, we shall defend our Island, whatever the cost may be, we shall fight on the beaches, we shall fight on the landing grounds, we shall fight in the fields and in the streets, we shall fight in the hills; we shall never surrender

This speech summed up the mood of the country. The determination to fight on, no matter what came over the Channel was a real one. However, what Churchill's speech also illustrated, consciously or not, was that there were layers of defence, from the coastal crust right into the centre of the country. The role that civilians would have played had the Germans come would have been immense. Unlike mainland Europe, the military and intelligence services had the opportunity to plan and recruit 'ordinary' civilians to assist in the nation's defence.

The narrative of ordinary citizens stepping up in the fight to defend their island has tended to be focused on images of old men lining the cliffs with a ragtag assortment of homemade or ancient weapons. There is a certain national pride in this perception, which has allowed it to continue and grow over the decades. However, as we have seen, it does not represent reality.

The early days of the LDV were somewhat chaotic; the almost spur-of-the-moment decision to create the force, the number of volunteers and the lack of equipment and uniform made it seem amateurish. It is these early days of the LDV that have coloured our impression of all of the British defences throughout the Second World War. This has been built on over the years since the end of the war. *Dad's Army* and the like have had a double impact on our impression of Britain during this period. There has been a real positive in that the civilians who volunteered have remained in the consciousness of the nation and were not forgotten as a side show that was never called upon. However, it has also tainted our perception, and this has influenced a national pride based on a brave but amateur force.

A reputation has associated itself around this pride, one of Britain 'playing with a straight bat', playing by the rules, no matter the cost to itself. The truth is, of course, that Britain has never been like that. Building and policing a huge empire during the nineteenth century could not have been achieved with such an attitude and this had not changed by the time the Second World War started. The narrative that has been built since the war gives a very different impression and is perhaps why the training and potential actions of the units this book has discussed often come as a shock to many who hear it for the first time.

The levels of ruthlessness, particularly those associated with the Auxiliary Units, Home Guard guerrilla sections and Section VII, could be seen as shocking. This reflects not necessarily the character of the civilians but their situation. The Auxiliary Units in particular understood that the main limitation impacting their role was time. Therefore, anything that could extend, or at least not reduce, the amount of time they could be effective would have been carried out. Whether this was the assassination of their own IOs, an elderly couple who witnessed the building of an OB, or anyone who was asking too many questions, undoubtedly, they would have been dealt with.

This gives us an insight into how effective these units might have been had the Germans come across the Channel. Both the Auxiliary Units and Special Duties Branch were anti-invasion forces. There was no expectation that they would operate for any length of time and so their impact on the enemy could only ever be short, so it had to be severe. Every eastern and southern coastal county would have had groups of heavily armed and extraordinarily well-trained civilians ready to disrupt the invading force, no matter the cost to themselves and potentially their families and local community. There were spies in the same areas, ready to report on the enemy's movements and numbers, to give those in command the opportunity to make informed decisions about counter-attacks and their future defensive strategy.

The fact that both of these groups tended to have static bases highlights how slender those training them thought their chances of survival were. The most incredible thing is that almost all of the veterans that have spoken were more than aware of this.

Delivering a short, sharp shock to the invading forces would undoubtedly have had an impact on the Germans. After experiencing sabotage and guerrilla warfare as soon as they made their way inland, it is no stretch to imagine that at every bridge, country house and airfield, at every turn in the road and every time they were on duty at night, there would be an expectation and fear that they might be next.

However, in occupied Europe, this fear manifested itself in the form of brutal attacks on the local population in revenge for or in anticipation of guerrilla action. German forces would have considered Auxiliary Units and Special Duties Branch terrorist cells. They would have been dealt with in the harshest manner, as would the local population. One just needs to look at the French village of Oradour-sur-Glane. On 10 June 1944, a Waffen-SS officer had been taken prisoner by the local resistance forces. As revenge, an SS Panzer Division (recently returned from the Eastern Front), sealed off Oradour-sur-Glane and ordered the men of the village into barns and sheds. Firing at the legs of the men so they were unable to move, they then set the buildings on fire. They placed all the women and children of the village in the church and proceeded to set it on fire too, machine gunning any of those trying to escape. In all, 642 civilians were killed. This is an extreme example and rare in Western Europe, but all too common on the Eastern Front. The impact of this type of revenge action on the respective units is, of course, unknown, but at the very least would have piled pressure and strain on individuals and teams, leaving them with a hugely difficult decision as to whether to carry on operations.

Since stories of the Auxiliary Units and Special Duties Branch first started coming out into the public in the early 2000s the word 'resistance' has been associated with them. This has misled some to consider them to be a long-term resistance and believe that they were the only organised resistance units recruited. Certainly, both groups would have resisted the invasion, but with neither expecting to survive more than two or three weeks, there was no expectation of undertaking an extended resistance. It would have been a suicidal effort to attempt to hold up the invading forces to allow the Regulars to gather themselves and counter-attack, led by information gathered by the Special Duties Branch.

Although, generally, the Home Guard shock squads/guerrilla sections would have had to wait a little longer for the Germans to enter their areas, as they were mainly based more inland, their role would have been similar to that of the Auxiliary Units but with less comprehensive training and fewer weapons. Their life expectancy is difficult to estimate, with some of those who spoke expecting to continue in a longer-term role; others, perhaps more realistically, anticipated a similar life expectancy as the Auxiliary Units. All of these units were under some form of military control, either GHQ or more loosely connected to Home Guard units. As anti-invasion forces this made sense. Anything that would be dealing with a post-occupation resistance had to come from the intelligence services.

As we have seen, other, even more secret, groups of civilians were also being recruited the length and breadth of the country to act in this post-occupation role. These groups should be considered the 'real' resistance forces and are much more in line with the resistance groups in occupied Europe. Fighting, monitoring and resisting an occupying force, trained by and led by SIS, (which had begun planning for such forces on mainland Europe and was using that experience to prepare Britain for the worst-case scenario), these cells of civilians were designed to hamper any move into an easy occupation for the Germans.

It seems as though more thought had been given to the longer-term survival of Section VII in particular. Wireless operators were given the ability to move their sets and change location, unlike those working with the Special Duties Branch who were restricted to one location. Although trained and prepared very much like the resistance forces on the European mainland, it is not clear how long they were expected to survive. Unlike mainland Europe, there was no easy base from which an invasion to liberate Britain could be launched from. Even if there was an unoccupied zone, the level of influence the Germans would have held over it would have been considerable (like Vichy France). Therefore, although trained to be operational over a longer period of time, it was still essentially a suicidal mission. It is difficult to see what success would have looked like for members of Section VII. Remaining active until any liberation came would have been highly unlikely.

It is clear that – despite the secrecy surrounding all of these civilian groups – they were all prepared to make the ultimate sacrifice for their country in its darkest hours. The type of people recruited meant that once they signed the Official Secrets Act, or had been sworn to secrecy, they were likely to take their role and stories to the grave, and so it proved. With so few individuals talking about their wartime experiences in these groups, and the authorities remaining equally as quiet, it is no wonder they have not received the credit and recognition that they so rightfully deserve.

It is only within the last few years that the Auxiliary Units and Special Duties Branch were granted the right to march at the Cenotaph on Remembrance Sunday – the Home Guard, the Bevin Boys and the Land Army all having been given the right many years before. The role that the Coleshill Auxiliary Research Team (CART) played in securing that honour for the few remaining veterans was pivotal, as is the continuing work of the group to find out more about these remarkable civilian volunteers.

We will probably never know the true number of civilians who volunteered for these various organisations. Very soon there will be no survivors to tell their tales and we will have missed the chance to understand the real story of Britain's defences during the Second World War.

For too long these brave, determined and modest civilians have been hidden within the story of Britain's war. For too long the nation has taken pride in an inaccurate and somewhat dismissive view of those volunteering to defend the country in its hour of need. In reality, men and women of all ages, from all backgrounds, across the country were preparing to make the ultimate sacrifice for their country, preparing to be utterly ruthless in their prosecution of their duties and to do all of this without telling a soul. Now is the time to look back with pride, and in some awe, at the reality and to be thankful that they were never called upon.

Investigating Service in Secret Units

These secret units are so compelling because there is little evidence as to who was involved. The prospect of a relative belonging to one of the groups is an intriguing one, but with so little tangible evidence remaining, what clues can people look out for to give them some indication of their relatives' involvement?

Physical traces

The very nature of these groups means there was never any large amount of physical material pointing to a person's involvement. No one from any of the groups described (with the exception of the Home Guard guerrilla squads) were entitled to the Defence Medal (which was handed out to members of other civilian groups operating in the UK, such as the Home Guard, Air Raid Precautions, Auxiliary Fire Service, etc).

One of the key pointers for families looking for proof of their relative's involvement in the Auxiliary Units is the lapel badge that was handed out to members of patrols in 1944. In the form of a shield with the numbers 203-202-201 embossed on it in the GHQ colours of red and blue, it is a distinctive item. However, unless you know what you are looking at, it is not obvious that this is associated with the Auxiliary Units. However, we know that some of the badges were never handed out, remaining for one reason or another with the group commander. Often those patrol members who had joined the regular forces later on in the war may not have received a badge, especially if they were not demobbed until after the war had finished.

So, whilst the lapel badge is a good piece of evidence not all Auxiliers received them.

The Auxiliary Units were the only group to receive such an item at the end of the war. However, the Special Duties Branch and Auxiliary Units did receive a stand-down letter. It does not appear to have been handed out as comprehensively as the badge and, as a fragile piece of paper, must have been ripped and destroyed over the course of the last 80 years in most cases. Like the badge, unless relatives know what they are looking at it, is not immediately clear that it is anything significant and, indeed, the Auxiliary Units letter could well be associated with the Home Guard. The documents that Elsie Rees had in her possession, discussing the returning equipment, are very rare (indeed possibly the only remaining example). Any paperwork associated with either group is very rare, but relatives should look out for any notes headed with the Coleshill House address or 'GHQ Auxiliary Units'. Many of these letters are also headed 'SECRET', which gives an indication that this might not be run-of-the-mill correspondence.

Elsie Rees's paperwork makes it clear that, in terms of equipment, the Special Duties Branch was comprehensive in the collection of all equipment it handed to civilians. It is unlikely, therefore, that there is anything remaining in the homes or possessions of Special Duties Branch personnel.

The Auxiliary Units, in contrast, seem to have been left with vast quantities of weapons, explosives and other equipment. This book has already described the efforts made to locate and destroy the Operational Bases were largely unsuccessful and it seems the same can be said for the collection of equipment. The list of explosives left over in the possession of Essex Area Commander, Captain Reg Sennitt, gives a real indication of the level of equipment left in the hands of Auxiliers after stand-down. Most of the Auxiliers who had explosives in their possession used them post-war – on their farms or even in the celebrations of VE Day. However, some families continued to find explosive material in the sheds and outbuildings of parents and grandparents, although this is getting increasingly rare. Any family members that do find suspicious-looking material should, of course, immediately notify the authorities. However, some of the devices

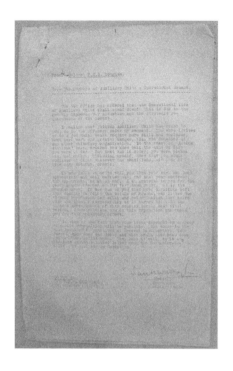

The letter from Colonel Douglas (the last commander at Coleshill House) to members of the Auxiliary Units. It makes it very clear that no public recognition will be possible. (British Resistance Archive)

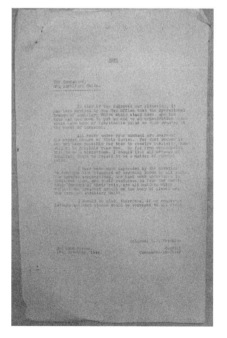

The letter from General Franklyn (C-in-C Home Forces) to Colonel Douglas in November 1944. He was impressed with 'their readiness to face the inevitable dangers of their role'. (British Resistance Archive)

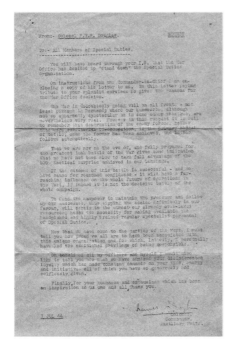

The stand-down letter from Colonel Douglas to the members of the Special Duties Branch. (Philip Smith)

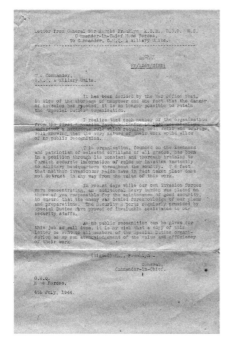

The letter from General Franklyn to Douglas hints at civilians compiling security reports on breaches of security in the run up to D-Day in June 1944. (Philip Smith)

associated with explosives are harmless and can point to a relative's involvement in the Auxiliary Units or even Section VII. Pull switches, pressure switches, time pencils, fuses and booby-trap devices are often found in toolboxes and, again, give a really good indication of a relative's involvement in some type of sabotage organisation.

Later in the war, as they came more into the regular army establishment and were given specific Home Guard and county insignia, the Auxiliary Units' uniform changed. Some members of patrols may have kept their uniform insignia (usually Home Guard shoulder insignia, county badge and either the 201, 202 or 203 badge depending on where they were based). Again, these are relatively rare to find but would give a very strong indication that a family member was involved at a late stage of the war at least.

These tend to be the main pieces of physical evidence and are often the first signs that a relative was involved in something other than the mainstream Home Guard. However, there are other areas in which relatives can look for clues.

Documentary traces

A good starting point for researching possible relative involvement is the staybehinds.com website. It is here that the research undertaken by CART is documented, with members of the public able to search by name, patrol, county and the Special Duties Branch radio network. Aside from this, the National Archives do hold some records about the Auxiliary Units and Special Duties Branch. Searching can be tricky, as they are not always labelled correctly or accurately (usually due to the highly secret nature of the organisations in question).

Correspondence between Gubbins, Churchill, Ironside and others are also available, but the most useful documents are the list of names of patrol members, their addresses and some other details that give absolute proof of a relative's involvement. The National Archives records, approximately WO199/3388-3391, include each county's relevant details (if you cannot get to the archives, then the CART website has all of the names listed). They are not listed in specific patrols, but just as names and addresses. This confirms they were in the Auxiliary Units but not which patrol they were in. However, if their address is included in the document, it can give a clue to their patrol through their proximity to a particular Operational Base.

However, the lists only include those men in the Auxiliary Units post-circa 1942. This means that many men who had joined in the early days of 1940 and had either left or joined the regular forces before 1942 are not included in these documents. It also means that there are potentially whole patrols that were created in 1940 but had been closed down by the time the lists were put together. This might give some explanation as to some of the gaps that are apparent when one looks at the distribution of patrols in the UK.

As you can see, even with documents in the National Archives, there is often no easy answer to whether a relative was involved in the Auxiliary Units. At least there are lists of names of those involved in existence. The same cannot be said for the Special Duties Branch (as far as is known at the time of writing) nor the potentially thousands of civilians involved in Section VII.

Post-war and recollections

The most common clues as to whether a relative was involved in any of these secret groups are their recollections. Too often, but perhaps understandably, tales told by those in these secret units have been dismissed by relatives in the years since the end of the war. A number of times I have spoken to a relative who has exclaimed that they wished they had taken these hints more seriously and asked more questions. It is entirely likely that any further questions would have resulted in a silence anyway, but even these snippets can provide some insight into their possible role.

Guarding against exaggeration or false memories (sometimes influenced by things they have seen, read or heard since the war) is of course important but sometimes even the smallest detail that a relative might have dropped in conversation can point to something significant. Listening out for or remembering certain phrases that often come up in discussion with veterans is a good first step. Often, instead of referring directly to belonging to one of these groups, veterans will refer to something else, hinting at its real role. For example, those in the Auxiliary Units describe belonging to a 'Special Home Guard', the 'Home Guard SAS' or 'doing something different with the Home Guard'. These types of descriptions can indicate service in the Auxiliary Units or even the Home Guard guerrilla forces but often point to something a little different in terms of what they were involved in. Mentions of silent killing or explosives can also indicate a role in one of these anti-invasion groups. Also, post-war strolls into copses where a father would disappear for a short time (or even taking sons and daughters to an air raid shelter in the woods) can obviously indicate an Operational Base.

In terms of Special Duties Branch, local rumours of 'spies' can often indicate a local cell, particularly when mentioned alongside wireless sets. Activity at night or taking part in special training (particularly for women) also highlights possible involvement in the Special Duties Branch.

Any female relatives who have knowledge about unarmed combat or talk about a special combat role during the war could be indicating involvement in a post-occupation force. As we have seen, women (and sometimes teenage girls) were trained by SIS to undertake acts of sabotage and assassination against occupying forces. As the regular army did not utilise women in any role involving combat, it is likely they were more aligned with the secret services.

Notes

Introduction

1   Hansard, https://api.parliament.uk/historic-hansard/commons/1940/may/22/local-defence-volunteers.

2   https://api.parliament.uk/historic-hansard/commons/1940/may/22/local-defence-volunteers, p. 243.

Chapter 1

1   John Warwicker, *Churchill's Underground Army* (Frontline Books, 2008), 17.

2   Malcolm Atkin, *Section D for Destruction* (Pen and Sword Military, 2018), 15.

3   Warwicker, *Churchill's Underground Army*, 31.

4   The National Archives, HS7/5, 'Notes and Lessons by Laurence Grand, 1946.

5   Warwicker, *Churchill's Underground Army*, 178.

6   Interview with Peter Wilkinson and Mark Seaman, 1993: IWM Audio, Cat. No. 13289, reel 5.

7   Joan Bright Astley, *The Inner Circle* (Memoir Club, 2007), 32.

8   David Lampe, *The Last Ditch* (Cassell and Company, 1968), 84.

9   Peter Williams Productions, *Secret Army*, Episode 1, 2003.

10 Malcolm Atkin, *Fighting the Nazi Occupation* (Pen and Sword Military, 2015), 65.

11 Testimony of Andrew Croft, British Resistance Archive.

12 Testimony of Nigel Oxenden, British Resistance Archive.

13 Lampe, *Last Ditch*, 68.

14 Nigel Oxenden (researched & compiled by Andy Taylor), *Auxiliary Units History and Achievement 1940–1944* (British Resistance Organisation Museum, 2000), 2.

15 Ibid., 3.

16 Ibid., 25.

17 Testimony of Bentley Patrol, British Resistance Archives.

18 Peter Williams, *Secret Army*, Episode 2 (Peter Williams Productions).

19 Adrian Hoare, *Standing up to Hitler: The story of Norfolk's Home Guard and 'Secret Army'* (Countryside Books, 2002), 235.

20 Testimony of Bob Millard, British Resistance Archive.
21 A. E. Cocks, *Churchill's Secret Army and other recollections* (Book Guild Publishing, 1992), 16.
22 Oxenden, *Auxiliary Units History and Achievement 1940–1944*, 3.
23 Testimony of Edward Batton, British Resistance Archive.
24 Donald Brown, *Somerset v Hitler* (Countryside Books, 1999), 69.
25 Testimony of Frank Blanchard, British Resistance Archive.
26 Hoare, *Standing up to Hitler*, 235.
27 Peter Williams Productions, *Secret Army*, Episode Two.
28 Testimony of the Icklesham Patrol, British Resistance Archive.

Chapter 2

1 Testimony of William Ratford, British Resistance Archive.
2 Bernard Lowry and Mick Wilks, *The Mercian Maquis* (Logaston Press, 2012), 79.
3 Interview with author, October 2021.
4 Ibid.
5 Lowry and Wilks, *The Mercian Maquis*, 79.
6 Somerset County Archives, DD/SLI/12/2/26.
7 Nigel Oxenden (researched & compiled by Andy Taylor), *Auxiliary Units History and Achievement 1940–1944*, (British Resistance Organisation Museum, 2000), 28.
8 Peter Williams, *Secret Army*, Episode 2 (Peter Williams Productions).
9 Alan Williamson, *East Ridings Secret Resistance* (Middleton Press, 2004), 86.
10 Interview with author, October 2021.
11 Testimony of Henry Hutchins, British Resistance Archive.
12 Arthur Ward, *Churchill's Secret Defence Army* (Pen & Sword, 2013), 93.
13 Ibid.
14 Testimony of Gilbert Smith, Fritham Patrol, British Resistance Archive.
15 Testimony of Bert Verney, Tawstock Patrol, British Resistance Archive.
16 https://www.staybehinds.com/coleshill/coleshill-house.
17 David Lampe, *The Last Ditch* (Cassell and Company, 1968), 80.
18 Lampe, *The Last Ditch*, 81.
19 Testimony of Bob Millard, British Resistance Archive.
20 Ibid.
21 Ibid.
22 Ward, *Churchill's Secret Defence Army*, 80.
23 Lampe, *The Last Ditch*, 79.
24 Testimony of Bob Millard, British Resistance Archive.
25 Interview with author, October 2021.
26 Testimony of Bob Millard, British Resistance Archive.
27 Somerset County Archives DD/SLI/12/2/26.
28 Testimony of Walter Denslow, British Resistance Archive.

29 Donald Brown, Somerset vs Hitler (Countryside Books, 1999), 99.
30 Ibid., 100.
31 Peter Williams, *Secret Army*, Episode 4 (Peter Williams Productions).
32 Testimony of Herman Kindred, British Resistance Archive.
33 Peter Williams, *Secret Army*, Episode 3 (Peter Williams Productions).
34 Ibid.
35 Ibid.
36 Interview with author, October 2021.
37 Geoff Elliot, *Colyton at War* (Colyton Parish History Society, 2007), 33.
38 Lampe, *The Last Ditch*, 110.

Chapter 3

1 Peter Fleming, *Invasion 1940* (Rupert Hart-Davis, 1957), 270.
2 Nigel Oxenden (researched & compiled by Andy Taylor), *Auxiliary Units History and Achievement 1940–1944* (British Resistance Organisation Museum, 2000), p. 6.
3 Personal interview with Fred Clarkson of Chardstock, with Martyn Allen (British Resistance Archive), 14 March 2017.
4 David Lampe, *Last Ditch* (Cassell and Company, 1968), 94.
5 Evelyn Simak and Adrian Pye, *Churchill's Secret Auxiliary Units in Norfolk and Suffolk* (ASPYE, 2013), 39.
6 Ibid., 40.
7 Bernard Lowry and Mick Wilks, *The Mercian Maquis* (Logaston Press, 2002), 61.
8 Ibid.
9 Somerset County Archives DD/SLI/12/2/26.
10 Ibid.
11 Ibid.
12 Ibid.
13 Bernard Lowry and Mick Wilks, *The Mercian Maquis* (Logaston Press 2002), 62.
14 Somerset County Archives, DD/SLI/12/2/26.
15 Interview with author, October 2021.
16 Oxenden, *Auxiliary Units History and Achievement 1940–1944*, 4.
17 Ibid.
18 Pelynt Patrol report, British Resistance Archive.
19 Interview with author, October 2021.
20 Oxenden, *Auxiliary Units History and Achievement 1940–1944*, 27.
21 Weapons-Explosives-Equipment Auxiliary Units, British Resistance Archive.
22 John Warwicker, *Churchill's Underground Army* (Frontline Books 2008), p. 130.
23 Oxenden, *Auxiliary Units History and Achievement 1940–1944*, 28.
24 Testimony of Nevern Patrol, British Resistance Archive.
25 Glenn Aitken Patrol report, British Resistance Archive.

26 Testimony of Trevor Miners, Perranporth Patrol, British Resistance Archive.
27 Oxenden, *Auxiliary Units History and Achievement 1940–1944*, 4.
28 Ibid., 12.
29 Ibid., 30.
30 Testimony of Gilbert Smith, Fritham Patrol, British Resistance Archive.
31 Testimony of Jonah Patrol, British Resistance Archive.
32 Oxenden, *Auxiliary Units History and Achievement 1940–1944*, 30.

Chapter 4

1   Nigel Oxenden (researched & compiled by Andy Taylor), *Auxiliary Units History and Achievement 1940–1944* (British Resistance Organisation Museum, 2000), 13.
2   Ibid., 15.
3   Ibid., 10.
4   John Warwicker, *Churchill's Underground Army* (Frontline Books, 2008), 93.
5   Oxenden, *Auxiliary Units History and Achievement 1940–1944*, 16.
6   Ibid., 13.
7   Testimony of Jim Holt, Crawle Patrol, British Resistance Archive.
8   Oxenden, *Auxiliary Units History and Achievement 1940–1944*, 17.
9   Testimony of Samuel Gilling, Sandford Levvy Patrol, British Resistance Archive.
10 Drake IoW Orders, British Resistance Archive.
11 Ibid.
12 Testimony of Len Escott, Jonah Patrol, South Wales, British Resistance Archive.
13 Testimony of Len Crackett, Acklington Patrol, British Resistance Archive.
14 East Anglian Auxiliary Units Badge document, British Resistance Archive.
15 Ibid.
16 Bruton Patrol, Somerset testimonial, British Resistance Archive.
17 Testimony of Leslie Bulley, Langstone Patrol, British Resistance Archive.
18 Interview with author, October 2021.
19 Testimony of Arthur and Gerald Dunford, British Resistance Archive.
20 Peter Fleming, *Invasion 1940!* (Rupert Hart Davis, 1957), 273.

Chapter 5

1   Austin J. Ruddy, *To the Last Round: The Leicestershire and Rutland Home Guard* (Breedon Books, 2007), 149.
2   Ibid., 49.
3   Malcolm Atkin, *To The Last Man* (Pen and Sword, 2019), 46.
4   'The Home Guard', *The Times* (15 August 1941).
5   Viscount Bridgeman, 'The Home Guard', *Royal United Services Institute Journal*, vol. 87, no. 546 (1942): 144.

6   S. P. Mackenzie, *The Home Guard* (Oxford University Press, 1996), 106.

7   Petherick to Grigg, 7 March 1942, The National Archives WO 199/363.

8   The National Archives, WO 199/361.

9   The National Archives, WO199/1869.

10 The National Archives, WO 199/364.

11 Tom Wintringham, *New Ways of War* (Penguin Special, 1940), 31.

12 Ibid., 73.

13 Ibid., 119.

14 Ibid., 119.

15 Charles Graves, *The Home Guard of Britain* (Hutchinson & Co, 1943), 79.

16 Mackenzie, *The Home Guard*, 75.

17 Graves, *The Home Guard of Britain*, 79.

18 Ruddy, *To The Last Round*, 143.

19 Ibid., 147.

20 Ibid., 145.

21 Ibid.

22 Ibid.

23 Ibid.

24 Ibid.

25 Interview with Derek Manning and the British Resistance Archive.

26 Ibid.

27 Ron Freethy, *Lancashire 1939–1945: The Secret War* (Countryside Books, 2005), 159.

28 Ruddy, *To The Last Round*, 145.

29 Defence of Britain Archive, https://archaeologydataservice.ac.uk/archives/view/dob/ai_full_r.cfm?refno=6725.

30 Family interview with author, May 2021.

31 'Sabotage Key Holders', *Leicester Mercury* (11 September 1964).

32 Atkin, *To The Last Man*, 52.

33 Ibid.

34 Bernard Lowry and Mick Wilks, *The Mercian Maquis* (Logaston Press, 2002), 113.

35 Ibid., 114.

Chapter 6

1   James Holland, *The War in the West* (Corgi, 2015), 350.

2   The National Archives, HS 8/214, 'Report VIII on the activities of D Section during July 1940', 4.

3   Malcolm Atkin, *Fighting Nazi Occupation* (Pen and Sword, 2015), 114.

4   The National Archives, WO 199/1194.

5   The National Archives, WO 260.9, 2.

6   Malcolm Atkin, *Section D for Destruction* (Pen and Sword, 2017), 20.

7   Douglas Mill Saunders, British Resistance Archive.

8   Arthur Douglas Ingrams, British Resistance Archive.

9   Evelyn Simak and Adrian Pye, *Churchill's Most Secret Special Duties Branch* (ASPYE, 2014), 7.

10 Ibid., 131.

11 Interview with author, March 2021.

12 Testimony of George Vater, British Resistance Archive.

13 Ibid.

14 Interview with author, March 2021.

15 Testimony of Jill Monk (née Holman), British Resistance Archive.

16 Ibid.

17 Simak and Pye, *Churchill's Most Secret Special Duties Branch*, 133.

18 Marjorie Sargeant, *Woodhall Spa: Past and Present* (Woodhall Spa Cottage Museum, 2006), 176.

19 Testimony of Beatrice Temple, British Resistance Archive.

20 Great Glenham OUT-Station, British Resistance Archive.

21 Smeaton OUT-Station, British Resistance Archive.

22 Captain Hugh May, *Chirnside 1* (Dudfield Publications 2014), 31.

23 John Warwicker interview with Stanley Judson, Imperial War Museum Ref. 29468.

24 Adrian Monck-Mason, British Resistance Archive.

25 Simak and Pye, *Churchill's Most Secret Special Duties Branch*, 120.

Chapter 7

1   Kate Ward, *Kenneth Martin Ward: Episodes in a Life* (British Resistance Archive), 17.

2   Evelyn Simak and Adrian Pye, *Churchill's Most Secret Special Duties Branch* (ASPYE, 2014), 15.

3   Ibid., 17.

4   The National Archives, WO 199/936.

5   Imperial War Museum, Ref. 14819/2.

6   Imperial War Museum, Ref. 29468.

7   Ibid.

8   Memoirs of Roy Russell, British Resistance Archive.

9   Monthly Notes to IOs No. 5, July 1943.

10 Simak and Pye, *Churchill's Most Secret Special Duties Branch*, 90.

11 Bernard Lowry and Mick Milks, *The Mercian Marquis* (Logaston Press, 2002), 119.

12 *Open Country*, BBC Radio 4, 8 January 2004.

13 Memoirs of Arthur Gabbitas, British Resistance Organisation Museum.

Chapter 8

1   The National Archives, WO199/1194.
2   Nigel Oxenden, *Auxiliary Units History and Achievement 1940–1944* (British Resistance Organisation Museum, 2000), 11.
3   Monthly Notes for IOs No. 6, August 1943, British Resistance Organisation Museum Archive.
4   General Franklyn to Commander of GHQ Auxiliary Units stand-down (4 July 1944), British Resistance Archive.
5   John Warwicker, *Churchill's Underground Army* (Frontline Books, 2008), 185.
6   Warwicker, *Churchill's Underground Army,* 185.
7   Roy Russell's memoirs, British Resistance Archive.
8   Captain Ken Ward, Imperial War Museum audio tape 29472.
9   Joshua Levine, *Operation Fortitude* (Collins, 2012), 238.
10 General Franklyn to Commander of GHQ Auxiliary Units stand-down (4 July 1944), British Resistance Archive.
11 Colonel Douglas to members of Special Duties Branch (7 July 1944), British Resistance Archive.
12 Ibid.
13 Letter to Mrs Rees re. return of equipment (20 July 1944), British Resistance Archive.

Chapter 9

1   Keith Jeffery, *MI6: The History of the Secret Intelligence Service* (Bloomsbury, 2010), 361.
2   Ibid.
3   Ibid.
4   Malcolm Atkin, *Fighting Nazi Occupation* (Pen and Sword, 2015), 145.
5   Peter Attwood, *Burton House* (Matlock Civic Association, 1999), 6.
6   Atkin, *Fighting Nazi Occupation*, 146.
7   Attwood, *Burton House*, 6.
8   Ibid.
9   Atkin, *Fighting Nazi Occupation*, 148.
10 Austin J. Ruddy, 'Resistance GB', *Britain at War Magazine* (March 2015): 48.
11 Correspondence with author, July 2021.
12 Ibid.
13 Ibid.
14 Ibid.
15 John Warwicker, *Churchill's Underground Army* (Frontline, 2008), p. 184.
16 Ibid., 185.
17 Correspondence with author, December 2021.

Sources

Secondary Sources

Atkin, Malcolm. *Fighting the Nazi Occupation*. Barnsley: Pen and Sword, 2015.

Atkin, Malcolm. *Section D for Destruction*. Barnsley: Pen and Sword, 2018.

Atkin, Malcolm. *To The Last Man*. Barnsley: Pen and Sword, 2019.

Attwood, Peter. *Burton House*. Matlock: Matlock Civic Association, 1999.

Bright-Astley, Joan. *The Inner Circle*. Durham: Memoir Club, 2007.

Brown, Donald. *Somerset Versus Hitler*. Newbury: Countryside Books, 1999.

Cocks, Albert. *Churchill's Secret Army: 1939–45 and Other Recollections*. Market Harborough: The Book Guild Publishing Ltd, 1992.

Elliot, Geoff. *Colyton at War*. Colyton: Colyton Parish History Society, 2007.

Fleming, Peter. *Invasion 1940!* London: Rupert Hart-Davies, 1957.

Freethy, Ron. *Lancashire 1939-1945, The Secret War*. Newbury: Countryside Books, 2005.

Graves, Charles. *The Home Guard of Britain*. London: Hutchinson and Co., 1943.

Hoare, Adrian. *Standing up to Hitler: The Story of Norfolk's Home Guard and Secret Army*. Newbury: Countryside Books, 2002.

Holland, James. *The War in the West*. London: Corgi, 2015.

Jeffery, Keith. *MI6: The History of the Secret Intelligence Service*. London: Bloomsbury, 2010.

Lampe, David. *The Last Ditch*. London: Cassell and Company, 1968.

Levine, Joshua. *Operation Fortitude*. London: Collins, 2012.

Lowery, Bernard and Mick Wilks. *The Mercian Maquis*. Eardisley: Logaston Press, 2012.

Mackenzie, S. P. *The Home Guard*. Oxford: Oxford University Press, 1996.

May, Hugh, Stanley Blackmore, T. R. N. Walkford and D. Hunt. *Chirnside* 1. Axminster: Dudfield Publications, 2014.

Oxenden, Nigel. *Auxiliary Units History and Achievement 1940–1944*. British Resistance Organisation Museum, 2000.

Ruddy, Austin J. *To The Last Round: The Leicestershire and Rutland Home Guard*. Derby: Breedon Books, 2007.

Simak, Evelyn and Adrian Pye. *Churchill's Secret Auxiliary Units in Norfolk and Suffolk*. ASPYE, 2013.

Simak, Evelyn and Adrian Pye, *Churchill's Most Secret Special Duties Branch*. ASPYE, 2014.
Ward, Arthur. *Churchill's Secret Defence Army*. Barnsley: Pen and Sword, 2013.
Warwicker, John. *Churchill's Underground Army*. Barnsley: Frontline Books, 2008.
Williamson, Alan. *East Ridings Secret Resistance*. Haslemere: Middleton Press, 2004.
Wintringham, Tom. *New Ways of War*. London: Penguin Special, 1940.

Newspapers/Magazines/Broadcasts

Open Country. BBC Radio 4, January 2004.
'Sabotage Key Holders', *Leicester Mercury*, 11 September, 1964.
Ruddy, Austin J. 'Resistance GB', *Britain at War*, 2015.
Secret Army. Peter Williams Productions, 2003.
'The Home Guard', *The Times*, 15 August, 1941.

The National Archives

WO 199/1194
WO 199/1869
WO 199/361
WO 199/364
WO 260/9

Imperial War Museum

Ref. 14819/2
Ref. 29468

Parham Museum of British Resistance Organisation

Monthly IO Notes

Somerset County Archives

DD/SCI/12/2/26

Interviews

Ken Welch. Interview in Mabe, October 2021.
Joyce Harrison. Remote interview, various dates 2021.

Coleshill Auxiliary Research Team (CART)

One of the main sources used throughout the book is the British Resistance Archive. The archive is compiled and run by CART, a group of volunteer researchers who look into the Auxiliary Units and Special Duties Branch. Much of what is included in the archive has been added to the website www.staybehinds.com with members of the public able to search by name, county, patrol, scout section, locations, radio networks and more.

There is a huge amount of information available on the site, with background information on both the Auxiliary Units and Special Duties Branch, their training, HQs, weapons and tactics as well as a report on each specific patrol, with details (where known) and images of their Operational Bases. The work done by CART has enabled many families to confirm or indeed find out for the first time that their relatives were involved in these secret organisations.

As well as helping families find out more about their relatives' roles during the war, CART also looks to locate and record the sites of Operational Bases, Special Duties Branch bunkers and wireless sites. Its work has allowed a much better understanding of both groups as well as helping to change the initial approximation of numbers of civilians involved.

Its work is ongoing, with new information coming in all the time. It is a fantastic group of dedicated and hugely knowledgeable volunteers who should be applauded for the huge amount of work undertaken during their 'spare' time to create such a valuable resource for the public.

Index